USING SELF PSYCHOLOGY IN PSYCHOTHERAPY

USING SELF PSYCHOLOGY IN PSYCHOTHERAPY

edited by

Helene Jackson, Ph.D.

JASON ARONSON INC.
Northvale, New Jersey
London

THE MASTER WORK SERIES

Library of Congress Cataloging-in-Publication Data

Using self psychology in psychotherapy / edited by Helene Jackson
    p. cm.
  Includes bibliographical references and index.
  ISBN 1–56821–044–2 (softcover)
  1. Self. 2. Psychotherapy. 3. Self Psychology. I. Jackson,
Helene.
  RC489.S43U85   1991
  616.89'14—dc20   90–1236

Printed in the United States of America. For information and catalog write to Jason Aronson Inc., 230 Livingston Street, Northvale, New Jersey 07647-1731. Or visit our website: http://www.aronson.com

To David, Jonathan, Robin, and Jessica

Contents

PART III. APPLYING SELF PSYCHOLOGY
IN DIFFERENT SITUATIONS

Acknowledgment

I wish to thank all the authors who contributed to this volume. Without their cooperation and generous support this work could not have been completed.

Many thanks also to Jason Aronson for his enthusiasm, confidence, and friendship, all of which have been invaluable in the formulation and completion of this book.

Above all, my gratitude to Abe Berger, for his abiding patience, understanding, and encouragement.

Introduction: Putting Self Psychology to Work

Helene Jackson

In recent years, Heinz Kohut and his followers have moved psychoanalytic therapy away from its primary concern with intrapsychic conflict to a focus on psychological deficiency. Today, the clinical concepts of self psychology so permeate our thinking about psychotherapy that it is hard to imagine a therapist who doesn't draw upon it in practice. It provides an additional model of psychic structure (the cohesive self), an expanded view of the therapeutic relationship (self–selfobject milieu), and consequently, different interventions (empathy, mirroring, understanding, and explaining) rather than traditional interpretation.

The work of Kohut and his colleagues challenges Freud's basic assumption that individuals are continually battling with the powerful, often dangerous and conflicting demands of id, ego, and superego. Rather, they see the individual struggling to establish and maintain an all-encompassing cohesive self throughout life.

From a self-psychological stance, narcissistic issues transcend any specific diagnosis. They come alive and can be observed during all phases of treatment. Goals of treatment shift from cure through uncovering unconscious conflict to the re-activation of the process of normal development and the building of various functions and structure of the self. Classical analytic therapists view change as occurring through interpretation and reconstruction. Self psychological therapists view change as occurring in the surround of an empathic milieu, fostered by the use of the therapeutic interventions of acceptance, understanding and explanation. Psychic structure is acquired in the context of the therapeutic self–selfobject relationship with its inevitable (but manageable) frustrations and gratifications.

The overall empathic effort is to discover and understand the patient's perception of the narcissistic injuries he experienced in the past. Extended periods of mirroring allow the patient with narcissistic deficits to risk self-examination and awareness. Since all individuals need sustenance from selfobjects throughout life, final separation and complete ego autonomy are not the therapeutic goal. The ultimate aim of treatment is the internalization of the structure and function of a cohesive self.

Heinz Kohut expanded on psychoanalytic ideas to create a model of the mind that brought a different perspective to the understanding of how individuals organize and make meaningful their internal and external worlds. In the process, the language of this new approach moved away from the vocabulary of ego psychology.

Learning self psychology, one is introduced to concepts such as mirroring, idealizing and twinship transferences, self, selfobject functions, self–selfobject relationships, and transmuting internalizations. Familiar terminology takes on new meaning. Specifically, narcissism is no longer seen as the primitive source of mature object relations, but as a separate, continuous line of development that unfolds in the context of self–selfobject relationships throughout life. Drives are no longer seen as the instinctive, compelling force behind human behavior. Rather, it is the whole self, in which the drives are but one aspect, that is the regulator of the individual's self-esteem.

Self psychology offers a new perception of how pathology develops. It emerges, not from intrapsychic conflict, but from the pervasive absence of empathically responsive selfobjects in the child's inner and outer world. In response to such deprivation, the child is obliged to take over, abruptly, the functions of the parent(s). Depending on the level of development, the child attempts to reconstitute the self in any manner feasible. Once this precipitous process is set in motion, the child desperately clings to defensive structures that serve to prevent feelings of vulnerability, humiliation, and shame. These protective strategies, while initially adaptive, can result in feelings of emptiness and fragmentation, and may lead to a broad range of psychopathology.

In psychotherapy, resistance and defense are not seen as processes mobilized against the drives, but as processes summoned against vulnerability and the threat of fragmentation. The maintenance of a cohesive self is the major motivating force. The curative factor is not interpretation, but a variety of specific types of transference in which selfobject deficits are mobilized and spontaneously emerge to assist the normal thrust of development.

Our goal in this book is to familiarize mental health professionals with this new and different approach to human behavior and demonstrate its implications for treatment in various stages of development and in a broad range of situations. The structure of the book and its individual contributors are outlined here.

In Chapter 1, Lynch defines the concept of empathy and its central role in self psychology. He traces the normal growth of the self which transforms over time. The meaning of core constructs, such as the grandiose and idealizing self, and the mirroring, idealizing, and twinship transferences, are explained.

Major points are:

1. Kohut's concept of empathy differs from support or sympathy. It combines both cognitive and affective elements.

2. Classical interpretations, based primarily on the therapist's intellectual understanding of the patient's productions, are often experienced as narcissistic injuries.

3. It is through the therapist's empathic attunement that the patient's inner life is understood and explained.

In Chapter 2, Nicholson traces the single line of narcissistic development, from its initial form in which the self is completely dependent on selfobjects in the environment, to a more highly developed, mature sense of self in which self-esteem and cohesion are relatively independent from the external world. She distinguishes healthy from pathological narcissism, both developmentally and diagnostically, and contrasts the diagnosis of narcissistic character disorder with other character pathology.

She emphasizes:

1. Normal needs for mirroring, idealizing, and twinship are not, in and of themselves, pathological.

2. It is the pervasive, intense and compelling need for mirroring, idealization, and sameness, that reflects severe and pervasive damage to the self.

Susan Donner in Chapter 3 shows how Kohut's theory grew out of his practice experience. In treating patients he found a great disparity between interventions informed by traditional psychoanalytic theory and what he believed to be the therapeutic needs of his patients. Rather than attempting to fit the patient into the theory, he revised and modified his traditional assumptions until they became more consistent with his clinical observations. In a case example, Donner demonstrates how self psychology underscores the importance of listening and focusing on the subjective meaning of the patient's experience and feelings.

Important implications for practice are that:

1. The central, most accurate source of understanding is the patient, not the therapist. The patient and the therapist work together, with the therapist offering optimal responsiveness.

2. There are three elements of an interpretation: acceptance, understanding, and explanation. Interpretations are offered tentatively, often in the form of a question, rather than as a statement of fact.

3. Genetic material emerges in the selfobject transference. It is through the transference that the patient develops the capacity for empathy, tolerance, and respect for self and others.

In the second and third sections, self psychology is examined as it applies to treatment of patients of different ages and in different situations. For purposes of illustration, patients who have specific diagnoses are presented and discussed. However, it is consistent with Kohut's ideas to emphasize that the narcissistic issues presented in the following chapters are found in all age groups and in every diagnosis.

Young reviews in Chapter 4 the psychological construct of selfobject as it impacts on the quality of children's developing relationships and their potential for either emotional development and the formation of a cohesive self, or a self disorder. He describes the treatment of sexually victimized children to illustrate how the therapist's responses within the treatment relationship can mitigate selfobject deficits:

1. The therapeutic relationship with a child (as with an adult) is a selfobject relationship through which disorders of the self may be reactivated and repaired.

2. Each type of transference (mirroring, idealizing, twinship) that emerges in treatment represents a particular kind of deficit resulting from the child's earlier failed selfobject relationship(s) with parents.

3. Intervening in the environment (teachers, guidance counselors, etc.) can help the child's milieu to become more receptive and responsive to the child's needs.

4. Separate treatment of the child's immediate selfobject milieu (family) can improve the capacity of the selfobjects to respond empathically to the child.

In Chapter 5, Elson views adolescent pathology as an attempt to reestablish a sense of a cohesive self that has been disrupted due to parental inability to tolerate the adolescent's development demands. The adolescent's compelling need for selfobject reorganization is a product of changing cognitive and affective capacities. It can be seen in the seemingly rebellious attempts to shift from dependency on parental to peer selfobjects. From this perspective, therapeutic focus is on the adolescent's mirroring, idealizing, and twinship needs, rather than on oedipal conflicts and a retreat from the demands of puberty.

In a detailed case illustration, Elson demonstrates the following:

1. Pathological types of parental narcissism can obstruct the adolescent's capacity to use selfobjects outside the boundaries of the family.

2. Underachievement, feelings of low self-esteem, and serious acting-out behaviors can be seen as reflections of self disorders.

3. The normal thrust of development is propelled by a nonthreatening therapeutic approach that promotes a selfobject transference in which the adolescent can merge with the tranquil and comforting strength of the therapist.

Solomon discusses the achievement of intimacy as the major developmental task of adulthood in Chapter 6. Adults for whom early relationships were faulty are particularly susceptible to narcissistic injury in intimate relationships with others. Consequently, most adults seek treatment because of problems in relationships. Solomon presents a self psychology model for the diagnosis and conjoint treatment of adults who have narcissistic deficits.

In two case examples, she identifies major issues in working with adults in conjoint therapy:

1. Selfobject transference reactions taking place between therapist and patient also occur in other close relationships.

2. Therapeutic focus is on process rather than content.

3. The therapist provides safety and protection by being empathic, active, establishing rules, and setting boundaries.
4. Confusing or destructive communications are decoded and explained. They are understood as a partner's efforts to protect against narcissistic injuries.

Lazarus reviews in Chapter 7 the fundamental developmental tasks of maintaining self-esteem as well as physical and emotional integrity in the face of the tension and losses that are the inescapable consequences of growing old. From the perspective of self psychology, these threats to the self are experienced as narcissistic injuries. Lazarus demonstrates with clinical examples various self psychological responses to manifestations of self pathology in the elderly.

1. The therapist, as an empathic selfobject, acknowledges and understands the older patient's pain and threats to the sense of self.
2. The therapeutic self–selfobject milieu allows the older patient to recover self-esteem, grieve for the losses of previously significant selfobject relationships, and establish new connections that can provide selfobject functions.
3. The therapist must understand the older patient's need to idealize the therapist as a self-survival strategy rather than as an emotional defense against hostility.

Part III is on the application of self psychology in different situations. In Chapter 8, Ornstein views the state of the self as primary. Pathogenic conflicts are seen as undesirable by-products of a self that is vulnerable to fragmentation. Consequently, attention to the condition of the self is fundamental in all types of psychopathology and in all forms of treatment. Ornstein describes the central role of empathic interpretations. In the case of Ms. Clark, a woman diagnosed as having a borderline condition, Ornstein illustrates the following:

1. The therapist's empathic observation is required to understand how the therapist is being used or experienced by the patient, to identify the type of selfobject transference, and to respond in ways that allow the patient to feel understood.

2. Empathic interpretations are the best therapeutic response regardless of the type of therapy or severity of psychopathology.

3. Empathic interpretations can effect structural change in ways that produce an authentic restoration of the self.

Lawrence Josephs, in Chapter 9, brings a self psychological approach to the treatment of a patient who has schizophrenia. This perspective differs significantly from both the ego psychological and conflict/defense approach to this profound disorder. Josephs views paranoid and grandiose delusions as concrete metaphors for the patient's past traumas and disappointments. These psychotic processes are efforts to convey the intense feelings that such abuses generate. They may also function to restore a sense of self in which the patient feels valued, special, and accepted. Josephs sees the use of primary process as an attempt to communicate feelings of defeat and frustration as a result of receiving inadequate or inappropriate responses when using ordinary language. In the case of Mr. N., a schizophrenic patient, Josephs identifies some important therapeutic concerns.

According to Josephs:

1. The therapist must unfailingly empathize with the patient's subjective experience and focus on the adaptive aspect of the patient's behavior.

2. The selfobject relationship must be allowed to develop. In this process, the patient's sense of self is augmented, leading to an increase in the capacity for reality testing and a higher level of functioning.

3. Attempts to reality test should be kept to a minimum as they may be experienced as an assault on the integrity of the patient's self. In addition, they may activate defensive measures such as schizoid withdrawal, passive compliance, and/ or a negative transference.

In Chapter 10, Patrick compares Kohut's approach to the severely disturbed narcissistic patient with that of Kernberg, specifically in their formulations and treatment of narcissistic rage. Contrary to Kernberg, who focuses on the development of the negative transference, Patrick views narcissistic rage reactions as serving multiple, interrelated functions: (1) communication of self-object needs, (2) narcissistic repair, (3) revenge upon a nonempathic selfobject, (4) restoration of selfobject bonds, (5) creation of a more responsive selfobject, and (6) working through past experiences of loss and deprivation. From a self psychological view, the patient's attempts to achieve these functions are at the root of two forms of regressive rage reactions often seen in treatment, criticism, and intimidation.

According to Patrick:

1. The inequity of the therapeutic relationship and the feelings of helplessness that are engendered by it are the most intolerable feelings for patients who have severe narcissistic deficits.

2. An onslaught of criticism by the patient is an attempt to reconfigure the balance of power in the relationship. Patients use intimidation when they feel they must demonstrate their superiority. In this way, they disavow their feelings of helplessness. For some patients, these behaviors may be the only way to maintain the therapy.

3. Understanding the therapeutic milieu as the source of the narcissistic rage can help restore the patient's narcissistic balance enough to avoid further regression and allow them to continue working in therapy.

In Chapter 11, Deitz uses self psychology to guide the treatment of patients who have experienced loss and narcissistic injury. He contrasts Kohut's view of aggression with the classical analytic approach. The latter viewed the core of depression as the patient's unconscious rage which has been displaced from the lost object and redirected to the patient's ego. On the contrary, Kohut's formulation of depression focuses on the patient's inability to intrapsychically reactivate in the present the loss of function that the object served in the past. In this view, rage is not at the source of depression, but is adjunctive to it.

In the case of Mr. R., some important issues in the treatment of a depressed patient emerge:

> **1.** Treatment addresses itself to both contemporary functioning and past history. Listening carefully to the patient's productions, the therapist focuses on the lost relationship(s) to identify the ongoing function the missing object(s) performed for the patient.

> **2.** Rage at the therapist reflects a rupture in the idealized transference and the patient's experience of fragmentation. Unlike the techniques used in classical psychoanalytic therapy to stimulate rage, self psychological techniques function to repair the rupture and restore the patient's sense of self-cohesion.

> **3.** Once those aspects of the self that the lost object had provided for the patient have been identified, the patient can begin to take over that function, and the depressive symptoms can remit.

Levin, in Chapter 12, applies self psychology to the diagnosis and treatment of alcoholics. Kohut viewed narcissistic disturbances as central to the pathology of addictions. From this perspective, drinking is viewed as a pathological compromise that attempts to make up for critical deficits in self structure. According to Levin, the concept of the grandiose self is most relevant to the understanding of alcoholism. Similar to Winnicott's concept of the "false self," this primitive structure has split off, intellectually and emotionally, from the alcoholic's sense of reality. The ensuing sharp division between the grandiose self and the capacity for reality-testing explains the simultaneous existence of both the pompous arrogance and the extensive low self-esteem so often seen in individuals suffering from addictions.

In his detailed case example, Levin identifies the therapist's major tasks when working with patients who abuse alcohol:

1. Maintaining an attitude of active rather than passive listening.

2. Empathizing with the alcoholic's suffering.

3. Addressing the genetic determinants of psychic structure deficits.

4. Understanding and explaining the idealizing and mirroring quality of the transference to the bottle.

5. Calling attention to the patient's need to control relationships with others and with the therapist (at the appropriate time).

6. Helping patients experience their feelings rather than using alcohol to anesthetize them.

In Chapter 13, Wagner views child abuse and neglect as a parental dysfunction that results from a breakdown in the child–parent (selfobject) relationship. She reviews parenting as a developmental phase that can either proceed along expectable developmental lines, or can become arrested. She perceives parents who abuse their children as having severe developmental self deficits resulting from their own internalized dysfunctional selfobject configurations. Consequently, these parents are severely threatened by their child's demands for selfobject fulfillment. In her case vignette, Wagner illustrates that:

1. The development of the mirroring, idealizing, and twinship transferences are of primary importance in the treatment of parents who are abusive.

2. The therapist's nonjudgmental acceptance and understanding of the parents' previously unmet needs provides an "experience near" phenomenon that asks no more of the parents than they are able to give.

3. Through parents reexperiencing their own childhood parental selfobject failures the parents' capacity for empathic attunement and responsiveness is increased.

Barth reviews and examines self psychological concepts in Chapter 14 that are relevant to the understanding and treatment of patients who have eating disorders. Three case examples demonstrate the critical importance of the sense of self in developing symptomatology. The role of resistance and empathy in the therapeutic work is also considered.

Barth identifies three major tenets of self psychology that contribute significantly to the treatment of eating-disordered individuals:

1. Symptoms are adaptive. They serve to attenuate feelings of fragmentation, disorganization, confusion, and self-hatred while they help to maintain a stable sense of self.

2. Pathological behavior can be reflective of efforts to adapt to a maladaptive environment. The therapist must be noncritical and accept that the patient's resistance reflects attempts to maintain a cohesive sense of self.

3. The therapist's focus on empathy and experience-near understanding provides a milieu in which the meaning of the patient's symptoms become clear without the imposition of theoretical bias or interpretations in the classical sense.

Mental health professionals who are familiar with the concepts of self psychology will find the following chapters useful in expanding their treatment ideas as they apply to different age groups and different situations. For those who are unfamiliar with self psychology, this material will provide new, different, exciting, and effective ways of thinking about patients and intervening in the treatment relationship.

PART I
UNDERSTANDING SELF PSYCHOLOGY

1

Basic Concepts

Vincent J. Lynch

This chapter provides an overview of the major contributions to psychoanalytic theory and practice made by Heinz Kohut.

THE CENTRALITY OF EMPATHY

Among Kohut's early writings the most crucial is his article "Introspection, Empathy, and Psychoanalysis" (Kohut 1959), in which he begins to explore the inner psychological world in a new way. Although the inner world of thoughts, feelings, wishes, and fantasies cannot be physically seen or touched, we observe them in *ourselves* through the process of introspection, and in *others* through the phenomenon of empathy. Kohut uses the phrase "vicarious introspection" to define the human capacity for empathy. Through empathy the individual observes vicariously the internal experience of another.

Kohut points out that if we observe only the concrete aspects of a human interaction without introspection and empathy playing a part in our understanding, we fail to take into consideration the important psychological dimensions of the interaction:

> . . . we can measure the deviation of the skin above the eye to the minutest fraction of an inch, yet it is only through introspection and empathy of the inner experience that we can begin to understand the shades of meaning of astonishment and disapproval that are contained in the raising of an eyebrow.
>
> [Kohut 1959, p. 464]

It is the therapist's *scientific use* of his or her human capacity for empathy that provides that which is curative in the psychotherapeutic experience. Kohut (1982) also stressed that empathy is "a value neutral method of observation attuned to the inner life of man" (p. 395).

The capacity for accurate empathy is composed of affective and cognitive components. Empathy is *not* used to satisfy or gratify the needs of another. It is *not* the same as sympathy or support. Rather empathy *informs* the individual as to what is needed or yearned for by the other. In the psychotherapeutic experience the therapist's empathic understanding of the patient's inner experience *guides* and *informs* the therapist as to what is yearned for and needed. The therapist takes the cognitive and affective understanding of what is being communicated and *explains* that which is understood. The curative role of empathy occurs through that process of *understanding* and *explaining* that results from the therapist's empathic immersion into the internal world of the client. As the client's internal world and deficits are understood and explained by another (that is, the therapist), new "compensatory structures" are built and the client slowly over time replaces his or her former enfeebled self structure with a stronger, more cohesive self structure. This gradual process of taking in the therapist's explanations has been referred to by Kohut as the process of "transmuting internalizations." In self psychology "understanding" refers to the process by which therapists place themselves (vis-à-vis empathic immersion) into the intrapsychic reality of the patient.

Only after doing so, can the therapist communicate or "explain" his or her understanding of what the patient is relating. This "explaining" process is somewhat different from the idea of "interpretation" in psychoanalysis. Traditionally, "interpretation" refers more to an intellectual explanation of material the patient presents. The self psychology concept of "explaining," however, refers to the therapist's intellectual and affective understanding of the patient's material, and this understanding can be obtained only after a period of adequate empathic immersion.

THE CONCEPT OF THE SELF

The idea of "self structure" and the "psychology of the self" is central to Kohut's theory. What is meant in this use of the term "self"? It has a specific meaning in Kohutian theory, referring to a psychic structure that is "the core of our personality." The Dutch analyst Treurniet (1980) wrote, "The self is the universe of conscious and unconscious feelings which the individual has about himself as the center of experience and initiative" (p. 325). The self does not replace the tripartite structure of id, ego, and superego. Rather it serves a supraordinate function. The concepts of id, ego, superego are "experience-distant," while the "self" is an "experience-near" structure. It is attentive to the quality and quantity of real experiences with real people in the real world.

It is crucial to grasp the concept of self if one wishes to analyze Kohut's ideas. His theories of narcissistic character pathology, narcissistic vulnerability, metapsychology, and the more recent elaboration of the self disorders all have as their underpinning reference the concept of self.

THE DEVELOPMENT OF THE SELF

The understanding of how the self develops and changes over time, as well as how deficits in the self can occur, is most useful in the treatment of the "mid-range disorders," most especially the narcissistic disturbances. It is also possible to use the psychology of the self to see how narcissism (which fuels the self in a variety of ways) continues and is transformed over time throughout life, rather than just being a "way station" between autoerotism and object love as earlier theorists had believed.

According to Kohut, the rudimentary self of the child begins to develop at about 18 months. At that time the child has a set of very powerful narcissistically based needs that must be responded to in certain ways for normal development to proceed. The three sets of these needs (or three "poles" of the self structure) have to do with a set of needs pertaining to the "grandiose" sector of the self structure, the "idealizing" sector of the self, and the "twinship" sector.

THE GRANDIOSE SELF

With regard to the grandiose sector of the self, the individual self structure of the child, beginning at about 18 months and continuing through the childhood years, has intense needs to receive confirming (or mirroring) responses from others regarding his or her greatness. The child may seek to be the center of attention, may actively seek the praise of others for his or her accomplishments, and has yearnings to be seen as the apple of the parents' eye. These yearnings for confirmatory or mirroring responses exist most strongly in relation to selected significant others in the child's life. Most often these selected people of importance will be the parents but may also include other significant people (or objects) in the developing child's psychosocial network. These significant others, who hold the promise of providing the much sought-after confirming/mirroring responses of greatness or specialness (as well as those who fulfill idealizing functions to be described later), have been described by Kohut as "selfobjects." This interesting term was developed by Kohut to describe the ways in which these important objects really function as a part of the self, supplying the much needed responses of mirroring and idealizing that assist the self structure to develop and flourish.

It should be emphasized that it is not the role of the self-objects to eternally or limitlessly gratify the child's selfobject need for mirroring and idealization. Instead, at times it may be necessary to set limits to curb a child's expanding demands to be exhibitionistic or demands to be the center of attention. This is where empathy enters the picture. In normal development, the selfobjects need to be receptive to the needs of the child to have his or her greatness validated or to provide an idealized function. However, the selfobject needs to be empathically attuned to the inner world of the child in order to respond in ways that are ultimately in the developing child's best interests. Sometimes it may be in the child's interest to actively gratify the yearnings while at other times it may be more in the child's interest to curb or frustrate the sought-after responses since, if gratified, they might lead to excessive excitability or danger. This process of empathic attunement informs the selfobject as to what kinds of responses may be in the child's interest; it is empathy that guides which response is made.

This process of at times gratifying the selfobject needs while at other times not gratifying the needs has been described by Kohut as the process of "optimal frustration" of selfobject needs. It is this alternating combination of gratification and frustration over time that helps the child's self to move from archaic manifestations of mirroring needs (for example, exhibitionism) and archaic manifestations of idealizing needs (for example, perceptions of the selfobject as omnipotent) to manifestations of more mature levels of self development. It should be emphasized at this point that Kohut does not feel that "perfect empathy" is needed at all times for the parental selfobjects to be able to assist the child's self structure to develop and mature. Indeed, it is expected at times that there will be empathic failures between the child and his or her selfobject world. However, if, on balance, there are more instances of accurate empathic attunement than empathic failure, there is a good likelihood that a normal, mature self structure can form and develop.

THE IDEALIZING SELF

As for the idealizing pole of the self structure, Kohut postulates that, in addition to the child's need for "confirmatory, mirroring" recognition of one's greatness from the child's world of selfobjects, the child also needs to be able to extensively idealize selfobjects in his or her world. To be able to participate in the perceived strength and stability of selfobjects, the child needs an available source of strength which can be turned to (and merged with) at times of anxiety, or fear. This kind of idealized merger with the selfobject provides a certain level of calmness and reintegration to the self structure of the child, especially at times when the child's self structure may have been somewhat fragmented as a result of some trying experience, failure, or upset in his or her world. The idealized selfobject "restores" the enfeebled self of the child to a new level of cohesion or maturity. Over the long term, this kind of idealization can gradually help the child internalize the idealized selfobject image and assist the child, in later years, in the formation of internalized goals and ideals for itself.

As a result of empathic attunement and optimal frustration on the part of the selfobjects to the child's needs for confirmatory, mirroring responses of his or her greatness (the grandiose sector of the self) as well as being able to engage selfobjects in idealizing merger at times of stress (the idealizing sector of the self), the "rudimentary self" gradually shifts away from archaic demands for selfobject responses. As this occurs, the archaic manifestations of grandiosity (for example, exhibitionism) slowly, over time become transformed into healthy ambitions for oneself, the enjoyment of activities, and a zest for life. Similarly, the archaic manifestations of idealization (the selfobject's omnipotence, omniscience, and so forth) become slowly transformed into internalized values, goals, and strengths.

This is what happens in normal growth and development. In short, these two poles or sectors of the self structure become transformed from the archaic into more mature manifestations.

Kohut believed that the mature self is pulled by one's ambitions and led by one's ideals. It continues to grow and change throughout adolescence, adulthood, and old age. Selfobject needs remain throughout life, but they shift and change through the life cycle. The self, then, endures throughout life.

When normal growth and development of the self structure is impeded in significant ways (as a result of chronic empathic failures by selfobjects), certain midrange disturbances—especially narcissistic disturbances—are likely to develop.

Self psychology also has espoused some different ideas regarding the place of aggression and anger in human development (Kohut 1977, p. 144). While classical psychoanalytic theory views aggression as a separate drive, partly biologically based, self psychology views it differently. Self psychology sees anger and aggression in general as by-products or "disintegration products" that develop as a result of significant, hurtful, empathic failures on the part of selfobjects.

PATHOLOGICAL DEVELOPMENT OF THE SELF AND ITS TREATMENT

The person who experiences pervasive empathic failures in one or all sectors of selfobject needs is likely to develop a disorder of the self structure. The most frequently occurring self disorder is that of the narcissistic personality disturbance, which may be severe (the narcissistic personality disorder) or may be more mild to moderate (narcissistic features). In any event, those with disturbances in this area present with a definable syndrome that includes vulnerabilities in the area of self-esteem regulation, and hypersensitivity to failures, criticism, rebuffs, and disappointments. As treatment progresses with these patients, the nature of the transference is likely to be a mirroring or idealizing transference. The area of the self structure with the most deficit (or unmet selfobject need) will show itself through the type of transference that develops. If there is a strong need of the patient for "confirmatory or mirroring" responses from the therapist, one can assume that much of the work to be done will have to do with issues relating to the grandiose sector of the self. Similarly, if the nature of the transference develops in areas pertaining to idealizing others, it is safe to assume that much of the work will relate to the idealizing sector of the self. It is not uncommon for the patient to be so defended from these yearnings that the therapist may initially see opposite manifestations in the transference. For example, rather than actively seeking confirmatory responses, the patient may be self-effacing and filled with humility or, rather than actively seeking to idealize the therapist, there may be an initial period when the therapist is devalued or demeaned. In short, whether the transference material is overtly mirroring or idealizing or is the complete opposite, such rapid transference responses are likely to occur in work with patients who have narcissistic disturbances. They give us important clues about the core deficit of the self.

MIRROR TRANSFERENCES

Kohut has categorized mirror transferences into three types, depending on the level of narcissistic formation. These include (1) the merger-mirroring transference, (2) the alter-ego or twinship mirroring transference, and (3) the narrower mirroring transference.

Merger-mirroring Transference

The merger-mirroring transference reflects the most primitive level of narcissistic pathology. With this type of patient, the therapist is experienced as part of the patient's grandiose self and the therapist is thought of *only* as an extension of the self. Patients with this level of pathology expect total control of the therapeutic situation, and indeed of the therapist. They often feel that their specialness makes them deserving of special favors and special consideration in areas such as fees, times, and scheduling. When the therapist sets limits and boundaries, the patient may fly into a rage. Over time, however, (and this may be a period of years) the patient can gradually feel that these needs are understood if the therapist can accurately and empathically point out (or mirror) the hurtful, deprived feelings that are indeed at the source of the patient's rages. As can be expected, these patients are difficult to work with. Therapists often find themselves angrily rejecting their excessive demands.

Alter-ego Twinship Transference

The second level of mirroring transferences is the "alter-ego twinship" transference. This transference emerges in treating a more mature type of narcissistically disordered patient. In this situation one sees a less archaic emergence of the grandiose self. There is a greater degree of separateness between patient and therapist (and indeed in relation to other objects in the patient's life as well). This person has the capacity to develop and to sustain some degree of reciprocal object relatedness, but often goes through life establishing and then breaking up a series of relationships with others. Life becomes a search for the "perfect twin," that partner who will experience all things in the same manner as the patient. When disappointments occur (as will be the case for all of us at times), these individuals experience them as confirming evidence that the object can no longer serve as the perfect twin and, typically at such points, they will end the relationship. In treatment, this type of narcissistic patient experiences the therapist in this twinship fashion, assuming that the therapist will always share the same views about the world as the patient.

In the course of treatment, the patient inevitably experiences the therapist as having different views, failing to be the perfect twin. At such points, the patient's rage and hurtful feelings will emerge, often manifest in the wish to terminate the therapy. This can be viewed as a repetition of the patient's lifelong search for the perfect twin as well as of the desire to abandon relationships when the partner cannot live up to the wishes and fantasy of twinship. The elaboration of this conflict and the therapist's empathic understanding of this struggle can assist the client in gaining greater insight, understanding, mastery, and resolution over this developmental arrest.

Mirror Transference in the Narrower Sense

The third level of the mirroring transference and the most mature of the three is the "mirror transference in the narrower sense." Here, the therapist is genuinely seen by the patient as separate and distinct. Nonetheless, the patient seeks the therapist's admiration and praise, in the constant quest for total approval and narcissistic gratification. Those times when the therapist fails to affirm the patient's narcissistic yearnings often result in severe narcissistic injuries, which, if not addressed, may seriously endanger the therapeutic relationship.

THE IDEALIZING TRANSFERENCE

The idealizing transference refers to the transferential response in which the therapist is experienced as all-knowing, all-loving, and omnipotent—the embodiment of the longed-for, perfect, and idealized parent. Narcissistic persons often experience their therapists in this fashion early in the treatment. Contrary to the classical analytic view in which idealization represented the patient's defensive attempts to ward off fears of destruction, Kohut viewed the idealizing transference as reflecting the patient's need to participate in the strength, stability, and the calmness of the selfobject. In the transference the therapist becomes the yearned-for "idealized parental imago." This idealized parental imago is the child's view of the parent as omnipotent, omniscient, and always stable. In treatment, the patient who develops "idealizing transferences" is expressing the deficit in self structure that reflects insufficient experiences with an idealized parental imago at times of stress, failures, disappointments, and hurt.

Kohut's article, "The Two Analyses of Mr. Z." (Kohut 1979), highlights the dimension of the idealizing transferences. He discusses two analyses, each four years in length, with the same patient. The first analysis was carried out along classical lines. The patient improved in many ways, but a few years later resumed treatment due to an increase in symptomatology (difficulties in sexual functioning). In this second analysis, Kohut approached the patient using concepts derived from his new psychology of the self.

Kohut describes interesting differences in the two treatments. For instance, in the first analysis the patient reported a dream where he was watching a doorway at his home. The patient's father, carrying several packages, was attempting to come through the doorway. In the first analysis, Kohut interpreted the dream as referring to latent castration fears, that Mr. Z. was attempting to keep his powerful, threatening father outside the doorway at some distance.

From the perspective of self psychology, Kohut had a very different understanding of this dream. He felt that, in the dream, the patient was trying to have his admired, beloved, longed-for, idealized father *enter into* his life. The packages carried by the father in this new understanding of the dream dealt with the longed-for gifts and attributes that the father had been unable to provide, considering his emotional limitations. This new level of interpretation, namely, working with Mr. Z. around the idealized parent–imago theme, sheds new light on the importance of Mr. Z.'s father and his inability to provide his son with an idealized parent–imago. The analysis progressed in new ways as a result of this self psychological perspective.

CONCLUSION

In a self psychology approach to narcissistic disturbances, the therapist consistently helps the patient uncover and "keep alive" all manifestations of the mirroring and/or idealizing transferences. The goal is not merely to remove symptoms or to educate the patient about the source of distress. Rather, the goal is to rehabilitate the self structure to a new level of health and maturity. To do that, the patient needs to verbalize and experience fully the core deficits of the self structure (as exemplified in the kind of transferential response which develops). The therapist needs to take the transferential response and remain empathically immersed with the patient to learn fully about the nature and extent of the deficits and their genetic origins. Through the process of understanding and explaining, the therapist helps the patient achieve a new and lasting level of strength and maturity for what once was an enfeebled, vulnerable psychological self.

2

Narcissism

Barbara L. Nicholson

Narcissism was defined by Freud (1914) as the withdrawal of libidinal cathexes from others with simultaneous redirection toward the self. In this way, he differentiated object–libido, or love of others, from ego–libido, or love of the self. This implied that as more psychic energy was directed toward the self, less psychic energy was available for relationships with others. Consequently, narcissism became a pejorative term and remained so until recently when the newer theories of self psychology expanded the concept of narcissism to include healthy forms of narcissism as prerequisites for developing and maintaining self-esteem and self-cohesiveness.

From self psychological perspectives, narcissism exists on a continuum from healthy to more pathological forms. In healthy narcissism, self-confidence and self-esteem develop in conjunction with stable and growth-producing relationships. An individual with healthy narcissism experiences a manageable degree of self-doubt when faced with the minor disappointments and frustrations of everyday life. All individuals are subject to narcissistic injuries, or to regressions in their feelings of self-esteem. For example, in vulnerable states any individual may withdraw interest in others and become self-absorbed. However, these feeling states usually pass; the regression is temporary and the individual recompensates when the crisis is averted.

Pathological narcissism is evidenced by an unstable self-concept, with grandiose fantasies of self-importance, a sense of entitlement, and an inability to see others except as need-gratifying objects. Individuals who experience severe narcissistic difficulties exhibit major vulnerabilities in self-esteem and self-regard. They are unable to utilize self-esteem and self-confidence in times of stress.

Individuals with narcissistic difficulties have a need to protect themselves from shame and humiliation. They characteristically utilize defenses of grandiosity, devaluation of others, and entitlement. Depending upon the extent of the deficit, such defenses protect the individual from various degrees of fragmentation of the self. Narcissistically impaired individuals seriously limit their capacity to form empathic and meaningful relationships.

In addition, individuals with severe narcissistic difficulties experience contradictions between feelings of grandiosity and omnipotence at one extreme and feelings of inferiority and insecurity at the other. The intensity and the extent of these contrasting feeling states are a measure of the severity of the narcissistic pathology.

Healthy narcissism helps individuals maintain self-esteem and is a necessary prerequisite for growth. Individuals with extensive narcissistic vulnerability are inhibited in such growth. The transformation of infantile narcissistic grandiosity into healthy and realistic ambitions and goals is important in the course of human development. It allows for relationships with others to be empathically grounded as evidenced by genuine interest in and concern for others.

This chapter has two purposes. It clarifies the concept of narcissism from both a developmental and a diagnostic perspective, and it examines and contrasts narcissistic character disorders with other types of character pathology.

DEVELOPMENT OF THE SELF

From a self psychological perspective, development begins with the nuclear self. This nuclear self is expanded into the tripolar self through the progressive development of three lines of early narcissism: grandiosity, idealization, and twinship. The first pole is early grandiosity and exhibitionism, which become transmuted into goals and ambitions. The second pole is early idealizations, which become transmuted into ideals and values. The third pole is the need for another to be the "same as" or "like" the self.

The development of the tripolar self occurs through the interaction of the young child with selfobjects. Selfobjects are defined as objects experienced as part of the self or in the service of the self. The selfobject relationship refers to an intrapsychic experience rather than to the interpersonal relationships between the self and important others. It refers to the mental representations that are necessary for the sustainment of self-esteem and self-cohesion.

Normal infantile narcissism is gradually transformed via the process of transmuting internalization. In transmuting internalizations, significant aspects of important selfobjects are internalized and transformed according to the specific needs of the developing child. When small frustrations occur, the gratifying responses of mother are internalized. Thus, the child becomes able to internalize the functions that the parent had originally performed. When this process occurs repeatedly in small increments, adequate structure is developed; the functions of the parents are taken in and transmuted into the child's sense of self and self-competence. Self psychological theory considers this normal growth.

Empathic shortcomings are unavoidable. However, if there is gross failure on the part of the selfobjects to respond appropriately to these shortcomings, then adequate structure will not develop. This results in narcissistic character pathology. If initial nurturing is deficient, the self will develop without a sense of cohesiveness. The intense reliance on selfobjects protects against fragmentation or loss of cohesiveness. The narcissistic character disordered person is unable to internalize the functions of selfobjects, thereby leaving him or her vulnerable to impending feelings and/or fears of fragmentation or disintegration. Kohut (1984) felt that disintegration anxiety was synonymous with a fear of loss of humanness or psychological death.

Thus, the narcissistic character disordered person is a result of continuous unempathic responsiveness: a failure of selfobjects to understand the wishes and/or needs of the developing individual. Empathic failures may occur in either the mirroring, idealizing, or twinship lines. The internalization of these functions for a successful self experience is thwarted. The result is a lack of self-cohesiveness, a lack of the experience of being at one with oneself, and an inability to utilize one's own resources in times of stress.

DISORDERS OF THE SELF

Self psychological theory views all psychological difficulties as disorders of the self. Narcissistic impairments may range from psychotic states to neurotic states. The extent (severity) and the location (mirroring, idealizing, and/or twinship needs) of the disorder are a result of unempathic responsiveness on the part of selfobjects to the developing child.

Kohut and Wolf (1978) describe clinical syndromes that are a consequence of these developmental failures. The definition of these syndromes are helpful in clinical work because they illustrate the types of experiences any individual may go through. These forms of self disorder may not always be observable in precise form; various mixtures may be observed in any person at a given time regardless of the severity of the self disorder. "A person may exhibit one or another of these self experiences sequentially, and often in close proximity" (p. 418).

Kohut and Wolf (1978) further define narcissistic disturbances by providing a typology of patterns of observable behaviors. Although they warn the clinician of the limitations of utilizing these typologies without understanding the underlying causes of the behaviors, they feel that a typology aids the clinician in understanding the significance of manifest behaviors of the self disorder. These character types represent the direction of selfobject needs which any individual may utilize to fulfill circumscribed areas of weakness of the self.

CLINICAL SYNDROMES
OF DEVELOPMENTAL FAILURE

The Fragmenting Self

The fragmenting self is caused by unresponsiveness on the part of childhood selfobjects which would aid the emerging self to integrate early experiences. Such integration is critical in the development of self-cohesion. The fragmenting self reacts to narcissistic disappointments by the loss of feeling cohesive and at one with oneself. This can occur at all levels of self disorder when self-esteem has been taxed for long periods of time or after a series of failures that shake self-esteem (Chessick 1985). Such blows can lead to a self experience of fragmentation, the degree of which will vary depending on the preexisting state of the self.

While all people will sometimes experience a sense of not being themselves, less structured individuals may severely lose their sense of cohesion in times of stress. When self impairment is not severe, symptoms will include a minimal amount of emotional and intellectual disorganization, "gait and posture will be less than graceful and movements will tend to be clumsy" (Kohut and Wolf, 1978, p. 418). However, in narcissistic personality disorders reactions to even minor disappointments produce fragmenting symptoms of greater severity. There is a marked difference in physical appearance; such persons may be disheveled and disorganized, and may become disoriented. Hypochondriacal symptoms may emerge, but disappear quickly when the patient reestablishes an empathic connection with the selfobject. In treatment situations, an unempathic response must be acknowledged and worked through. In this way, the self/selfobject connection between therapist and client is reestablished and the fragmenting symptoms begin to disappear.

The Overstimulated Self

The overstimulated self is a consequence of consistent, inappropriately excessive responses from childhood selfobjects with regard to grandiose and/or idealizing fantasies of the developing child; childhood grandiosity is not neutralized into developmentally phase-appropriate ambitions and goals. The overstimulated self is unable to experience excitement and pleasure in successful achievement; creativity is often impaired. Such individuals experience painful tension and anxiety regarding their fantasies of greatness. They defend against this anxiety by shielding themselves from situations that place them in the limelight.

When ideals have been excessively and inappropriately responded to, enthusiasm and vitality are lacking. This leaves an individual unprepared to pursue healthy goals and ambitions. A firm sense of a self that can learn from others and integrate experience into their unique self experience does not develop.

A patient may experience acute discomfort if the therapist recreates such overstimulation in the therapy. This may occur if the therapist is overly supportive of and enthusiastic about the patient's accomplishments before the patient is ready to recognize such accomplishments as truly deserving of praise. If grandiosity and idealization are not recognized as defenses for a fragile self, the therapist may inappropriately support these defenses rather than allow the patient to gradually work them through in timely fashion. The fragile self would remain fragile. Such an intervention on the part of the therapist would result in a break in the therapeutic bond, but the bond will be reestablished when the reasons for the client's discomfort are understood and genetically interpreted.

The Overburdened Self

The overburdened self is closely related to the overstimulated self. It is the result of unempathic responsiveness on the part of childhood selfobjects to the need for merger with the calming and soothing functions of the idealized parent. When calming and soothing functions are not transmuted and internalized into self functions, the world is viewed as a hostile place, deplete of calming and soothing selfobjects. In such instances, anxiety is intense. In treatment, suspiciousness and paranoia may result when the therapist fails to respond homeopathically to the patient's need to merge with the calm of the therapist. When the narcissistic injury is attended to and the patient–therapist bond reestablished, these symptoms disappear.

The Understimulated Self

The understimulated self is created when selfobjects do not provide stimulating responses to childhood needs over prolonged periods of time. This results in individuals whose experiences are boring and who lack vitality and a zest for life. Such individuals are prone to seek any outside excitement to create in themselves a feeling of being alive. Symptoms of the understimulated self include addictions, perversions, compulsive masturbation, and social hyperactivity, all of which are utilized in an effort to stimulate themselves.

In treatment situations, the therapeutic alliance is often broken by an unempathic response from the therapist. Interventions that do not take into account the functions that acting-out behavior serves for the understimulated personality may be seen as an unempathic response. Only when the importance of the maladaptive behavior is understood as an attempt to avoid fragmentation will the bond be reestablished and the therapeutic work resumed.

CHARACTER TYPES

Mirror-hungry

Mirror-hungry personalities constantly search for selfobjects who will mirror their sense of self-worth and self-esteem. Individuals with mirror-hungry personalities have not sufficiently acquired the structure to feel secure within themselves. They need to elicit admiration from sources outside the self in the service of enhancing inner feelings of cohesion and decreasing feelings of worthlessness. The intensity of the need for admiration and confirmation results in a constant search for selfobjects from whom they can elicit such responses. In this way, the depleted self will be bolstered, allowing the person to regulate and maintain self-esteem. The mirror-hungry personality is never satisfied with the degree of confirmation and admiration they receive. Therefore, they constantly search for others who will continue the cycle of confirmation that the self cannot provide.

Ideal-hungry

The ideal-hungry personalities search for selfobjects with whom they can merge so that their needs for both calming and soothing functions can be met by persons outside the self. Individuals with ideal-hungry personalities have not sufficiently acquired the means to calm and soothe the self. They thirst for others "whom they can admire for their prestige, power, beauty, intelligence, or moral standards" (Kohut and Wolf 1978, p. 421). Without such persons, ideal-hungry individuals feel worthless and lack values and ideals, which seriously compromise their ability to reach realistic goals. The ideal-hungry personality is never satisfied for any extended period of time with the idealized selfobject. When disappointment occurs, one idealized selfobject is replaced with another.

Alter-ego-hungry

The alter-ego-hungry personalities quest for a selfobject who appears to be like the self, thereby confirming the self experience of belonging, of being a part of a twinship. They have not had the opportunity to experience themselves as being like others and always feel out of place in the social world. The need to feel a likeness with other people confirms that the self belongs and is the same as others. As with the mirroring and ideal-hungry personalities, the search is never ending. When the person discovers that the likeness is not complete, that the other is not the same as the self, the search for another selfobject begins. Although some persons may be able to form lasting friendships, most alter-ego personalities will fill the inner emptiness created by the disappointing self-object with a series of selfobject replacements.

The mirror-hungry, ideal-hungry, and alter-ego-hungry character types should not be considered pathological in and of themselves. They are variations of normal selfobject needs. The location of the deficit determines an individual's characteristic stance through which they attempt to alter specific selfobject needs. On the other hand, the contact-shunning and the merger-hungry personalities exhibit greater pathology.

Contact-shunning

The contact-shunning personalities avoid social contact and any form of intimacy in an attempt to ward off rejection and to defend against the feared merger that they desperately yearn for. The self withdraws out of a fear of fragmentation and loss of cohesion. The intensity of the need for human intimacy is so frightening that isolation presents a more palpable solution to their difficulties. Since the childhood selfobjects were not able to provide needed support, affirmation, and acceptance, contact-shunning personalities defend against further rejection and loss by withdrawing into themselves. In this way, they avoid both disappointment and the possibility of fragmentation.

Merger-hungry

Conversely, the merger-hungry personalities search out selfobjects who will provide the structure to the self that they lack. They are unable to distinguish themselves from their selfobjects and thus are not able to maintain clear boundaries nor a solid sense of self. The selfobject is utilized to enhance and bolster the self functions. Merger-hungry personalities are unable to distinguish their own functions from those that they borrow from their selfobjects. Since thoughts, feelings, and wishes cannot be distinguished from those of the selfobject, the selfobject serves the function of maintaining cohesion for the injured self.

There has been a greater extent of unresponsiveness in early

development for the contact-shunning and merger-hungry personalities than there has been for the mirror-hungry, ideal-hungry,
and alter-ego hungry personalities. Consequently, the damage to
the self is more severe.

NARCISSISTIC CHARACTER DISORDER

Symptomatology

Theorists (Adler 1981, 1986, Basch 1984a,b, Kernberg 1975,
Kohut 1971, 1977, 1984, Modell 1975, 1976, Rinsley 1982, 1984,
Tolpin 1980) who have investigated narcissistic character pathology agree that individuals who suffer from narcissistic character
disorders evidence extreme sensitivity to criticism, failure, disappointment, and minor slights. To avoid such painful feelings, they
protect themselves through maladaptive defenses (Kernberg 1975,
Kohut 1971, 1977, Modell, 1975) that make them appear healthier,
more mature, and more socially appropriate than they actually
are. At times they may be quite charming and charismatic; at other
times arrogant and indifferent. Underneath this façade of health,
they constantly seek tribute, approval, and recognition to bolster
their low self-esteem. There is an extreme contradiction on the one
hand between their grandiosity and inflated self-concept, and on
the other hand, their constant need for praise and total acceptance.

Interpersonal relationships tend to be superficial, remaining
on a need-gratifying and exploitative level. Persons who suffer
from such narcissistic pathology both envy and idealize those from
whom they expect narcissistic supplies while devaluing those who
cannot offer them such nurturing. Often, they devalue those whom
they had previously admired, utilizing the defense of splitting.
They tend to view others as all good or all bad.

Such individuals experience a sense of entitlement. They feel
that they should be treated as special, yet they are unable to give to
others in return. If they don't receive the attention they demand,
their self-esteem is injured. Their humiliation and shame, when not
treated as special, elicits rage. Kohut (1971) viewed rage reactions
as a defensive protection against threats and injuries to the self.

Stolorow (1986) explained that the hostility of these individuals indicates both extreme fragility of the self-experience and acute fear of fragmentation. The urgency of the need to restore self-esteem and self-cohesiveness is demonstrated by the intensity of the rage.

Narcissistic patients have defects in their sense of self-worth, in their interpersonal relationships, in their social adaptation, and in their ability to genuinely love other human beings.

Kohut and Wolf (1978) divide narcissistic character disorders into narcissistic behavior disorders and narcissistic personality disorders. In the former, symptoms include perversions, addictions, and delinquency. In the narcissistic personality disorders, symptoms include hypochondria, emptiness, boredom, and depression. In both groups, patients range from manifestly disturbed, functionally limited people to socially well-functioning, but privately painfully distressed people (Tolpin 1980). In severe forms of self pathology, symptoms are more extreme and lead to feelings of emptiness or temporary enfeeblement.

DIFFERENT VIEWS OF PSYCHOSIS

This section will present the traditional and self psychological views of psychotic states, borderline personality disorders, and neurotic disorders. These will then be compared and contrasted with narcissistic personality disorders.

The Traditional View

Psychosis is a "gross impairment in reality testing and the creation of a new reality" (DSM-III-R 1987, p. 404). It is an active attempt to reconcile inner experiences with the external world. Psychosis is manifested by detachment, denial, and misrepresentation of objective situations. The world is seen as a projection of fantasy. Adaptation to the environment is difficult, if not impossible. Object relations are of no concern, as the capacity for empathy and sharing experiences with others is absent. All psychic energy turns inward.

In psychotic individuals, the ability to differentiate internal from external stimulation is severely impaired. There is an over-sensitivity to stimuli. Ego boundaries are shaky, resulting in fusion and identity confusion. Thought processes are disturbed as are affective states. Major problems with thinking can include hallucinations, delusions, concrete thinking, incoherence, and many other symptoms. Disorders in perception include hearing, seeing, and altered body states. Affects are often blunted, indifferent, or shallow. There are hopelessness and emptiness as well as inappropriateness of affect. Anxiety tends to be catastrophic and overwhelming.

Psychosis is biogenetically determined. Although other factors may be involved in the development of psychosis, there is clearly a defect in part of the developing system or a defect in the process of organization. Early difficulties in development, family dysfunction, life stresses, and traumatic experiences can often contribute to or exacerbate these conditions.

Self Psychological View

Kohut considers psychotic states to be primary disorders of the self. The psychotically organized personality is marked by permanent or protracted breakup, enfeeblement, or serious distortion of the self. This individual lacks the organized defensive capabilities of the borderline personality. The psychotically organized individual has not experienced, or has withdrawn from, affectively maintained relations with selfobjects.

Some psychotic individuals have active psychotic symptoms, while others, although the core of the personality is psychotically organized, are able to maintain a façade of normality. Thus, in some instances, a psychotic core coexists with sectors of the personality that are cohesively organized.

Psychotic states are caused by pervasive, prolonged failure on the part of the childhood selfobjects to meet the developing needs of the child. Patients who experience psychotic states have been exposed to serious damage to the nuclear self and no reliable or substantial defensive structures can be formed to cover the defect (Chessick 1985).

Psychoses can be either organically, constitutionally, or experientially based. When the mutual cuing necessary for development is missing, relations with others do not develop normally. Transmuting internalizations, learning from the empathic responsiveness of the selfobjects, and modulation of grandiose and idealizing fantasies do not occur.

Thus, the core of the self, the center of self-cohesion, is never developed. These patients lack the defensive structure to organize and order experience. The self does not develop into a cohesive, organized center of the personality. Since there is no self/selfobject bond, there can be no unfolding of a selfobject transference in therapy. Kohut believed that compensatory structures could not be developed in psychoanalysis since the central chaos of the self would preclude the activation of a transference. Because of the extensive withdrawal from others of these patients, a nuclear self would not develop in treatment.

Kohut (1984) believed that a positive therapeutic relationship could be developed within a sustaining, empathic selfobject milieu. The breakdown of defensive structures that have ordered experience would be too painful, and essentially destructive. Thus, the goal of any treatment should be to strengthen these defensive structures. While a nuclear self will not develop, the patient can utilize the therapist as selfobject to create new defensive structures and to support already existing ones.

The therapist must allow for a merger selfobject transference wherein the therapist mirrors, idealizes, and offers alter-ego support to bolster the patient's positive self experiences. Educational activities, a milieu environment, and empathic responses will lend support to the fragmented self and allow this self to strengthen over time.

DIFFERENT VIEWS
OF BORDERLINE PERSONALITY

The Traditional View

Borderline refers to a particular kind of stable, pathological personality organization. "The essential feature . . . is a pervasive pattern of instability of self-image, interpersonal relationships, and mood. . . ." (DSM-III-R 1987, p. 346). Borderline personality structure is neither typically psychotic nor typically neurotic but occupies an area between these two categories. Kernberg (1975) describes it as stable instability or organized chaos.

There is general agreement that the borderline personality arises out of a developmental impasse that initially occurs in early childhood. It develops during separation–individuation when the individual does not separate adequately from the primary caretaker. During early development gross problems with maternal and paternal care exist. These may be actual or subtle insofar as the primary caretaker may be physically or emotionally absent or unable to differentiate from the child.

One of the most apparent deficits of the borderline personality is the primitiveness of object relations. In essence, such individuals have no satisfactory connections with others. These patients are unable to form intimate relationships because they are afraid of merger, of being unable to distinguish themselves from others.

Relationships tend to be dyadic, but such relationships are not based on the other as a love object, but rather for their need-gratifying qualities. Most relationships are experienced as fluctuating and stormy.

Borderline individuals have a rigid system of primitive defenses, including splitting, projection, projective identification, and denial. Splitting is an essential defensive operation that underlies all of the other defenses. This is an active process of keeping apart self and object representations. There may be sudden and complete shifts in feelings about any particular individual. There are also repeated and extreme oscillations between contradictory self images.

Affects are intense and unmodulated. This results in impulsive behavior, rage at others and at self, and chronic diffuse and free-floating anxiety. Lack of impulse control is chronic and ego syntonic. Enjoyment, creativity, and the achievement of goals are limited. In times of stress the borderline personality may regress toward primary process thinking.

The Self Psychological View

Kohut (1977) considers borderline personality disorders within the range of primary disturbances of the self. For Kohut, the borderline disturbance is marked by a potential for protracted disturbance of cohesion, which is defended against by maladaptive behavioral mechanisms. Well-developed defensive structures serve to hide a central emptiness of the self or intense hostility and rage.

Kohut felt that borderline conditions are similar to the psychoses, and included both schizoid and paranoid disorders among the borderline states. He viewed these conditions as permanent distortions of the nuclear self. Tolpin (1980) emphasized that although these conditions may be characterized by some psychotic-like symptoms, the availability of defensive structures prevents "massive deterioration and the subsequent self and reality distortions that mark a manifest psychosis" (p. 302).

In early development, a nuclear self was not developed. Thus, these patients suffer from "permanent or protracted breakup, enfeeblement or serious distortion of the self . . . covered by more or less effective defensive structures" (Kohut 1977, p. 192). Defensive structures protect the patient from the feared closeness with selfobjects. The fear of merger could produce loss of cohesion, and, therefore, loss of a sense of self.

Kohut holds an essentially pessimistic view of the treatment potential of the borderline personality. Since closeness to others creates fears of fragmentation, he feels that these patients would not be able to enter into a transference relationship with the therapist. Such an in-depth relationship would produce overstimulated or chaotic affect states in an otherwise well-defended, but fragile, personality structure.

He does, however, view the term borderline as relative. In more structured borderline states, the possibility of successful treatment depends upon the therapist's ability to remain empathic despite ". . . the serious narcissistic injuries to which he is exposed" (Kohut 1984, p. 184). In addition, the therapist must encourage the patient, via the selfobject transference, gradually to explore the underlying causes of his vulnerability.

Tolpin (1980) classifies borderline disorders as fluid, ranging from the psychoses to the neuroses. His spectrum is based on the quality of the self structure, ranging from the healthier to the more severe personality disorders. He defines "border" borderline patients as those "who have a self that is better organized than the self of the true borderline patient" (p. 307).

These patients have developed cohesive segments of their personality due, at least in part, to positive self/selfobject interactions in early childhood. These experiences provided some degree of nurturance, attunement, and empathic responsiveness. However, the nuclear self of these individuals is less organized and more easily subject to fragmentation than is the more structured self of the narcissistic personality.

Because of these positively-toned selfobject experiences, these patients may be able to form what Kohut (1984) terms a "pivotal" selfobject transference (p. 206). Such a transference is based on the least traumatic and most empathic childhood selfobject experiences and can lead to the strengthening of compensatory self structures.

However, treatment of these patients may be difficult because of their ". . . oppositional tendencies or the extremeness of their reactive rage which, because of their intensity and lability, may severely tax the understanding, equanimity, and effectiveness of the therapist" (Tolpin, p. 307). Thus, for treatment to be successful, the therapist must remain empathically responsive despite repeated narcissistic wounding.

DIFFERENT VIEWS OF NEUROSIS

Traditional View

DSM-III (1980) deleted the category of neurosis. No consensus could be reached as to whether the term neurosis should be used descriptively (to describe painful symptoms) or as an etiological process (unconscious conflict which creates anxiety). This anxiety leads to the use of defense mechanisms, which, in turn, lead to symptom formation. DSM-III suggests that the term neurotic disorder should be used to describe symptoms while the term neurotic process should be used to describe etiological processes. This would clarify the ambiguity that presently exists.

Freud originally utilized the term neurosis both descriptively and etiologically. During early childhood, conflict arises between the ego and the id. The ego resolves the conflict by creating stable defenses against the expression of the sexual and aggressive drives or drive derivatives. This works for a time, but a subsequent conflictive event or series of events destroy this equilibrium and the ego is no longer able to control the drives effectively. A compromise solution results. The compromise formation is called a neurotic symptom.

Freud further presents a theory of psychosexual development, which includes the oral, anal, phallic, and genital stages of development. The phallic phase has also been called the oedipal phase. Freud believed that between the ages of 4 to 6 years, all children develop unconscious conflicts, resulting in what he called the Oedipus complex. He discovered that incestuous fantasies toward the parent of the opposite sex were common. Combined with these fantasies were feelings of jealous rage against the parent of the same sex. The Oedipus complex was thought to be the nucleus of all psychoneurosis. Without the working through of oedipal conflicts, mental health would be unattainable.

From an object relations perspective, individuals with structural neurosis have successfully completed the stage of separation-individuation and have achieved object constancy. Thus, neurotic individuals have a clear sense of identity, a firm sense of self, well-established ego boundaries, and stable self and object representations. They possess a capacity to tolerate anxiety and depression as well as a capacity to delay gratification. In addition, there is a capacity for forming and maintaining reciprocal and growth-producing relationships.

A neurotic individual experiences conflict interpersonally. There is a range and flexibility in the use of defenses with the higher level defenses of intellectualization, sublimation, and rationalization the most readily used. There is clear differentiation of past from present. Impulse control is well modulated with an ability to tolerate unpleasant affect, including depression and anxiety.

Individuals who have acquired neurotic structure experience more circumscribed conflicts; these are internal and ego dystonic. They have a self-observing ego and a motivation to change. Neurotics may temporarily regress under extreme stress. However, boundaries remain intact; reality testing is not impaired. The neutralization and internalization of good and bad, love and hate, demonstrate a capacity to tolerate ambivalence.

Self Psychological View

Kohut viewed neurotic conditions as secondary disturbances of the self. These disorders were defined as reactions of an undamaged self to the vicissitudes of life. The capacity for a wide range of emotional response exists in these individuals. A strong self experiences and tolerates wide swings of self-esteem in response to victory or defeat, success or failure. A firmly established neurotic self is not immobilized by dejection following failure or expansive fantasies following success. Because a cohesive self is established with clearly delineated boundaries, the self recompensates in times of stress.

Kohut (1977, 1984) maintained that neurotic disorders arose from difficulties in development during the oedipal period. He felt that patients with these disorders did not develop structural neurosis because of overstimulation and premature excitement but because of the failure of selfobjects to gratify specific childhood needs during this developmental phase.

Self psychological theory suggests that these patients are understimulated or neglected rather than overstimulated. As a result, they are not able to deal with emotional needs in times of crisis (Basch 1984a, p. 10). The threat of reexperiencing the disappointment of unempathic selfobject responses causes them to avoid situations that could offer a fulfilling creative–productive future.

The child enters this developmental period with a cohesive self created by optimally frustrating selfobjects. Up to this point, the child has not encountered traumatic rejections in its "need to be confirmed in vitality and assertiveness by the mirroring selfobject, to be calmed and smoothed by its idealized selfobject, or to be surrounded by the quietly sustaining presence of alter egos" (Kohut 1984, p. 23).

However, empathic shortcomings thwart this development. The normal childhood self becomes fragmented and weakened and creates defenses which serve to avoid fragmentation and protect cohesiveness. Since the cohesive self is thought to be the center of vitality, healthy assertiveness, and affection, these are the attributes that are threatened by empathic shortcomings of parental selfobjects.

If parental figures are not in tune with the child's needs, then further development of a firm self experiencing joy in healthy affection, vitality, and assertiveness will be thwarted. Ambitions and goals will not be fully realized. In addition, conflict may arise over the expression of healthy sexuality and aggression in adulthood.

In the psychotherapy of neurotic patients, the therapist provides a selfobject milieu that includes mirroring, idealizing, and alter-ego empathic responses. Within the context of this selfobject transference, the basically undamaged self firms up. The transference reactivates the unresolved conflicts created by minimally unresponsive childhood selfobjects. As a result, the patient's ego functioning improves as maladaptive defenses and resistances are understood and interpreted.

DIFFERENTIAL DIAGNOSIS

In the practice of self psychology, diagnoses are not formulated by assessing symptoms, the severity of manifest behaviors, or the degree of social and/or relationship difficulties. Rather, differential diagnosis is based on the degree of cohesiveness of the self, the structural organization of the personality, and the type and intensity of the selfobject transference that develops in treatment.

Correct assessment can only be made after a prolonged period of treatment. The type and intensity of the selfobject transference is thought to be the most reliable diagnostic tool for self psychologists. In addition, the therapist must recognize his own countertransference reactions and his empathic limitations.

Assessment is based on the "interaction of two participants in an extended diagnostic or treatment process" (Tolpin 1980, p. 308). Honesty, dedication, sensitivity, and empathic responsiveness on the part of the therapist are crucial. Kohut (1977, 1984) points out that the curative factor in self psychology is the development and sustainment of the selfobject transference. It is only after prolonged periods of empathic responsiveness that patients will be able to utilize explanations and interpretations.

In assessing the cohesiveness of the self, the psychotically structured personality has serious damage to the nuclear self, and therefore no cohesive self has been formed. It lacks the defensive capacities that would provide shelter from fragmentation and disintegration. The psychotically organized individual is subject to regression to active psychosis when the positive selfobject milieu fails to support the fragile self.

In contrast to the psychotic person, the borderline personality has a "well-developed peripheral layer of defensive structures" (Kohut 1984, p. 8). These structures are subject to fragmentation, and, therefore, the borderline personality withdraws affectively from others to prevent merger and/or regression, or merges with others to prevent the experience of total aloneness. Although most clinicians are in consensus about the manifest behaviors and specific features of the borderline personality, Tolpin (1980) suggests that behavioral groupings and personality types may vary, and often seem to have little in common, except for their inaccessibility to treatment. Despite the blatant symptomatology in the borderline patient, these persons have developed a cohesive self and a nuclear self that is more structured, less subject to fragmentation, and more successfully organized than has the psychotically-organized individual.

In contrast to the prior two diagnostic entities, the narcissistic character disordered patient has established a nuclear self in early development. The structure of the self remains incomplete but is more resilient and less subject to fragmentation or disintegration anxiety than is the psychotic or borderline individual. The self reacts to narcissistic injury with only "temporary break-up, enfeeblement, or disharmony" (Kohut and Wolf 1978, p. 416).

Kohut divides this diagnostic entity into narcissistic personality and behavior disorders. The core of the self is essentially the same, although symptoms and behavior are dramatically different between these two typologies. Since both groups are more resilient, they are also more amenable to treatment.

The neurotic individual is significantly more structured than any of the other diagnostic groupings. In neurotic states, the self is cohesive, whole, and subject to minimal fragmentation or disintegration. The self is more or less firmly established in childhood, and is considered a secondary disorder of the self. Since the self is structurally undamaged, neurotics react to narcissistic injury with resilience. However, in times of stress the self may be temporarily inhibited from pursuing goals and ambitions. As conflicts are worked through in treatment, the self will be able to pursue creative–productive strivings (Kohut 1977).

CONCLUSION

Heinz Kohut and later self psychologists have introduced a new theory of human development, assessment, and treatment intervention to the field of psychoanalytic psychotherapy. The essential feature of this new theory is that all psychological disorders are considered to be disorders of self-esteem, self-cohesion, self-identity, and self-worth. Self psychological theory proposes that the development of the self is central to all developmental processes; that other psychological functions develop separately but in relation to self development. The self is considered at the core of all human functioning and, therefore, is a separate line of development from the line of the development of object relations.

Development takes place within an interactive matrix of mother and infant, in an environment of optimal gratification and frustration. At the onset of development, the infant connects with the mothering figure as a selfobject, one who is considered by the infant to be part of the self, or working in the service of the self. Kohut contends that selfobjects are important figures, who provide essential functions for all individuals throughout the human life cycle regardless of the degree, location, or intensity of the self pathology. These functions are synonymous with the three lines of development of the tripolar self, that is, the mirroring, the idealizing, and the twinship functions.

In addition, these functions mirror the needs and wishes of every individual but vary in degree and kind depending upon the state of the self. In more severe pathology, the need of an individual to merge with selfobjects or the need to isolate from selfobjects are included in this conceptualization. These five characteristics are categorized as character types.

The self psychological clinical syndromes, on the other hand, provide a typology of observable behaviors. These behavioral syndromes are also a result of unmet selfobject needs to the developing self in both infancy and childhood, and are evidenced in adult narcissistic difficulties. Together, the character types and the clinical syndromes are viewed as diagnostic and assessment tools. However, self psychology differs from other theories of assessment and treatment insofar as these tools are not considered reliable in and of themselves. Only after an extended period of treatment, and after a positive self/selfobject transference has developed, can a reliable assessment be made. The nature, the location, and the intensity of the selfobject needs in the transference provide the most reliable assessment measure. The character types and the clinical syndromes provide further information for such an assessment.

Thus, from a self psychological perspective, differential diagnosis and assessment stem from the transference and are always regarded as measures of self disorders, or narcissistic difficulties of all individuals. Narcissistic disorders range from neurotic to psychotic states of the self. Differential diagnosis is based on the degree of self-cohesion, self-worth, self-identity, and self-esteem of patients in treatment.

In summary, narcissistic disorders are a part of the human condition. Whereas all individuals have some degree of difficulty with self-esteem regulation and self-worth, the degree of this difficulty is reflected in the degree of psychological difficulties experienced. Narcissistic character disorders are in the lower range of self disorders, as are the borderline and psychotic conditions.

Individuals who experience these difficulties will be more subject to narcissistic injury, or injury to self-cohesion, than will individuals who do not exhibit this degree of functional and behavioral pathology. Thus, Kohut and his colleagues have provided the field of psychoanalysis with a nonpejorative and human theory of development and treatment, which has become very useful to contemporary psychotherapists.

3

The Treatment Process

Susan Donner

The recognition that there is frequently a great deal of leeway in the degree of concordance between one's theoretical base and the therapeutic actions one chooses has been remarked on by many in the psychotherapeutic field (Henderson 1988, Stern 1985). For some disparity is a sign of positive flexibility. For Kohut the disparity between what he thought his patients needed and what drive theory dictated confronted him with an untenable misalliance. His solution was to revise basic assumptions of psychoanalytic theory (Kohut 1971, 1977, 1984). Because the therapeutic directives that emanated from classical drive theory resonated poorly with the psychological realities that his patients presented, Kohut (1979) formulated a new theory, self psychology.

Though self psychology preserved features from its parent theory, it also broke with it particularly around implications for therapeutic intervention. Above all, Kohut organized a theory intended to increase listening skills and to hone the therapist's and patient's ability to focus in on "experience near" (Kohut 1980,

p. 485) phenomena in the clinical encounter. Self psychology takes as its therapeutic arena of concern patients' subjective experiences and their meanings. Efforts are aimed at the process of entering that domain with the client. Theory serves primarily as a guide to the process. In self psychology theory is more a handmaiden to practice than the other way around. Consequently, all the major constructs within self psychology theory lend themselves easily to a translation into aspects of a coherent therapeutic approach. Because the theory has been discussed in an earlier chapter, only its implication for treatment will be dealt with here.

Though not exclusively so, most theory in self psychology has been explicated within an analytic framework. Although the goals, the intensity of transference, and some of the tools differ between analysis and psychotherapy (Elson 1986), many self psychologists have recognized the relevance of the theory to psychotherapy (Kohut 1987, Ornstein and Ornstein 1984). This chapter deals exclusively with treatment as it applies to psychotherapy.

As the self is seen as the supraordinant psychic configuration within self psychology, treatment in the most general sense addresses the state of the self. This includes the extent, both structurally and experientially, to which the self is whole, cohesive, vital, authentic, in conflict, continuous in time and space, and is able to pursue its goals and beliefs. All symptoms (unless behaviorally induced), developmental deficits, intrapsychic conflicts, and relational and behavioral difficulties are attributed to underlying self issues in need of a new developmental impetus. A disruption in the growth of the self is held to be the fundamental and overriding determinant of the problem.

TREATMENT SUMMARY

The process of treatment that focuses on the self and how aspects of the environment are experienced proceeds as follows: catalyzed by a connection of empathy between client and therapist, the client's thwarted selfobject needs are reactivated. These needs take as their focus one or more selfobject transferences to the therapist. Through a three-step process constituting empathic interpretations, acceptance understanding, and explanation (A. Ornstein 1986), the frustrated needs of the self via the selfobject transference become apparent. Within the evolving psychotherapeutic matrix, the client's selfobject needs meet with both optimal "frustration" (Kohut 1984, p. 70) and "optimal responsiveness" (Bacal 1985, p. 202). These responses promote a process of "transmuting internalizations" (Kohut 1987, p. 124) that enables a client to draw more successfully on internal functions that previously could only be provided externally. More cohesive, flexible, vital, and enduringly self-regulating structures emerge from the process of transmitting internalizations. This enables the individual to live in a less archaic selfobject milieu that more lastingly sustains the self from within and without (Kohut 1984, p. 66). One's ability to pursue what is uniquely important to oneself is buoyed by a deeper self acceptance, self ownership, and empathy toward the self.

The preceding explanation of treatment, what Kohut (1984) called cure and Elson (1986) calls healing, is a summary of the unfolding therapeutic process. Unfortunately, this theory is obscured, like many, by unnecessarily cumbersome terminology. The remaining task of this chapter will be to expand on the steps outlined in the summary and to make the relevant concepts more linguistically accessible.

EMPATHY AS A THERAPEUTIC TOOL

Empathy was the therapeutic tool first mentioned because of its centrality in a self psychological psychotherapeutic approach. The place of empathy within the theory of self psychology is perhaps one of the most controversial (Kohut 1984, D. Berger 1987). In my opinion, it is also one of the most crucial. In any therapy in which relationship serves as the crucible for change, empathy is imperative, as it is the connection that sparks the relationship. Without empathy there is no meaningful relationship and no access to experiences and data by which the self becomes known. Only empathy can offer a convincingly safe invitation to a meeting attended by patient and therapist in which the subjective world of the patient creatively unfolds. As such, empathy is a prerequisite for all other therapeutic interventions.

The establishment of an empathic bond is descriptively simple but operationally an achievement. It requires an active and open listening stance on the therapist's part. Equally necessary is a willingness to accept, without judgment and narrowly defined bias, the patient's subjectively processed views on reality. Such views must not be challenged but taken on their own terms.

What the therapist hears from "placing himself imaginatively into the center of the patient's inner world" (empathy) (Ornstein and Ornstein 1984, p. 4) should be continuously reflected back to the client. The tentatively offered understanding is given expectantly, carrying the message that only the client can confirm it or reject it. The client is then viewed as the most accurate source of understanding. Repeated experiences of feeling empathetically heard and understood increase the power that the patient invests in the therapeutic process and more specifically in the therapist. Though there are always major social components that contribute to power dynamics between therapist and patient (Dvorak-Peck 1987), here I am referring to the power that adheres to a selfobject transference. Once feeling understood, the patient invests the therapist with the ability to respond to his or her particular constellation of unmet developmental needs. The therapist is imbued with the parts of the self that cannot successfully function autonomously. A selfobject transference is thus established via empathy.

Before addressing more specifically the therapeutic implications of the selfobject transference, let us consider other ways in which empathy serves a therapeutic function. What does the putting of one's self into the subjective experience of the other offer? On a level that can be trite or profound, it allows the recipient of empathy to feel understood in a way that connects the person to others. Though not a self psychologist, Carl Rogers (1987) succinctly gets to the essence when he states: ". . . it [empathy] brings even the most frightened client into the human race. If a person can be understood, he or she belongs" (p. 181).

Empathy is a message, and a particularly powerful one when coming from a selfobject (Bacal 1985), that one is a human among humans. The most disavowed thoughts and affects previously held by a client to be out of the realm of "normal" or acceptable human experience can, in the context of empathy, be brought into the thinkable sphere of self experience. As such, an immersion in a therapeutic relationship characterized by sustained empathy can increase ownership of self and expand the range of self experiences that fall within one's concept of humanness. This achievement inevitably expands one's ability to view others through a more empathetic lens.

In life and in therapy, empathy or its lack establishes in part the parameters around which one's internal world can be incorporated into a relational context. Every therapist has encountered individuals who treat their inner life as foreign, forbidden territory, off limits to themselves and certainly to others. This is not necessarily repression of particular material though it may be, but it often represents a characteristic lack of permission within a relationship to draw upon internal realities as a legitimate means of exchange. When the private domain of inner experience cannot be shared, it tends to be excluded from what one assumes to be common human experience and contributes to psychic isolation (Stern 1985). The isolation extends both inwardly and outwardly. Empathy can alter such a patient's relationship to his or her inner life and in doing so frequently renders it available to intimate encounters with others. Over time a patient experiences hundreds of mini-exchanges in which inner meanings, superficial and deep, take shape and empathetically reconnect and connect the patient with the self and with the therapist. For many patients a new set of possibilities arises in terms of being with self and being with the other.

ESTABLISHMENT OF
A SELFOBJECT TRANSFERENCE

The most pivotal role accorded to empathy in the treatment scenario of self psychology is that it is the glue that establishes, holds, and rebuilds when fractured, the selfobject transference. The establishment of a selfobject transference is the second step in the process of treatment referred to in the initial summary.

The reactivation of a patient's unique selfobject constellation in the form of a selfobject transference to the therapist is the sine qua non of therapeutic work within the self psychological framework. It is crucial that this "contextual unit" (Schwaber 1980) be established, and that as a part of the "immediacy of the surround," the therapist becomes empowered to contribute to a shaping of problematic aspects of self experience (p. 215). Once the selfobject transference is in sway, the patient, by psychic necessity, will ask the therapist in a variety of differential mediated ways to function as part of the patient's missing self (Baker and Baker 1987). What is asked for and the ways in which it is asked for will constitute the most therapeutically useful aspects of the selfobject transference.

The functions the patient looks to the therapist to provide, usually out of awareness, will most likely be related to one or more of the three major selfobject states that Kohut has described as inherent in human development. They are the grandiose exhibitionistic self—the need to experience narrowing, affirmation, and acceptance, the idealized parent imago—the need to merge with the calm, strength, wisdom, and greatness of others, and the alterego twinship—the need to feel that one is like another.

The major therapeutic task of the therapist, achieved with the active aid of the patient, is to establish a dialogue in which the selfobject transference can be experienced and understood. For the therapist this means not interfering with the manifestations of the transference but simply allowing them to be until such time as they are more firmly established and thus can be convincingly dealt with. For different therapists this poses different challenges. For example, some find quite threatening the demonstration of idealizing needs on a patient's part. When confronted with externally unrealistically exalted views of himself/herself, many therapists are too quick to deflate the patient's overevaluations and to remind the patient of one's many limitations. Because it isn't primarily about the therapist in the first place and more important, because it is a sign of a pressing need on the patient's part, to do so is a therapeutic mistake. The idealization will diminish as the

patient better understands the need and has begun to develop
alternatives for dealing with it.

INTERPRETATION

Once the conditions have been created for a therapeutic dialogue
in which the selfobject transference has developed, the next therapeutic goal is an interpretive one (Kohut 1984, A. Ornstein 1986).
Empathetic interpretation remains within self psychology a fundamental therapeutic tool. Though it shares this therapeutic mandate
with a more classical drive theory approach, there are also important differences in the uses of interpretation that differentiate it
from a classical approach.

Unlike those offered within the formulations of drive theory,
interpretations are targeted not so much at conflictual drive derivatives as at selfobject needs, defenses, and manifestations. Interpretations of the reactivated selfobject needs within the treatment
relationship are the focus of the work rather than the vicissitudes
of aggressive and libidinal instincts.

The manner in which interpretations are given, as well as the
content at which they are aimed, also are a point of divergence for
self psychology. Interpretations are not authoritatively visited
upon passive/receptive patients. The patient is assumed to be the
expert on himself/herself and as such is not viewed as a source
resistance (Kohut 1987). This does not eliminate the necessity for
recognizing defensive stances on the patient's part or for working
toward important experiences that are not within awareness. It
simply is an attitude that affirms that ultimately the therapist and
the patient are partners in a process and that the relative approxi-
mate correctness or incorrectness of an interpretation can only be
ascertained from within the patient. It also implies a recognition of
the fact that as a patient feels more understood, the momentum of
unfolding material will accelerate.

This approach to interpretation is an empowering one for
patients. An interpretation is always made as a tentative statement
and never as a declaration of fact. The tentative statement is often
followed by a question that conveys to the patient some variation

on a theme such as "Is this correct? Does this sound like what you have been getting at? Is that a helpful way of putting it? How might you say it that gets more accurately at what you are experiencing?" Not only does this checking back place the power to decipher inner meaning where it belongs—with the person whose subjective meaning it is—it also reinforces an interpersonal process in which one person who has been given power by the other says in effect, "'You can come to trust the validity of what comes from within you on its own terms. You can, over time, know what is within you, claim as your own your thoughts, feelings, and reactions, and know that they are as real as anything else is real." The affirmation of and authority over one's own inner experience is developmentally a part of the formation of self. Within therapy, interpretations can be offered in a way that powerfully facilitates a process that for many has come to a halt.

Another aspect that differentiates the ideas about and uses of interpretation in self psychology from other psychodynamic approaches is the conviction that not all aspects of interpretation have to be operative in order for them to be therapeutically effective (Kohut 1984). The third element of interpretation, that of explanation in which meanings are extended to include genetic components, may not always occur. Even without explanation—which is recommended wherever possible—structure building can occur. Empathetic acceptance and understanding can sometimes alone contribute to an appreciable shift in selfobject need, propel previously thwarted idiosyncratically determined strivings toward health, and increase one's ability to take an empathetic stance toward the self.

A belief within self psychology that all human beings struggle inherently toward health colors the manner in which interpretations are made. However disturbing the behavior, however outrageous the demand or unproductive the defense, all are viewed as a necessary attempt to preserve and protect a fragile self trying to survive and to find the best ways at its disposal to do so. All are interpreted accordingly. This does not mean that either client or therapist is spared from coming to grips with painful experiences that must be endured. It does mean that interpretations do not confront clients with a view of themselves that is inherently destructive. Neither are patients viewed as saddled with excessive biological drives pitting them inevitably against the superior constructed demands of society. In spite of the fact that many interpretations will be disturbing to patients, they are offered in a framework that in its totality offers a more assuring view of human nature than one in which we are doomed inevitably.

Empathetic interpretations consist of three components that are intermingled in a spiraling fashion as treatment proceeds (Ornstein and Ornstein 1984). They are acceptance, understanding, and explanation (A. Ornstein 1986).

ACCEPTANCE

Acceptance is self-explanatory. However, the simplicity of the concept should not be confused with ease of realization. Acceptance implies that everything that the patient experiences and expresses must be treated moment to moment as that which simply is. Condemnation, judgment, confrontation, and externally imposed views of health all militate against the achieving of true acceptance. They also catapult the therapist out of an immersion in the inner life of the patient and place him/her in a more foreign position, that of an external observer.

Because none of us is free from bias and we probably engage in judgments many times daily, creating a mode of genuine acceptance necessitates vigilance in our clinical work. In understanding the place of acceptance in treatment, it is important, however, to be clear that it does not connote the condoning of any particular behavior or actions on a patient's part though some patients may regard acceptance as such. If, however, the therapist confuses acceptance of inner experiences with the approval of particular actions, permission will become a substitute for interpretation. So too will unjustified authority take the place of truly empowering and enabling therapeutic processes.

Acceptance is conveyed by several means: an active listening stance, reflective responses that let the client know what has been heard and that closely duplicate the language and content of what the client has actually said, tone of voice, facial expression, body language, and also attention to how the expression of certain material influences the patient's state of mind.

For most patients acceptance alone is not enough. Though to be able to see that what is, *is*, is an achievement, it is incomplete. The understanding of what *is* requires that a context be constructed around it in order to help it make sense. To state that one is sad, for example, usually means to be sad about something and the something calls for some exploration.

UNDERSTANDING

Understanding manifests itself as a bringing together, in a shared manner, affectively meaningful knowledge about the patient that illuminates in the present something about the patient's experience that has previously remained without a point of reference. The tentatively stated understanding, such as "It seems you became sadder as we began to talk about terminating," will be followed, if close enough to what the patient is actually experiencing, by an affirmation offered in the form of a quickening evolution of related material.

Understanding frequently strengthens the first stage of an interpretation—that of acceptance. This is most powerfully true when selfobject needs experienced in the transference are understood. Adult patients are easily shamed by the nature of their selfobject wishes and the acceptance of them comes reluctantly. When discovered in their earlier forms, and although they arise out of normal developmental imperatives, patients may tend to view them as childish and unreasonable. This is particularly true when they are attached to a therapist with whom they believe they should not experience such things.

Marianne

Consider the following example: Marianne, a bright professional woman in her early thirties who had been seen for a little over two years began to discuss the fact that between sessions she rarely thought about what we had talked about during our sessions. She further confessed, and confession was her style, that she did not want to think about our exchanges except when we were in session. This was an involved bright woman for whom therapy had come to mean a great deal. I also had ample reason to believe this was not a reflection of her lack of interest or disappointment in what was happening. I accepted what she said with curiosity and took great care not to reinforce her characteristically negative view— that perhaps she was a "bad client" unmotivated and someone in whom I would not remain interested. Because she always attributed the most self-effacing motives to almost everything she experienced, I was concerned that she first accept what she was describing and then be able to understand it. It was not until I offered a potential understanding of what this was about that she could accept the legitimacy of her wish not to work actively outside of the session.

Her need, oversimplified here, that explained her perplexing behavior, was also for her a source of shame. Actually only the explaining stage of our interpretation ultimately relieved her of the intensity of her shame. Though her intense selfobject transference to me had elements of both the idealizing and mirroring needs, it was the mirroring needs that were most compelling. Marianne, initially quite estranged from herself, came to treasure (and sometimes dread) our dialogue and looked to me to help her express and make real some of the most basic parts of her self. Whatever she experienced that could not be shared or confirmed in my presence lacked conviction and validity. To experience alone anything that she tried to name or identify also frightened her and, worse, exposed her to a lonely emptiness. The process of understanding all this confronted her with other vulnerability, however. As she began to put together a picture of the way in which she experienced needing me, her sense of autonomy was disturbed. A usual response was to tell me it made her feel like a baby, and she didn't much like the baby. Gradually her wish to feel validated in her inner experiences and her need for help in making them less overwhelming became more tolerable to her. They began to make sense. Equally important, she could accept them as needs that at one point or another mark all human beings.

The gradual understanding significantly softened her initial disdain for her need as well as her behavior of not thinking about the substance of our work outside of the therapy sessions. She came to accept it, not only because I could accept it, but because together we could understand it.

The intensity of Marianne's selfobject needs for basic mirroring also lessened as it was understood. There seemed to be something in the understanding, as well as in mirroring that I did provide in reality, that loosened her own abilities to provide more of this for herself. She increasingly processed for herself reactions occurring outside of our sessions and proudly began to be more in charge of her own psychological reality. Accompanying the change was a shift in her desire to ask others in her life to know her and respond to her, where true intimacy had previously not been very present.

EXPLANATION

The final aspect of the empathetic interpretive process is that of explanation. This is not something that occurs in every treatment course. Kohut (1984) in his last writing about cure saw this stage as enhancing the other two but, though ultimately preferable, not necessary in every case.

An explanation deepens that which has been understood. Though it is the level of exchange that is the most cognitively mediated and most distant from the immediacy of a patient's present experience, it is a means of access to fuller, more meaningful insight into the nature of one's difficulties (A. Ornstein 1986). An explanation puts into a dynamic and earlier genetic developmental context in which the present meaning began to evolve, that which is understood about the patient. Daniel Stern, a psychoanalyst and infant researcher with an appreciation of self psychology, maintains that literal points of origin can never be found. He suggests for integrative purposes that patients be assisted to discover/create a "narrative point of origin" (Stern 1985, p. 258). The narrative point of origin, always subjectively real, serves as a genetic developmental metaphor that helps organize a context in which earlier visions of present needs and difficulties can be appreciated.

Without a genetic explanation Marianne's attitude toward her identified selfobject needs manifest in her reluctance to reflect on anything outside of my presence remained a source of painful embarrassment and self disgust. Over time, however, she alternatively empathetically and punitively reclaimed within herself a frightened, confused, and lonely little girl who used to panic in the face of any strong emotional experience. Though anger and envy were the hardest to allow, almost any emotion allowed to see the light of day was perceived as a threat to important selfobject ties.

As she looked back in the face of wondering why she needed me around to own almost any of her feelings, she could rarely recall any instances in which she was asked what she thought or felt. Times of grief, expectation, disappointment, and shame were unshared both within the family and between members. Attitudes and feelings were proscribed and prescribed. In the midst of a large family that described itself as close, Marianne felt isolated from herself and others. Family homeostasis also, in retrospect, seemed fragile and her parents, particularly her mother, were overburdened. Marianne experienced her emotions as threatening the balance both within herself and within the family. As best she could, she conspired to have as few emotions as possible. The result was long periods in which she felt emotionally deadened and other shorter periods in which she experienced threatening emotional upheaval.

Bit by bit we began a process of linking that which she sometimes felt intensely with me and dared not feel alone to events and relationships in the past in which she had had fleeting responses that seemed too threatening to herself and to her family. As the lonely, frightened child appeared more and more in the sessions and began to want what she wanted and feel legitimized, understood, though frequently frustrated in the wanting, Marianne became more emotionally alive and available to herself. Furthermore, as she grieved that loss of what she hadn't had, she developed empathy toward aspects of herself that previously she simply wanted to discard and deny.

Marianne moved in the explaining phase in ways not open to her in the understanding phase. She not only understood what she needed but understood a context in which those needs made sense. Understanding how her particular wishes, anxieties, and defenses against them came to be made them much more acceptable. In a way, it allowed her to become a better mother to herself.

Although I did not fundamentally fulfill Marianne's needs or compensate for what she had never received, together we were able to treat her needs differently. Consequently, she could claim what was and had been, mourn what was lost, and most significantly, alter her relationship to herself. Though the explanatory aspects of our interpretations are not to be entirely credited, they did release a momentum that the others did not.

ENVIRONMENTAL AND SOCIAL FACTORS

Rarely included in an explanation of genetic antecedents, but always in fact shaping the meaning system of a patient, is a myriad of environmental and social factors. Any genetic reconstruction that aims at deepening one's understanding of an empathy toward self should attend to the ways in which gender, race, ethnicity, and class have shaped, most particularly within the immediacy of the family, the evolution of self experience. Such factors are not extraneous and in fact when sensitively listened for have very "experience-near" implications (Donner 1988). Not to include them is to limit the scope of meaningful understanding and insight.

EVOLUTION OF STRENGTHENED
PSYCHIC STRUCTURES

As mentioned in the initial summary, one product of a selfobject transference within the psychotherapeutic relationship is the establishment of new or more solid internal psychic structures. The functions invested in the selfobject transference must be internalized as part of the self. Concomitantly, the patient's ability to meet his or her needs with more sustaining and mature selfobject ties develops. Both of these evidence new structural capabilities.

Strengthened selfstructures arise in treatment by means of what Kohut (1984) referred to as "transmitting internalizations" (p. 4). Functions needed by the self but provided by the other, if done in a manner consonant with the very particular needs of the self, are transmuted into the self and become part of intrapsychic functioning. When internalized, these functions are shaped by the client in a process of assimilation and accommodation, rather than interjected whole as though something belonging to someone else is taken in unchanged. Such functions include the ability to regulate and organize one's own emotional life, the monitoring and soothing of tension and stress down to tolerable levels, the ability to energize one's own ambitions, goals, and values, and the ability to regulate one's own self-esteem.

Most self psychologists conceptualize transmuting internalizations as occurring almost exclusively at times of optimal frustration (Kohut 1984). Howard Bacal (1985) challenges the notion that change is the inheritor exclusively of frustration and offers the concept that change occurs also as a result of "optimal responsiveness" (p. 202). The term includes responses both frustrating *and* gratifying. Because I believe that much that occurs in therapy is inherently gratifying in a growth-producing way, I am including the concept of optimal responsiveness as part of the change process.

The material that follows is an exploration of the way in which optimal frustration contributes to change. Optimal frustration is not something that a therapist needs to deliberately introduce into the treatment situation. Frustration is inherently part of any human relationship and the therapeutic one is not exempt. At the most obvious level, therapy is frustrating because it cannot compensate for patients' previously unmet needs. Equally significant is the fact that empathy is always imperfect.

If the channel of empathy that resonates between patient and therapist is the catalyst for inducing the selfobject transference, its inevitable failures disrupt the transference. If the disruption is not overly traumatic, it can be constructively managed to facilitate change.

The concentrated "intuneness" of the therapist with the patient's psychological world inevitably falls short. Something is said or neglected to be said that breaks the client's feeling of being understood. Lack of attentiveness, external judgments, jarring confrontations, or constructions of the patient's experiences that are badly misconstrued all occur. The patient is then confronted, hopefully in manageable doses, with the reality that the therapist is not a part of the self but quite outside and that the therapist is not the wished-for omniscient power. If the ensuing disappointment is not too great and the task in which the patient is then forced to manage on his or her own not too far from a possible grasp, then the patient, as children do in normal development, will draw upon the self to provide the function that previously had been expected of the therapist. For example, with some externally provided experiences of being understood, in the face of an uncharacteristic failure on the part of the therapist a patient might well be able to go on and understand him- or herself in a way the therapist could not. Toward the end of treatment with Marianne, she was able to say to me in a manner that demonstrated a new ability, "No, that isn't quite what I mean. This is what it was like for me. . . ." When my statements of understanding were off the mark she recognized it. More important, she could then go on and state for herself a level of understanding that I had been unable to offer. She stretched where I failed.

Failures in empathy also provide an opportunity for optimal responsiveness. The way in which a therapist handles such failures, whether objectively or subjectively real, is paramount. When the empathetic break occurs, both patient and therapist may find themselves faced with what seems like an inexplicably intense response. The response may be anger, intense disappointment, actively devaluating behavior, a sense of deflation, or dramatic and sudden withdrawal. The intensity of the response to something that observationally may seem quite minor serves as a clue that the selfobject tie has been disrupted and that the event has evoked something psychically meaningful. This is an opportunity to discover with readily available affect something very significant about the self. Usually this means an opportunity to learn something about a patient's selfobject needs, which have suddenly been pushed into awareness. Acceptance, understanding, and explanation may converge at such therapeutic junctures. Empathetic breaks may pave the way for some of the most meaningful empathetic interpretations, which, when appropriately offered, become part of the most effective aspects of the armamentarium of optimal responsiveness.

Another form of optimal responsiveness involves the meaning to a patient of having responses to empathetic failure met with a genuine attempt on the therapist's part to understand instead of being met with defensiveness, anger, blame, belittling, or withdrawal, so frequently the case in life. That empathetic failures occur is not likely to be a surprise for patients, at least consciously. No one is ever the recipient or bearer of perfect empathy. What may render the experience of being misunderstood intolerable is that the reactive disappointment, deflation, or anger may find no room for expression within one's important relational matrix. The developmental exclusion of such normal responses from a relational context obviates the ability to process one's own experience, validate it, and move on. A tension is created between one's authentic emotional life and the felt needs of the other upon whom one is dependent, to whom one is attached. Marian Elson (1986) refers to this as the "trauma of unshared emotion" (p. 45). This readies the stage for a relational propensity in which others are seen as uncaring and the needs and responses of the self are viewed as burdensome and dangerous. Repeated experience in therapy in which one's responses to disappointment are treated as legitimate and further understood, I believe potentiate structure building as much as "optimal frustrations." If self psychology holds to the connection that a developmental thrust is within us all waiting only for well-matched environmental releasers, then it is contradictory to assume that only correct dosages of frustration push us ahead.

An incident with Marianne illustrates the change inducing convergence of optimal frustration and optimal responsiveness in the face of an empathetic failure. The critical incident in her therapy followed a fairly lengthy therapeutic history of faithfully attended weekly sessions. Up until that time Marianne had been unable to question the validity of almost anything I said or did and conversely questioned the validity of almost everything she did. ("I shouldn't be feeling this" was a very typical response and not one intended to disarm any anticipated responses on my part.)

The actual event was that I did not show up for an appointment. I made a mistake in the appointment time and was elsewhere when she came to my office. Her initial response was one in which she feigned my innocence and her blame. Guilty and unsure of the factual elements of the misunderstanding, I let her be the one who misunderstood. I let her protect me and take the blame.

What ensued was a missed appointment followed by very obvious emotional inaccessibility on her part. After our first conversation, initiated by me, about the missed appointment, she dropped the subject. Her demeanor, however, was changed. I had begun to reconstruct in my own mind what had happened and was sure that I had allowed her to assume responsibility for something I in fact had done. I commented on how she seemed quite different, mentioned the missed appointment, and further commented that we both had quickly allowed her to be the party who had mistaken the time. As I inquired as to what she might be feeling about this as well as observing that she seemed withdrawn, she made what seemed to me, in the face of much success together, a remarkable statement. She said she had considered saying nothing and never coming back! I registered her statement (not easily) and inquired about the way in which she felt let down and angry. She had talked of anger many times previously but it never appeared in live form between us before.

The missed appointment was bad enough, though forgivable, she told me. What seemed not forgivable was that I would save myself at her expense! Beyond feelings of being misused and manipulated that any patient would have under those circumstances was Marianne's all-too-familiar pattern of denying her own experience to meet the perceived needs of those in her family, something they seemed to let her easily do. For her, my failure in empathy was not really the missed appointment or even just that I let her take the responsibility for it. More germane was the fact that I had done so in the face of painfully shared knowledge that she had reluctantly entrusted to me. I had reason to know what my action might mean to her and I had acted in spite of it. She felt betrayed and that I had re-enacted with her a deeply dreaded and very emotionally familiar scenario.

The event and its multilayered meanings dominated our work together and reverberated throughout her therapy for a long time to come. Though the event and my initial handling of it went beyond what I would consider optimal frustration and optimal empathetic failure, it happened within the context of a strong therapeutic relationship and a strong selfobject transference that was able to absorb the shock of it. My owning up to my part and a genuine concern and interest in accepting, understanding, and explaining the intensity of her response constituted a restorative optimal responsiveness in the face of a serious empathetic failure. The level of empathetic "intuneness" was enhanced on my part and on hers toward herself. Our work deepened. Marianne's "trauma of unshared emotions" became, as we explored why leaving had been her only initially envisioned response, a more central and powerful part of our work. In time her emotional life, regardless of its affective valence, became a more empowering source in the pursuit of what was important to her.

CONCLUSION

It is important to consider that although interpretation occupies a central role in the therapeutic approach of self psychology (Kohut 1977, 1980, 1984, A. Ornstein 1986) it is clear that it is not its only tool or even as central as Kohut once thought it to be. Certainly insight is not valued as the primary vehicle for change (Baker and Baker 1987). Interpretation is only potent when offered within "the creation of a new kind of experience . . . within the transference relationship" (p. 1). Though the idea of "corrective emotional experience" proposed by Franz Alexander has been vociferously discredited, in Kohut's final work he did not feel a need to distance himself from the concept. He made it very apparent that he did not believe in a corrective emotional experience in the way Alexander envisioned it. Yet therapy constructed upon self psychological understanding does offer a different kind of experience to both client and therapist and extends what Carolyn Saari (1986) refers to as an internalization of a new edition of what one takes as possible between self and other (p. 171). Within self psychology this also means firming up the self in the new edition of selfobject relationships. Kohut (1984) himself ended his career by saying that if he was charged with the following: ". . . that I have finally shown my true colors . . . and demonstrated that I believe in the curative effect of the 'correctional emotional experience' . . . so be it!" (p. 78).

PART II

APPLYING
SELF PSYCHOLOGY
IN DIFFERENT
AGE GROUPS

4

Children

Thomas M. Young

To help children with emotional problems, the therapist must understand both the significance of himself and that of others in the child's environment as selfobjects. This understanding guides the therapist's use of himself in the treatment relationship with the child and also leads to interventions designed to correct or at least alleviate specific forms of empathic failure within the child's current selfobject milieu.

A selfobject, according to Kohut, is a psychological construct. It refers to the experience we all have in certain relationships where the other person (object) fills in for our self by providing us with certain essential psychological functions. The other person may provide us with a sustaining, joyful, mirroring response to our ambitions, embrace or envelop us as a calming source of idealized strength, or supply us with an affirming feeling of belonging, of essential sameness. These relationships supply psychological functions that eventually we are able to provide for ourselves most, though never all, of the time. Selfobject relationships also are special relationships in a psychological sense because it is within them that we learn how to provide these psychological functions for ourselves.

In this chapter, selfobject relationships are viewed as the formative interpersonal context for the development and disturbance of emotions in children. Correlatively, the treatment relationship is viewed as a selfobject relationship also, through which arrested or distorted emotional development may be corrected.

SELF PSYCHOLOGY

Initially, Kohut articulated a conception of the self as bipolar, one pole of which harbors the person's ambitions, the other his ideals. Ambitions and ideals are connected by a "tension arc of psychological activity" through which skills are developed from basic talent that, in turn, makes possible the further expression of ambitions and pursuit of ideals. "This tension arc is the dynamic essence of the complete, nondefective self; it is a conceptualization of the structure whose establishment makes possible a creative, productive, fulfilling life" (Kohut 1984, pp. 4–5). He developed this conception as an alternative to the tripartite (id, ego, superego) structural model of the mind set forth by Freud.

Kohut developed this alternative conception in order to improve his empathic understanding of his analysands. He referred to it as a more "experience-near" metapsychology for understanding complex mental states. If an individual's interpersonal environment facilitates the pursuit of his ideals through the development of his talent into skills that are applauded and rewarded, he experiences himself as cohesive in space and continuous in time: vigorous, harmonious, joyful, and productive. On the other hand, if the individual's environment does not facilitate this pursuit, the development of the self suffers. And the specific nature of the suffering appears to be closely related to the specific nature of the environment's failure to facilitate the process.

In the context of conducting psychoanalyses, Kohut witnessed the specific nature of his patients' suffering through their attempts to use the relationship with him as an opportunity to reactivate their need for the specific responses others in their environment had failed to provide them in the past. Through his own empathic immersion in the complex psychological life of his patients, he had the repeated experience of their making use of him as if he were an extension of themselves; either as a source of joyful, self-sustaining mirroring of their ambitions or as a calming, self-soothing source of idealized strength. Later on he distinguished a third way, as a self-validating source of essential likeness and belonging (Kohut 1977, 1984). His patients' attempts to use him for mirroring, soothing, organizing, validating, strengthening, and inspiring themselves was so powerful that they seemed to overlook his separateness from them in the process. It was the force and persistence of their efforts to use him as an extension of themselves that led him to develop the term selfobject. With it he could focus his thinking on the role of selfobjects in the development of the selves of his patients and in the development of their emotional disorders. Correlatively, he could understand more clearly how his role as a selfobject in the transference aspects of the therapeutic relationship contributed to the success of the treatment.

It is the selfobject relationships that are essential for the development of a cohesive, vigorous, joyful, and productive self. These relationships are with other people: parents, aunts, uncles, grandparents, siblings, teachers, coaches, friends, neighbors. Collectively, Kohut referred to them as the selfobject "milieu," "matrix," or "surround."

Each type of selfobject relationship corresponds to one of the three basic needs of the bipolar self. "Mirroring" selfobject relationships involve people who reflect back in a joyful, sustaining way our (frequently grandiose) ambitions for ourselves. "Idealizing" selfobject relationships are ones in which we merge, psychologically speaking, with others in terms of what they represent for us as ideals, and in doing so, share in their (idealized) strength. "Twinship" selfobject relationships involve people who, because they are like us, provide us with an affirming sense of essential sameness and validate our sense of belonging. While it may be tempting to equate mirroring with mother–child, idealizing with father–child, and twinship with peer relationships, that is unnecessarily limiting. Any important relationship can become the vehicle for any of these selfobject functions at any stage of psychological development. Indeed, this is one of the therapist's tasks: to discern which type of selfobject response the patient needs at which point in treatment.

While it is important to understand how selfobject relationships can firm up each pole of the self and promote the continuing development of skill from talent, it is important also to envision how failures in these selfobject relationships can lead to the kinds of emotional disorders that require treatment. Mirroring failures can lead to feelings of enfeeblement rather than vitality. Idealizing failures can lead to feelings of fragmentation rather than self-control. And twinship failures can lead to feelings of estrangement and self-doubt rather than belonging and self-confidence.

So, for example, a relationship with someone who can understand our ambitions to master a particular task, achieve a goal, or be a certain way leaves us with a foundation of self-esteem, feeling firm and vibrant. In contrast, when just such a selfobject relationship is needed but not available, the result can be feelings of enfeeblement and depression.

Similarly, a relationship with someone whom we admire and look up to because of his or her competence, strength, and equanimity can leave us with a residual sense of strength, calm, and self-control. This may be especially important whenever we are facing a challenge to master a particularly arduous task or perform well at something new. In contrast, the absence of such a relationship when it is needed can result in our feeling weak and fragmented.

The third kind of selfobject relationship derives from the self's ever growing constellation of skills from talents and our need to experience the reassuring presence of someone else like us, that is, someone with whom we feel essentially alike in terms of what we can do. Having such a relationship can result in our feeling in harmony with ourselves and competent in the world. In contrast, the absence of such a relationship when it is needed can result in our feeling estranged and inept.

SELFOBJECT RELATIONSHIPS
AND THE DEVELOPMENT OF EMOTIONS

The explicit link between Kohut's psychology of the self and the development and disturbance of emotions in children is provided by Basch (1976, 1984). Drawing upon the work of Silvan Tomkins (1962–1963), Basch shows how affective behaviors in small children—autonomic or involuntary behavior—acquire order, organization, and meaning. This takes place through an interactive process between the child and his caretakers; it encompasses a rather extended period of time and a progressively broader range of situations and experiences as the child grows older. In this process, affects become emotions—"subjectively experienced states . . . always related to a concept of self vis-à-vis some particular situation" (Basch 1976, p. 768).

So, for example, the affective behavior classified as "distress–anguish" by Tomkins (crying, arched eyebrows, corners of the mouth turned down, tears and rhythmic sobbing) is viewed by Basch as signaling the child's "inability to organize [new] stimuli into meaningful patterns" (Basch 1976, p. 763). If the child's caretaker provides comfort by surrounding him in embrace and giving words and meaning to the affect ("Ooh, that barking doggy *scared* you, didn't he?"), the child begins to learn that his sense of self can be shaken by exposure to distressing new stimuli but that the affective arousal can be given a meaningful name (afraid) and that he can restore his sense of psychological balance when it is threatened in such situations by finding someone (a selfobject) who can understand his distress, help him organize what he has experienced, and make it meaningful.

We can think of emotion, then, as having three component parts: the affective (neocortical) foundation, the cognitive (cortical) overlay, and the self (psychological) as organizer of the experience. The latter is the most fundamental. For it is the inner life of the emerging nuclear self of the child that caretaking selfobjects must be able to grasp empathically. That is, they must be able to (1) understand the child's initial distress signal, (2) provide the right kind and amount of soothing, (3) find the appropriate words and images to give meaning to the stimuli, (4) introduce the explanation(s) with a timing and sequence suitable to the child's own rhythmicity and pattern of acquiring new information, and (5) remember the importance of the encounter over subsequent days, weeks, and months so that further self-strengthening communication can take place "spontaneously," for example, around dogs in picture books, dogs on television, dogs seen out the window, pretending to be a puppy dog . . . to continue the example. Several authors have described this kind of interactive, sequenced process based on infant observational research. The centrality of the infant's evolving active self in cuing the caretaking environment for the purpose of organizing affect into subjectively meaningful experience (emotion) has reinforced the importance of Kohut's emphasis on the empathic quality of self-selfobject relationships. Readers are referred to the work of Demos (1988), Lichtenberg (1983), and Stern (1985), for further details.

Since each child's emerging sense of self is unique, not every child will respond to dogs (or any other new stimuli he cannot organize meaningfully) in exactly the same way. Nor will every child benefit from the same response from the caretaking selfobject. The *empathically attuned* response is critical. It is, after all, understanding (by way of an empathic immersion in the child's emotional life) that makes it possible for us to comprehend the specific nature of his selfobject needs.

When the caretaking selfobject's responses are not attuned empathically, when understanding is absent, the child is in effect abandoned to the experience of self-threatening distress. His only recourse is to give it his own meaning, which, however distorted it may seem, also will be constructed in terms of his fragmenting sense of self. If the empathic failure endures, the child is deprived of an experience of acquiring self-regulating abilities. The child will react, then, to subsequent, similarly experienced stimuli in a manner designed to protect his precarious sense of self and restore some semblance of emotional balance, cohesion, and harmony. Some children will retreat emotionally into a depressed state or seek to soothe themselves through isolated and repetitive masturbatory or pain-inflicting behavior. Others will attempt to organize their experience by way of some bizarre (to us) incorporative fantasy. Still others may attempt to obliterate either the perceived cause of their distress or those who fail to organize it for them, or both. It is these behaviors of children that we refer to as signs of emotional disturbance. Arrests or disruptions in the development of the self yield disturbing sequelae of emotion and protective reaction that will be invoked whenever external stimuli threaten the child's sense of self in similar fashion.

This view of the development and disturbance of emotions in children is particularly relevant to children with neurocognitive insufficiencies (Palombo and Feigon 1984) or temperaments that lead to dissonance (Chess and Thomas 1984) in selfobject relationships. On the caretaker's side, understanding the child is made much more difficult. The capacity to provide the child with needed selfobject functions is diluted by uncertainty as to exactly what the child needs and how to provide it. On the child's side both the capacity for cuing caretakers and for assimilating their selfobject functions is diminished or distorted in ways that are enfeebling, estranging, and fragmenting.

IMPLICATIONS FOR CHILD TREATMENT

The treatment implications of the self-psychological perspective on the development and disturbance of emotions in children are twofold. It influences how the therapist uses himself as a selfobject and it guides the therapist's understanding of and intervention in the child's selfobject milieu.

Three case summaries are provided below. The first illustrates how the therapist discerns the child's needs in the context of the treatment relationship and uses himself to provide both understanding and needed selfobject functions. The second illustrates how one therapist can do so for a mother and child treated separately with the result that their relationship with each other becomes more attuned, particularly to the child's needs. The third illustrates how the therapist can attempt to modify a child's selfobject milieu in a systematic way so that it is predisposed to be more responsive to the child's needs as they arise.

For the child in treatment, the relationship with the therapist is an opportunity to reactivate arrested developmental needs for

mirroring, merger with an idealized source of strength, and twinship. The child's hope is that the therapist's empathic capacities
will lead to attuned responses to his needs and the acquisition of
self-regulating abilities. The therapist's task is to understand the
selfobject needs presented by the child and to respond accordingly.
Kohut (1984) stated that in his clinical work with adults, they
typically presented the least arrested or disturbed of the three basic
selfobject needs first, moving on to the more arrested or disturbed
one(s) later in the process of treatment.

I have found this to be true consistently in my own clinical
work with children. Some will seek a mirroring response initially,
telling or showing me aspects of themselves so that I can admire
their wonderfulness. This often serves as a prelude to their attacking me, my toys, and any accessible piece of office furniture
because they have been unable previously to secure an adequate
merger with a source of idealized strength. (For example, with a
parent who has moved out of the home or become emotionally
unavailable even though physically still present.) Others will seek a
merger with an idealized view of me initially as a prelude to
displaying their need for extended mirroring. (For example, by
attempting to avoid treatment, and, even when present, participat-
ing in listless, self-depreciating play, and complaining of boredom.) Still others will initiate a twinship type of relationship as a
prelude to seeking either one or both of the other types of relationships as treatment continues. (For example, by directing me first to
build or draw alongside them, as they are doing, but separately,
followed by the precipitation of a crisis of frustration from which I
am to rescue them.) Rather than interpret their behavior to them,
which seems to have a narcissistically injurious effect, I try to
grasp the statement they are making about themselves and their
selfobject needs and respond accordingly.

For example, if the child cheats or changes the rules in order
to win at a game we are playing, I compliment him on how clever
he is at figuring out a way to win. If the child begins to attack me
or himself physically, or even the toys and furniture, I restrain him
physically, saying only that I can tell he is feeling very bad but that
I am going to protect him, me, and the things in the room by
holding him. Or, if the child presents himself in a pseudo-adult

fashion, for example, by bringing food and announcing that we are going to have a picnic, I express delight, assume that we are going to have a twinship session, and proceed to converse with him about his day, his school, his friends, his pets, favorite toys, or what his room at home looks like, sharing rather freely whether I have or have had toys, pets, or experiences similar to his.

The challenge in each session is to grasp the inner meaning of the play for the child in terms of the selfobject function(s) he wants me to supply and then to supply them.

Micky

Micky, at age 7, had been seduced, along with two other boys his age, into sexually molesting play, by a 13-year-old boy in the neighborhood named Vinny. Vinny had held a toy pistol to Micky's head (that Micky thought was real at the time) while ordering him to suck his penis. This took place some three months after Micky's father, Lou, had separated from Micky's mother, Sally, and moved out of the family home.

Micky's behavior at home and in school became problematic. At home, he became both obstinate and physically aggressive with his mother; depressed and socially withdrawn from other children his age. He also began to soil his pants after going without a bowel movement for longer than usual. At school, he provoked and disobeyed his teacher, was unable to complete his assigned work, and initiated bathroom- and sex-talk with other children. His mother brought him to the Children's Center for treatment.

Lou and Sally, although amicable toward each other and very concerned in a collaborative way about Micky, were most striking in their relatively anergic, rather enfeebled presentations of themselves. They had never gotten legally married, although they had been living together for twelve years; they had "sort of wanted to have children" but had not planned to have Micky; their daily schedule of living seemed more the by-product of their assigned shifts at work than of any ideas they had about how they wanted to live. Micky, it was said, "had never had a schedule" and his visitation pattern varied as his parents' shifts changed.

In playing with me, Micky initially devoted himself in an intense very businesslike fashion to constructing a powerful vehicle out of Lego-like materials. My only assigned role was to build and mount the engines—the more, the better. Despite my compliance, he became visibly exhausted within thirty–forty minutes of working on this construction and he would ask to have his mother join us. This I allowed, even though she began to talk about herself and her problems rather than those of her son.

Following the third session, I asked Sally if she would like to see a colleague of mine for herself, a suggestion she welcomed eagerly and followed up on quickly. This conversation took place in Micky's presence. In the fourth session, Micky's vehicle-construction play became silly as he departed from constructing the vehicle and began building a wavering vertical tower. He then asked me if he could "karate chop" it. Since my understanding of his role for me was to supply motor-power-energy-strength to his play (and to him), I said, "Sure, like it was Vinny's dick?"

His facial response (surprised delight) was more expressive than any I had seen previously and he proceeded to destroy Vinny's dick, repeating the sequence several times during the fourth and fifth sessions. At points, he appeared to become overwhelmed by the force of his anger and I would hold him and tell him that we had to take care not to damage the toys or the walls. In the sixth session, he initiated play with molding clay in which he was attempting to construct a hydroelectric power station. My assigned roles were to (a) mold the generators, and (b) understand and appreciate how he cleverly maintained all the necessary connections of water pipe and electrical lines.

After three more sessions of this clay play, he suggested we build forts out of wooden blocks and staff them with army men. His instructions to me were that we were to be on the same side and that I should have a communication commander in continual radio contact with one of his commanders. He had *three* commanders, he explained, because of all his bazookas.

This vignette illustrates the pattern of the child beginning treatment in a fashion that initially seeks a mirroring response valuing his proficiency at building what was a rather complex vehicle. This, however, was but a prelude to his showing me (through his exhaustion) that what he was seeking was an idealized source of strength with whom he could merge, psychologically speaking, while he released his anger at the abuse he had experienced and worried about whether it had somehow changed him inside (the water pipes and electrical circuits) in some permanent way. Providing that selfobject function allowed him to pursue a less anxious, more age-appropriate game (the forts and army men) that began to establish the dominance of his command over his self-fragmenting rage.

> The accuracy of this interpretation of events seemed borne out when in the sixteenth session, just prior to his leaving for a week of overnight camp, he saw that I had an ace bandage on my ankle. When he asked about it, I told him that I had sprained it while playing tennis. His subsequent behavior in the session progressively deteriorated to resemble that of a petulant 2-year-old. Finally, I asked him if he was worried about me because of my ankle. "Yes, I'm worried," he said, and began to throw toys around the room. Telling him that I was just fine, I picked him up in a playful wrestle/hug in response to which he said calmly, "I want my hot chocolate now." He was composed and in control of his behavior until it became time for him to leave, when he became upset once more. Checking with his mother by telephone later that day, I learned that she had found herself wondering if some of his upset might be related to his upcoming departure for an overnight camping trip. She asked him if that was so and he said yes, immediately regaining his composure once more. Her understanding of this distress was enough. He was able to restore his own emotional equilibrium. This, I believe, is because he had succeeded in strengthening that self-regulating capacity in therapy. He no longer needed a selfobject to do it for him.

The second implication of the self psychological perspective for clinical work with children is that the therapist must concern himself or herself, often directly, with the adequacy of the child's selfobject milieu: that constellation of selfobject relationships in which the child is embedded on a daily basis.

In some instances, the selfobject relationships in question will be with other family members. But, especially as children grow older, these relationships can extend, as Wolf (1980) noted, to include people outside of the immediate family. The therapeutic issue, of course, is whether they can provide the selfobject functions needed by the child for the continuing development of his self, and if not, what to do about it.

Perhaps the first point we should address concerns the self psychological perspective on parents with respect to their child's emotional difficulties. Kohut was unambiguously clear that parents should not be blamed for their child's emotional disturbances. All parents want and do the best they can for their children. Many parents are handicapped, however, in their functioning as self-objects for their children by disorders of their own selves—something they are truly not "responsible" for in any moral sense.

Parents with disordered selves deserve therapeutic selfobject relationships of their own in order to reactivate their developmental arrests and acquire the psychological structure necessary to pursue their own program of action, including their role as parents.

Bob

Bob is a 10-year-old boy who along with his sister, Tamara, age 8, was sexually molested while on visitation with his father following the parents' separation pending divorce. At the time, the children were ages 7 and 5. Both children were brought by their mother (who was awarded custody) to the Children's Center for treatment. Bob's need for treatment was evident through his self-criticism, angry, destructive outbursts at home (toward mother and sister) and school (toward other children), and underachievement despite above average intelligence.

During my meeting with his mother, Jill, to gather detailed information on his developmental history, she began to tremble uncontrollably, experience shortness of breath and memory lapses while attempting to describe her relationship with her ex-husband. He had begun to drink heavily and beat her after they had been married for a year and continued to do so periodically until she left him nine years later. She said that talking about it made her feel like it was happening to her again. After she had calmed down, and in response to a question about whether she wanted to pursue some individual treatment for herself, she said that she often worried that her own fearful emotional state interfered with her being able to give her children what they needed from her as a mother.

After some discussion of the potential difficulties involved in having the same therapist for herself and her son and a discussion of the possibility with Bob to obtain his reaction, the author offered to see both of them for separate weekly individual treatment sessions.

The course of Bob's treatment over a two-year period has involved an initial phase of mirroring followed by an intense and prolonged phase of idealizing, within which his loss, rage, and disappointment over his father's behavior and subsequent absence required increasing his appointments to twice a week in lieu of residential treatment. The activities during this second phase included his testing my ability to keep him from trashing the therapy room, feed him candy upon demand, pursue and catch him when he ran away, carry him—once caught—piggyback fashion back to the office, and maintaining daily telephone contact when my travel out of town required missing his regular appointment.

This phase was followed by a return to one session per week in which he sought an alternating twinship/mirroring response from me. The activities during this latter period included model airplane and boat building, learning to throw, catch, and kick a football, exhibiting his prowess at baseball and on a skateboard, and learning to master electronic video games with me watching over his shoulder. For the most part, board games, drawing or painting, clay play, and conversation have never held his interest.

The course of his mother's treatment over the same two-year period began with her wanting me to function as a strong, idealized selfobject as she revisited the self-weakening trauma of her marriage, the separation/divorce, the suspicion and discovery of the sexual abuse, and its aftermath. This was followed by a reexamination of her past and present relationship with her parents in which she clearly sought a mirroring function from me, saying at one point, "I guess I keep trying to get from you what I wasn't able to get from them." Near the end of this phase, she said during one session that she found herself being more attentive and understanding of the children, yelling at them less and taking more time to arrange after-school, evening, and weekend activities for and with them.

In this case, the therapy was able to supply, over time, several selfobject functions for both mother and son with the end result that the mother became able to provide those functions she previously had wanted to but could not. Simultaneously, the son was able to use the therapist as a selfobject to reactivate his own selfobject needs and continue his self development despite both his father's and mother's emotional unavailability for doing so when he needed them. In time, he became able to make use of his mother as a source of selfobject functions without experiencing them as insufficient for maintaining his cohesion.

Other parents are handicapped not so much by self disorders of their own as by a lack of understanding as to how their child differs from themselves and by a related lack of information about the implications of this difference for communicating with their child. Schoolteachers and administrators, too, are handicapped in a similar fashion when the child does not respond to their direction as other children do. Although this latter point seems to be implicit in Kohut's thinking and has been addressed by some of those applying his work (Basch 1984, Shane 1984), it is most directly developed in the work of Chess and Thomas tracing the origins and evolution of behavior disorders through their New York Longitudinal Study of a sample of children from infancy through early adulthood (Chess and Thomas 1984, 1986).

Combining Kohut's elucidation of the importance of empathically attuned selfobject relationships for the healthy development of the self and emotional development with Chess and Thomas's emphasis on the importance of "goodness of fit" for optimal development provides a framework for assessing the adequacy of a child's selfobject relationships with his parents and teachers.

> As an example, a child may develop behavioral distress as a reaction to a new social situation in which functioning of a new kind is required. This is not an automatic signal to the parent to restore immediate comfort by withdrawing the child from the new demand. Rather, the parents should evaluate the best strategy which will make it possible for the child to master this new situation. This requires a judgment, based on the child's past experiences and an estimate of his current abilities and motivations, that the child can cope with the new expectations; with this, his efforts should be encouraged and assisted if necessary. However, if a judgment is made that the limitations of the child's capacities and/or the complexities and special demands of the new situation would result in

poorness of fit, so that mastery cannot be achieved at the particular time, then a different strategy is in order. A delay in the introduction of the new social situation until the child's level of functioning has expanded, or introduction of the individual elements of the complex social aggregate one at a time may bring about a goodness of fit and mastery, even if more slowly. [Chess and Thomas 1984, p. 21]

For the child therapist, this implies a role of consultant/ educator vis-à-vis the parents or other potential selfobjects. In this role, the therapist discovers in the therapy hour ways of understanding and expressing the child's unique constellation of goals, ideals, talents, and skills, and the quality of the dynamic tension among them, and then searches—through an empathically guided process of trial and error—for an attuned configuration of expectations, instruction, support, and reward. Once discovered, these can be conveyed, discussed, and modeled for use by the child's parents, teachers, neighbors, babysitters, and others in ways that are compatible with their desire to function as selfobjects in their respective settings (Young 1990).

Tommy

Tommy was an 8-year-old boy when he was fondled three or four times by the teenage nephew of his stepfather, Sam. Tommy's mother, Alice, and his biological father, Jack, had separated and then divorced when Tommy was 1 year old. Alice and Jack's marriage had been a stormy one, punctuated by Jack's drinking and emotional abuse of Alice and her desperate efforts to first please him (including getting pregnant with Tommy) and then retreat from him into what might be described as an enmeshed emotional relationship with both Tommy and his older brother, Jack Jr.

Alice left and then divorced Jack, only to fall in love with and marry Sam, who, it turned out, developed an addiction to alcohol and marijuana after they had had two children (Nicky and Sam Jr.). By the time the sexual molestation of Tommy occurred, Alice was considerably depressed and self-critical, believing that her first husband's continued criticism of her as an incompetent witch was true. Although she had pursued both individual treatment for herself, family therapy for her new family, and mediation counseling for herself, Jack Sr., Jack Jr., and Tommy, she still felt her life was out of her control and that things were getting worse. She brought Tommy to the Children's Center for individual treatment following the sexual abuse incident because of his escalating violent behavior at home and because his school had informed her that they were removing him from the Talented and Gifted (TAG) track that he was in and preparing to classify him as seriously emotionally disturbed in order to render him eligible for special educational services. In addition to these concerns, she reported that he was still wetting the bed each night, despite having completed a behavioral modification regimen designed to correct the problem. She was feeling particularly overwhelmed at this time because Sam had entered a residential treatment program for his substance abuse and was not living at home.

In his initial treatment sessions, Tommy demonstrated that he was indeed talented and gifted—above average in intelligence, verbally adept, quick to discern the essence of complicated interpersonal situations, and unusually well coordinated and accomplished at sports (soccer, basketball, gymnastics) for his age. He sought mirroring from the very beginning as he showed me how good he was at shooting baskets in the gym for several months. What conversation he was able to sustain about school suggested to me that he felt shamed and enraged that the school personnel—a guidance counselor in particular—treated him as though he was "retarded or weird or something."

I arranged a meeting at the school with the counselor and Tommy's homeroom teacher. At that meeting I learned that they were most concerned about his sexually precocious and provocative language. The guidance counselor in particular felt some pressure from Tommy's teachers to treat this problem and correct it. She and the homeroom teacher agreed to follow my suggestion that they not attempt to treat him but instead firmly prohibit that kind of talk at school, telling him that he should use his therapy sessions at the Children's Center to talk about those things. They further agreed to suspend the process leading to classifying him as emotionally disturbed and hold him accountable for academic performance commensurate with his ability. He responded almost immediately with a cessation of the sex talk and an improvement in his academic performance.

A few months later, when his stepfather returned to live with the family, his academic and interpersonal behavior deteriorated in a different way. He became aggressive with other boys and overtly defiant of his teachers. Knowing that his school performance had become a source of pride for him, I arranged another meeting at school—this time with Tommy present along with his homeroom teacher and the school principal. We arranged for Tommy to have access to a small room off the principal's office whenever his behavior became objectionable. At his teacher's direction, or on his own initiative by request, he could take his work to the small room and work by himself there until he felt he could regain control of his behavior in the classroom. He used the room once, at his own request, and never needed it again.

Following this, he expressed interest in the play therapy room and we spent several months of weekly sessions there during which he made up games that involved his dodging all my efforts to hit him with throw pillows followed by his mock killing of me with swords and karate blows. During one such session approximately a year afer he had begun treatment, he raised the subject of his having "night terrors," as he called them. I asked him if he was still wetting the bed at night ("yes") and did he think there was any connection between that and his night terrors. He did not know and I did not dwell on it. Instead, I asked him if he wanted to try to do something about the bed wetting and see if the night terrors stopped. He seemed eager to try so I suggested he ask his Mom to get him an alarm clock or clock radio and teach him how to set it for midnight. (He thought that when he wet, it was closer to morning than to when he went to sleep.) The plan was to try waking up at midnight, go to the bathroom, and then back to sleep. He was to keep track of whether he was wet or dry in the morning by marking it down on a calendar so he could tell me the following week how it had worked out.

I asked him if he wanted me to explain the plan to his mother and he said yes. When I talked with her, I emphasized that this was to be *his* experiment and that I thought she should help him set it up but then stay uninvolved whether it succeeded or not. I tried to explain to her that it seemed to me that he was most able to maintain control of his own behavior—both in sessions with me and at school—when he felt he was in command of a situation that he also thought he could manage. Fortunately, the experiment succeeded and, naturally, he proudly announced the results to his mother, who had no difficulty expressing her pleasure with him. She later told me that learning to help her children become more independent as they grew older was difficult for her and that she appreciated my helping her do so.

This case illustrates how appropriately calibrated expectations, instructions, supports, and rewards can contribute to the development of the self and emotional health rather than to the disturbance of emotional development through the enfeeblement of self. What appears to be a critical step in this approach to treatment is translating an appreciation of the child's selfobject need into terms (expectations, instructions, support, and rewards) that are comprehensible to the child on the one hand and yet both meaningful and acceptable to persons in the child's selfobject milieu on the other.

CONCLUSION

This chapter has applied some of the central ideas of Kohut's psychology of the self to clinical work with children. Specifically, it has described the role of others as selfobjects in the formation of a cohesive self and the development of emotions. It has shown further how prolonged empathic failure on the part of needed selfobjects can undermine the acquisition of a cohesive, vigorous, harmonious, and productive self in ways that are disturbing of emotional development. And it has illustrated three cases in which this theoretical perspective guides the clinician in his work with children, their parents, and other persons in the child's environment.

5

Adolescents

Miriam Elson

Every major changeover in life shakes up an image of the self and its world of selfobjects (Kohut 1977). There is, of course, no static period. What appears static is an imperceptible process of change, which at significant intervals intensifies in speed and becomes notable. Adolescence is one such period.

Prominent in adolescence is the rapid pace in physical growth. The bodyself matures slowly, yet its manifest stages are dramatic. The world of selfobjects responds to each phase with expectation. Parents look ahead with and for their offspring, musing nostalgically over what has been and what will not come again.

The adolescent's mind–body self responds to being enfolded in the larger vision of the world of selfobjects by transmuting their vision into a unique vision of that world. The stories woven by joyous parents in contemplating their daughter's or son's future become a self-function in facilitating the process of establishing idealized goals. Structure building occurs by reason of optimal frustration—the selfobjects are in tune with the individual's needs and wishes, but not quite. Hearing, listening, and taking in the vision offered by selfobjects, the adolescent will give that vision special emphasis and new direction.

In experience with extended family, neighbors, and playmates, the adolescent, through the process of optimal frustration, continues deepening, firming, and elaborating self structure. Response from the "widening world of selfobjects" (Wolf 1980) provides sustenance for the enhancement of native endowment. Mirroring needs—affirmation, confirmation, guidance—blend with the need for merging with the idealized wisdom and competence of a broadening range of mentors. Twinship and partnering needs are more obviously prominent in the early school years than at any other time except adolescence, when they are asserted even more vigorously. One has only to observe the intense bond of doing things together: This is what we are . . . this is what we do . . . and this is the way we do it.

The way we do it is almost more important than who is the swiftest or the strongest. Key expressions, rituals, typical dress, and possessions are sought and defended with an intensity that can bewilder and irritate parents. For the adolescent they are confirmation of a special place in the world. Increasingly, that unique self with its special place in the world will be enriched, defined, and confirmed as selfobject functions become the self-functions of more sophisticated monitoring of signal anxiety, greater strength in the capacity to self-soothe and thus to undertake the mastery of new tasks.

There is a vital, phase-appropriate thrust toward new selfobjects in peers, cult heroes, and ideologies (Kohut 1974, Wolf 1980, Wolf et al. 1972). The world of thought and the strength that lies in the mind become increasingly the focus of mastery and growth for some adolescents; for others, the focus is on body strength and prowess in athletics. For still others, both worlds are available. There appears a simultaneous intensifying and loosening of the ties to primary selfobjects. Parents are put on hold, needed yet resisted. Their opinions and judgments are sought after, but their suggestions may be abjured even when they coincide with and confirm the adolescent's deeply cherished longings. They are tested against the values and standards of selfobject peers, or older selfobject mentors, which in turn must be vigorously argued with parents. The process attests to the intense scrutiny to which the adolescent subjects external and inner world in the struggle for confirmation of the self as a center of perception and initiative.

There can be a refreshing and vigorous increase in the stream of ideas between the generations as the adolescent confronts cognitively and affectively, as if for the first time, those values, ideals, and goals that had earlier been laid down as psychic structure. Some they will jettison, others they will modify, and still others they will now include more firmly and enduringly as *their* values, *their* ideals, *their* goals (Elson 1984).

PARENTS AS SELFOBJECTS
FOR ADOLESCENTS

It is at the point of their children's adolescence that parents as selfobjects have the greatest need for flexibility and tensile strength in reviewing and expanding those enduring values and goals that are basic to a sense of continuity of the self in space and time. While much has been made of adolescent turmoil, the profound upheaval that parents experience in this transitional phase has been less noted. In the light of newer societal norms, parents must now examine within themselves the validity and importance of values, beliefs, and behaviors intrinsic to their own cohesive functioning.

Through each developmental phase, child and parents inform each other. Factors impinging upon the parent–child relationship are reciprocal and complex; they are not just unidirectional. The child influences the parent to nearly the same extent that the parent influences the child (Cohler 1980). This is the unique significance of the simultaneous ongoing process of the experience of self and other in parents and children.

Throughout the course of family life, there are periods of vibrantly intense joy experienced by parents and children alike, when each enhances a sense of radiance and power in the other.

There are equally intense periods of anger and despair. There may be times when the explosive force unleashed by the narcissistic needs and demands of one or both parents may be thoroughly distorting and destructive to the child, giving rise to severe breaks in empathy. Parental behavior may be excessively punitive and counterproductive to the adolescent's growth and development or unrealistic in relation to the adolescent's genuine interests and abilities. Anxiety, guilt, and depression may then hamper a necessary search for understanding and resolution of the impasse. Pathological forms of parental narcissism may perpetuate parental control long after the adolescent has signaled need for and capacity to forge a course and to use others in the expanding world of selfobjects for this purpose.

Out of their own needs, parents seek to halt development. History is strewn with the locked combat of parents and children in this arena, when the immaturity and rigidity of the parents' narcissism exact behavior from the adolescent that will exactly mirror the parents' needs. Unable to be free of a noxious merger, the adolescent cannot elaborate skills and talents that will permit the expression of ambitions in realizable goals stemming from centrally perceived initiative.

Parents may also be threatened by their adolescents' maturing adult form and may enviously compete for their beauty, power, and opportunity. In other instances they may misunderstand rebellious attitudes or behavior, which often cover regression and retreat. The battle is joined interpersonally rather than intrapsychically, as adolescents struggle against their archaic needs and the fear of engulfment and as parents cling more tenaciously to their former encompassing central position in the lives of their children. The selfobjects an adolescent seeks out to overcome this fear at times seem to represent in gross form the values exactly opposite to those that are central to parental self-esteem and have earlier seemed central to that of their preadolescent children. In other instances, fearing separation and the task of self-definition, adolescents may linger in a merger that does not permit that quickening opportunity for trusting and expanding their perceptions, for initiating a unique program of action that is the necessary task of these years (Elson 1984).

Disorders of the self in adolescence become manifest in low self-esteem, lack of goals, immobilization, or in dangerous acting-out behavior, such as substance abuse, delinquency, or perversions. The following excerpt from a three-year period of treatment will illustrate the deficits that are exposed and the understanding offered by self psychology to the process of filling in these deficits.

Tom

Tom, almost 15, was brought to the clinic by his parents, who felt themselves helpless to move him from his entrenched taciturnity. At home his typical day was spent sleeping or sitting before the TV; at school he moved from class to class "like a zombie." He had few friends and those he did have were, like himself, "deadwood" in classes.

In a joint interview with his parents, he sat silently, appearing vaguely uncomfortable when his frustrated mother, bursting into tears, exclaimed, "If he goes on this way I don't know what's going to become of him." His father patted her shoulder, proclaiming gruffly, "Aw, he'll snap out of it; it's just a stage."

An argument erupted between the parents, during which Tom's face took on something of a sneer and he shifted uncomfortably in his chair. The burden of the argument was that Tom's behavior was worsening, not getting better. His sisters, 12 and 10, gave no trouble; they did their homework, were into a variety of activities, and were good company. Tom just kept to himself, sleeping long hours or watching TV. He never did anything he was asked to do unless "you just shout at him!" His grades were "abominable" and getting worse. It was clear that his mother was responding with narcissistic rage to her loss of Tom as a selfobject. His father's attitude was bland. "You just make a big case of it. Like I tell you, he'll snap out of it; give him time." Tom appeared bored when his father spoke, but his face flushed.

In the course of the interview the intensity of feeling between the parents subsided, but it was apparent that Tom's father had agreed to therapy in order to appease his wife. He firmly believed that Tom was just going through a phase and would "shape up" after he did "some more growing."

His mother presented Tom's industry throughout earlier grades and middle school in glowing terms and expressed her great disappointment that he had ground to a halt "just when grades were so important." Efforts to draw Tom into the discussion were met with uneasy shrugs. He did not, however, resist the therapist's suggestion that he stay a while after his parents left so that together they could come to an understanding of whether therapy was in order.

Tom volunteered little information, appeared sleepy and yawned several times in the silence that followed his noncommittal responses to questions. It was the therapist's belief that Tom not only was expecting the therapist to react to him as his parents did, but also was in his way attempting to diminish intense feelings of being the center of attention. His attitude induced an inner state of exasperation and bewilderment in the therapist, who sought to engage this unwilling adolescent. Tentatively he suggested that it was possible Tom felt coerced and angry. Although he could not say whether he could help Tom, he would like to see if they couldn't work together to figure things out. Tom seemed to lose some of his sleepiness, but, with something of a sneer, asked, "Like those shrinks on TV?"

> **Therapist:** I don't know what programs you've been watching. (As Tom did not respond, he continued.) What's really important is our working together; we help each other in puzzling things out.
> **Tom:** Isn't anything to puzzle out. . . . I just don't get a kick out of anything.
> **Therapist:** That's just it; what's happened to the kick?
>   Tom volunteered his first half-smile.
> **Therapist:** I think it's worth trying to see what we come up with; I've worked with other kids who seem to have lost it.
> **Tom:** (After a pause) Well, for a while.
> **Therapist:** I don't think a while will help much, but it may give you a sense of how we work together and whether you want to go on.

Tom agreed to the proposed weekly interview. In the first few weeks the taciturn behavior of which his mother had complained was much in evidence. He was often late and lethargic. Comments volunteered by his therapist were met, for the most part, with a shrug. On one occasion, prompted by Tom's unusually disheveled appearance and the strong, sweetish odor of marijuana that emanated from him, the therapist commented that sometimes things hurt so much that it just felt better to pile the covers on and hope it would all go away. When Tom did not respond, the therapist asked how long Tom had been medicating himself.

> **Tom:** (Startled and uneasy) What do you mean?
>
> **Therapist:** The odor from your clothes is very strong.
>
> **Tom:** (Flushing) So what?
>
> **Therapist:** I think only you can say *what* is troubling you. I only know from my work with many young people your age that when things get to be too much, some of them turn to drugs to overcome those low times. They're really trying to treat a depression.
>
> **Tom:** Are you going to tell my folks?
>
> **Therapist:** What goes on is between us. The only time I change that agreement is when it seems clear that your behavior creates a danger for yourself or others. And I would take such a step only after telling you first why and when. Fair enough?
>
> Tom reluctantly agrees.

The therapist seeks to establish how often and for how long a time Tom has been medicating himself. His replies are not so much evasive as confused, and the therapist considers whether there may be a beginning thought disorder. He points out that when Tom medicates himself it is not possible to understand what prompts the low states. Tom protests that it is nothing special, but the therapist points out that the effect of self-medication is to dissipate painful feelings and therefore it seems as if there is nothing especially upsetting. He asks Tom's cooperation in trying not to medicate himself but to come in for an extra hour when he feels he cannot hold out. Tom agrees, but volunteers that his parents are always arguing about whether therapy does any good and about the expense. The therapist comments that even coming in to see him, then, probably adds to the bad feelings, and Tom, with a thoughtful, direct look at the therapist, agrees. The therapist asks whether Tom would like to have him see the parents again and prepare the way for sessions twice a week.

Whether or not to arrange to see parents again or at regular intervals is a matter of therapeutic judgment. The therapist had observed Tom's sneering when his parents began to quarrel in the first consultation. He had also observed Tom's discomfort, particularly when his mother burst into tears. He believed that the crucial issue was that of extending an empathic understanding of Tom's obvious discomfort but that a consultation now might help Tom by removing therapy from the arena of parental disputes.

Tom: Are you going to tell them about the pot?
Therapist: (Firmly and without taking offense) You and I have a clear understanding about that.

The consultation goes well. There is despair at home over Tom's grades, which are failing in three out of four subjects. His father is no longer taking the position that Tom is just going through a phase. The parents' problems with each other are faced more directly—his mother's excessive orderliness, his father's tendency to let things slide around the house, in his work. His father's defensiveness is much in evidence as well as his mother's disappointment in his father's achievement. She is openly envious of a younger sister whose husband has achieved more in the world. His father reminds her that they aren't too badly off, precipitating a long discussion accompanied by tears over their lost youthful aspirations. This ushers in memories of earlier good times and feelings they had about themselves and their world.

The therapist uses this opportunity to point out that Tom seems to have ground to a halt because the future may look frightening to him, full of adult problems he is not as yet equipped to handle. The parents together talk over how much he used to consult them, what good company he used to be, but that now he won't let anyone talk to him or help him. They are concerned about the few friends he has and that they seem to be such slouches. The therapist suggests that perhaps when he is with these friends he doesn't feel so bad about himself. He enables them to see that Tom's having ground to a halt is not willful rebelliousness but immobilization proceeding from depression. When Tom's emotional and behavioral state is viewed in this light, the parents become less exasperated and more concerned. Twice-weekly appointments are agreed to.

In the next few months, Tom misses appointments and reverts to bouts of self-medication. The therapist telephones and does not scold but firmly takes the position that Tom is doing all he can at present; it is hard to examine bad feelings and what precipitates them. Tom counters sneeringly, "You're the shrink, you ought to know." The therapist's response is that sometimes bad feelings are too deep for words and that at such times Tom must feel exasperated with the therapist's failure to provide answers. There is a long period in which Tom essentially comes in promptly and regularly but says very little.

> **Tom**: Well, my folks are paying for this so I guess I may as well come in and sit.

At one point, as he is leaving, he comments with a sigh that it feels good just to sit in the office with the therapist not hassling him. The therapist accepts this with a quiet comment, "I'm glad it helps."

In the next sessions, Tom begins to talk about his two friends and the fact that when he is with them, he doesn't feel so bad, or at least they all feel bad together. His mother objects to them, thinks they're a bad influence on him. He asks defiantly, "How does she know *I'm* not a bad influence on *them*?"

He comments rather sneeringly that Cynthia, his 12-year-old sister, came home with all As. "Mom was dancing all over the place," and that's what she used to do with Tom. But getting good grades at that school is no big deal. After a pause he adds that, again, it just feels good to be with someone who just accepts him as he is and doesn't hassle him about school and grades and what's going to become of him. He sits silently for some time, his eyes moisten, and he brushes the tears away, flushing. With sudden anger he bursts out, "I guess you think I'm just a kid." The therapist comments that "memories of earlier years help us to understand ourselves; they don't mean one is just a kid."

As Tom absorbs a sense of the therapist's interest and respect, he begins to talk about his earlier school years and interests.

"I used to get a kick out of things then." Taciturnity, surliness, cynicism, much in evidence earlier, have given way as Tom shares with his therapist his earlier enthusiasm in school activities. He offers himself and his activities to the therapist for admiration, at first shyly, and then with zest, as he recalls his excitement over each new project and the response of a particular teacher to them. When he moved to eighth grade, this teacher continued her interest, often stopping him in the hall to inquire about his progress. "I felt she was really interested in what I was doing and what it meant to me, not like my mom, as if I were a feather in her cap." Tom described the experience of being used as a selfobject by his mother for her own exhibitionistic needs, an intrusion that deprived him of a joyous sense of growing strength in shaping his ideas and his skill in expressing them. With some resentment and shame, he confided that his friends began to tease him about his teacher's interest in him. He began to avoid her also, ashamed of his earlier response and attachment to her.

It was difficult to determine from Tom's description whether his teacher had been too intrusive in her interests. She used to put her arm around him, something he didn't mind earlier: "Grownups were always doing that to me." But what a prepubertal child can tolerate becomes uncomfortable for the pubertal adolescent. Perhaps more striking was that Tom had been oblivious until teased by his friends. Somewhat slower than his friends in pubertal changes, he began to avoid old friends as well as to withdraw from a central position in his class. He was uncomfortable with his mother, shying away from her and shrugging off her embraces. She was always fussing with his sisters' hair and clothing. He remembered with deep flushing and considerable difficulty in expressing himself that she used to bathe him and then supervise his bathing for longer than most mothers. She was always inspecting him, his ears, his fingernails. Even his father would sometimes say, "Let the boy alone!"

Tom felt demeaned by his father's statement and withdrew from both parents. His mother became more intrusive as Tom tried to shrug her off, pursuing him with questions as to how thoroughly he had scrubbed himself; as Tom persisted in avoiding her, she would add, "You know what I mean?" He flushed very uncomfortably as he blurted out, after some hesitation, that his mother always used to wash the area around his anus and penis very vigorously. When, as he grew older, he began to push her away, she would let him wash himself but under her supervision. Occasionally his young sisters would barge in until he rebelled and began to lock them all out.

After particularly trying times, he would run into his bedroom and lock the door. His mother would say, "I know what you're doing in there." Since at one point this coincided with his attempt to soothe himself in what became compulsive masturbation, he was frightened and confused. Interrupting himself, he commented, "Aw, this is all just a bunch of garbage; I'm just a mess." His therapist replied that he could understand Tom's confusion and the intensity of his feelings about these early experiences. Perhaps he was fearful that the therapist would, like his mother in earlier days, think of him as a smelly little boy, or that, like his father, he would not be able to help him get to the root of things.

> **Therapist**: It's not garbage; you are not a mess. You and I together are trying to clear away your confusion about these experiences and your reaction to them.

Tom said that he was often the subject of arguments between his parents, his father taking his usual position that it was just a phase that all boys go through. His support did not work toward modulating the intensity of Tom's guilt and anxiety. After one particularly stormy session, his father agreed to talk to Tom in response to his mother's insistence that he would not listen to her.

His father's discomfort was obvious. Their discussion essentially terminated with his father's ruffling his hair and saying, soothingly, "That's my little guy." Since Tom was by now 13, he was enraged and his discomfort grew; his disappointment, resulting from further de-idealization of his father, intensified. At night he would have disturbing sensations in which it seemed to him that his body was too large for his bed, that his arms and legs were out of all proportion. He grew uncomfortable with his friends as their physical development became obviously more rapid than his own. His interest in schoolwork began to decline. He avoided activities he formerly enjoyed, finding some degree of companionship in three classmates with whom he began to turn on with pot. In the next few weeks Tom began to talk about these early experiences of turning on. "John could get the stuff any time. We used to go to his house and hang out. I didn't feel bad anymore; I just didn't care; it was great; just like floating. But when I came down, it was worse. I couldn't wait for the next time."

Pointing to his chest, he said it felt "like a heavy weight in there." He would sit slouched in his chair confiding that at least, when he was taking pot, the heaviness seemed to go away. He asked poignantly of his therapist, "Have you ever been depressed? Does it ever go away?"

Empathically in tune with this distressed adolescent, his therapist answered that he knew the feeling he was describing, and that initially their work together probably added to his pain. He pointed out that it was a little like an infection in which things had to be drained away before healing could take place. He had a lot on his mind that he had been unable to talk over and clarify. His well-meaning parents were unaware that Tom was no longer the small boy he had once been. Some mothers found it hard to give up that earlier close contact, and when "things get tough, we, too, long for that earlier time." He could understand Tom's efforts to soothe himself through medication, but since it didn't really help him get to the bottom of things, all it did was to drive him to turn on again and again. When things aren't cleared up they grow more intense. As his therapist absorbed Tom's feelings of distress, his sense of being at sixes and sevens, he was able to help Tom understand the state of fragmentation reflected in the sensation of his arms and legs being out of proportion.

Questions beginning "Could it be . . ." or "Is it possible . . ." allowed Tom to merge with the calming and soothing strength of the therapist. As Tom examined the feelings states that followed sharp breaks in his relationship with his parents, particularly his mother, he could identify precipitants for and consequent states of fragmentation. His natural sexual curiosity, linked with his mother's vigorous scrubbing and her concern with cleanliness, both stimulated him physically and provoked unmanageable anxiety associated with feelings of filthiness. At the same time, his father's laissez-faire attitude, which under other circumstances might have been helpful, left him more at the mercy of his mother's intrusiveness. His father's attempt to offer help more directly had dissipated when he took the easier outlet of regarding Tom as "my little guy." Tom's rage and frustration were understandable, since his difficulties did not represent a phase that he would outgrow but a struggle to understand and make some order of his conflicting wishes to be understood and cared for and, at the same time, to go beyond such needs.

The relationship with his therapist grew very intense. If there were a small delay in the time of the interview, or if Tom's path crossed that of another patient, there woud be recurrent states of feeling out of proportion. After occasional unavoidable cancellation of an appointment, he would become sullen and withdrawn. A petulant quality characterized his questions and responses; he was irritable and quarrelsome. He would attack his therapist, saying, for example, that he knew what his therapist was thinking about him but he was wrong. Tom confided with some shame and with difficulty that he found it hard to wait for his sessions; he felt whole when he was with his therapist. In the months that followed, Tom discussed with his therapist disturbing fantasies of sexual activities, intense absorption in his parents' relationship, curiosity about his sisters' development, concern about his own sexual equipment, and guilt about masturbation. He began to separate normal interest in exploring his body and testing his equipment from guilty, confused feelings of being dirty. Tom was increasingly able to monitor signal anxiety and to transmute the therapist's soothing by taking steps to soothe himself that did not include "turning on" or returning to driven sexual fantasy and masturbation. He expressed a good deal of curiosity about the therapist's life and outside interests; when appropriate, the therapist would respond factually, allowing himself to be used as a target of idealization as Tom sought and defined his own goals.

Tom was now well into his fifteenth year. He had grown several inches and broadened. There were longer periods of his seeming to be in charge and at ease with himself. At such times he would talk about his "kid sister," now 13, and the way she would come to him for advice. With his parents, there appeared to be an uneasy truce. But he quickly bridled when his mother sought to question him about his school work or activities.

As she had occasionally over the past eighteen months of Tom's therapy, his mother sought an interview with the therapist. She appeared depressed and confided that she thought she would like to undertake therapy for herself. Even though her relationship with Tom was still "like walking on eggs," she felt he had improved; his grades were at the top; she could see he felt better about himself. But she was beginning to have trouble with her middle daughter. She felt the problem was more with her own feelings about herself. She felt increasingly unsure and doubtful about her relations with her growing children. The therapist helped her to recognize that the process of gradually giving up the central position in their children's lives was difficult for most parents and, perhaps, for compelling reasons, particularly so for her. For this mother, individual therapy appeared to be an important step. The therapist was able to refer her to a woman therapist with whom she made a very effective therapeutic relationship. She smiled as she commented that Tom, in an unguarded moment, had once said to her, "Mr. T. never scolds; he just understands, but he also tells you where to get off."

Tom continued to work very intensively with his therapist. In his sixteenth year he became interested in an advanced course in constitutional history. He didn't think he would go into law as a profession, but "it wouldn't hurt to have that background," whatever he did. He was getting into heated arguments with his father about politics, challenging his passivity, stoutly defending his conviction that "there are things you can do to change what's going on in government." His father typically believed in letting things ride: "You can't change things overnight." Tom smiled ruefully as he shrugged his shoulders and commented, "When I was a kid, I used to think he had the answer to everything and I guess he did, for a kid." Tom began to quote, with admiration, an admired advisor to an advanced group of students, of which Tom was now a member. He was also increasingly attracted to a classmate who was "awesome" in her studies but "fun to talk to." What he liked about this girl and his advisor was that they didn't try to "shove their ideas" at him. They just "asked good questions that made you think about what you felt and what you were saying"; he added, with a flush, "like you."

In his seventeenth year, Tom was intensely caught up in school and related activities. He said that he would like to try cutting down on his hours. He needed the time, and, more important, he thought things were going okay. There had been a number of trying episodes, which Tom had handled well. As an example, the girl to whom he had been attracted, and whose way of thinking had pleased him, did not respond to his moves toward a closer relationship. She was happier with just being part of a group, doing things together. Tom was deeply dejected, experiencing doubts about himself. He struggled uncomfortably with the feeling that perhaps she could see through his asking for a date as just an excuse to "make out." But he was also able to relate this to his earlier feelings about his mother's intrusiveness and his fear that she could see through the door into his room. As he struggled to regain his self-esteem, he was both amused by his fears and at the same time able to free himself from such distortion. After several weeks he observed with some surprise and relief that things didn't throw him as much as they used to or for as long a time. "It just feels good when you listen to me. You don't tell me what to do and you don't tell me what I should have done. You give me space to think for myself."

In therapy he began to check out with the therapist, as "one guy to another," what the guys were saying and doing—"or rather, *saying* that they're doing"—in their relationships with girls. He still felt uncomfortably behind in his own experimentation, worrying about the strength of his masculinity. There were times when the "whole thing" seemed to be too much and he wanted to turn on or to crawl into bed and sleep it all away. He described uncomfortable fantasies of crawling onto his therapist's lap and being closely held. He dwelt longingly on those earlier times when his father had seemed such a big man to him; he had enjoyed being his "little guy" and would often sit on his lap. He recalled that he enjoyed roughhousing with his father, how excited he would get and how he would struggle against being pinned down. These memories

now triggered sensations of physical arousal, which both frightened and shamed him, though they were at the same time pleasurable. And these sensations could also be stimulated by the feeling
of being affirmed by his therapist.

The therapist offered his understanding that it was natural
for a little boy to enjoy the strength of his body, in all its parts, just
as now he was learning to enjoy and understand his maturing
body. Being understood in the present reverberated to those earlier
times when it felt good to sit on his father's lap absorbing his
strength. "When we work together and you feel understood, it's
like being held."

It was hard for Tom to accept the frustrating slowness with
which the process of defining his sexual tastes and proclivities
proceeded; he was envious of his friends and their exploits. He felt
comforted when his therapist commented, "But Tom, isn't it *your*
own time schedule, *your* body, *your* tastes?" Tom's eyes moistened
when he replied, after a struggle to regain his composure, "You just
don't know how good it feels not to be pushed. To have some
space."

There emerged more clearly periods of intense lusty feelings
toward girls, which would arouse anxiety in his relationship with
his younger sister. Since she was somewhat into "the same scene,"
he would become uncomfortable about the fantasies her nearness
triggered. With a combination of pride and concern, he reported
that she was very popular with his friends and that he kept warning
her about guys, trying to slow her down.

His mother began to consult him about his sister. In the midst
of reporting his reassuring comments to her—"It's just a phase;
give her time; she'll snap out of it"—he appeared startled and burst
into laughter. "Just like my Dad! I guess sometimes it *is* just a
matter of waiting and maybe with her it'll straighten out, but with
me, I know now I needed your help."

Tom's behavior with his parents was undergoing a change. In
place of his earlier withdrawal and later brittle irritability and
explosiveness with them, he reported pleasure, at times, in being
with the family. He had observed his mother's attempts to give
them all "more room." He said, rather shyly, that he thought she
was getting a lot out of *her* therapy, too. She seemed more content.

His parents were doing more things together. "She isn't after us so much."

As the school year drew to a close, Tom's vigor and zest in his studies and activities continued with only minor upsets. He enjoyed his friends, a different group from those of his earlier years and those of his depressed period. In class activities, he played an important role and was sought out by his peers. He used his therapy hours now mainly to work over and work through things that hadn't gone as well as he had hoped, looking for the reasons. He would be disappointed, even dejected, but he would recover and reengage himself in ongoing activities. He was also accepting of his own unique skills. When a close friend won an award in a science fair, he was genuinely glad for him while observing that he himself wasn't the kind of person who could work "all those long hours alone." He got his "kicks out of working with people . . . like you do." But he also differentiated his interests from those of his therapist by stressing that, for him, working with people would be in politics or in government. He wanted to change things; he wanted to make the world a better place—and it could be, he just knew it!

He blurted out that his girlfriend thought so, too, laughing in some excitement as he commented that he guessed he hadn't said anything about her. This was a beginning relationship, but one he felt hopeful about.

> **Tom:** I guess I wanted to keep it to myself until I was sure we'd hit it off.
> **Therapist:** You were concerned that I might pry, not let you handle your affairs on your own, as earlier you felt your mother intruded on you.
> **Tom:** I like the space you give me. You listen; you let me go until I'm ready to share if I want to share.

Tom was now actively engaged in the adolescent process with increasingly effective self-awareness. This awareness enabled him to use signal anxiety to alert internal regulation of self-soothing, of seeking and finding those selfobjects necessary to his sustenance, of enduring ambiguity and uncertainty as he sought to master those skills that would put him on the road to achievable goals. The zest with which he approached his life differed markedly from the immobilization of the young adolescent who had initially been presented by his parents for therapy. Termination now seemed clearly in order and a date was set toward which he worked. As the time for this approached, Tom was aware of sadness along with a sense of excitement.

> **Tom:** It's not like I'm depressed the way I used to be. I guess I'll miss coming here, miss being able to talk things over with you. It used to be everything I did I was always hearing your voice or wondering how you'd look at it. Now, lots of the time I just lose myself in what I'm doing. Even when things don't turn out so great, I'm thinking about how I can work it out; . . . not "wait till I see Mr. T."

He became engrossed in plans for college and graduation from high school. With his father, he visited several campuses. He struggled with uncomfortable feelings about whether he might choose his father's college because he still wanted to be "his little guy" or because of its genuine appropriateness for his interests. He was accepted by several colleges and felt a heady excitement about the way in which the world was opening up for him. He said, with a grin, he and his girlfriend had turned handsprings, "just like kids," when they were accepted by the same colleges. They weren't sure what their decisions were going to be, but Tom did not feel threatened by the possibility of a separation. They would still get together on holidays.

What seemed firm in Tom was this ability to work independently on his problems, as well as the capacity to seek out and work with mentors, parents, and peers. He felt in charge of himself, and when things did not go well he did not shrink from looking within and determining what initiatives were available to him. In their last therapy hour, Tom thanked his therapist, saying he knew he would miss him, wondering if he could drop by at the Christmas break to talk things over. His therapist replied that he would miss him, too, that he felt they had worked well together, and that he would be glad to see him.

THE ADOLESCENT'S NEED FOR
A COHESIVE SELF

Reflecting on the experiences of this adolescent from the vantage point of self psychology, what may be striking is the absence of focus on oedipal conflict. The therapist did not approach the problem of treatment from the viewpoint of libidinal theory, a retreat from the demands of puberty. Tom's need to medicate himself appeared rather as a driven attempt to reinstate a feeling of wholeness, to calm and soothe himself. In the treatment literature of adolescents, consideration of the oedipal conflict seems to overshadow all else, and most pathology is diagnosed and interpreted from the viewpoint of regression from oedipal issues, fixation at preoedipal levels, or neurotic pathology arising from faulty resolutions of the oedipal conflict. Kohut's depth immersion in the psychic life of his patients, and those patients whose analysis he supervised, led him to the conviction that the storms of adolescence proceeded from the failures of the selfobject milieu to respond to the whole developing child. In the therapeutic relationship what is reinstated is the thrust to complete growth when the self is phase-appropriately supported.

As a latency-age child Tom seemed to have had a well-functioning cohesive self. He seemed to take pleasure in his schoolwork and was apparently a child whose attractiveness and skills elicited appropriate mirroring from the selfobjects of his expanding world. He enjoyed the companionship of a group of friends and schoolmates. It was only later that the intensity of his mother's merger with her son became apparent, and Tom's lingering in that merger signaled deficits in his self structure as well.

The details of his mother's difficulties with his father can only be inferred from the glimpses of her competitive strivings with her more materially advantaged sister and her growing discontent. Unlike his wife, Tom's father did not feel discontented with the level he had reached. He had no burning desire to enhance his position or increase his possessions. From his wife's viewpoint, his lack of assertiveness seemed to be weakness; she wanted him to shape his abilities and productive efforts into more ambitious projects than the small business he owned and managed. He tended toward passivity and delay in tackling new projects. There were intimations of this in the early consultation with the parents and from comments Tom volunteered in his sessions about opportunities his father had bypassed, though he centered his disagreements with his father in the realm of politics.

In her increasing frustration, Tom's mother, to bolster her self-esteem, turned more and more to her son, overseeing his grooming, monitoring his school work more intensely at a time when his thrust toward adolescence dictated his need to free himself. Up to a point, he did not resent his mother's continued supervision until his own maturation and the intensification of her tenacious hold resulted in an explosive rupture. At the same time, Tom began to feel something amiss in the continued relationship with his eighth-grade teacher; he experienced humiliation particularly when his classmates teased him about this relationship.

As he became more alert to his slower physical development, he sought more actively to disentangle himself from the merger with his discontented mother. Because of her own incompleteness and fragmentation fears, his mother could not release her hold and respond with appropriate acceptance and pleasure to her son's independent strivings toward new selfobjects; nor could his father, lacking assertiveness, effectively encourage his son's struggle to free himself.

THE ADOLESCENT'S NEED
FOR SELFOBJECT PEERS

Adolescents need selfobject peers intensely; they seek and use selfobject peers as alter-egos, partners in the process of sharing their anxiety about changing body structure, as well as of defining and experiencing pleasure in their new freedom and power. Their need of parents as selfobjects undergoes a transformation as they seek new symbols and idols for confirming a sense of greatness and expanding idealized goals (Goldberg 1975, Kohut 1977, Wolf 1980). The symbols and idols of these years will go through many transformations and will bear little resemblance to earlier values and goals; this is a necessary process in firming and deepening psychic structure. Parents are still needed as available but not as intrusive selfobjects. In the failure of Tom's parents as selfobjects to respond to the whole self of this developing adolescent, Tom felt increasingly depressed, a sense of hollowness, emptiness. Left out and left behind by his earlier group of friends, to relieve his shame he turned finally to classmates whose feelings of low self-esteem matched his own. He turned away from former activities that had been an expression of his central nuclear self and sought to restore a sense of perfection and wholeness through a soothing drug.

Tom's therapist did not target the parents as culprits, nor Tom as victim. He viewed Tom's earlier sneering at his quarreling parents and his apparent boredom and flushing when his father reiterated his belief that Tom was going through a phase and would snap out of it as an expression of bitter disappointment in his formerly idealized parents. As his mother clung more desperately to Tom as a selfobject through whom narcissistic replenishment for her own undernourished self could be provided, Tom increasingly retreated. He found no strength in his father's easygoing acceptance. He withdrew from both parents and from the intense struggle to identify his own inwardly perceived and evaluated goals.

THE UNFOLDING TRANSFERENCE

Through his understanding of the unfolding transference needs for affirmation, the therapist now provided Tom with the opportunity to experiment zestfully with typical adolescent tasks, to fill in missing functions of self-esteem regulation. There was a long period of need to have the therapist perform a mirroring function, rekindling his earlier pleasure in himself and his power. Tom exposed his reawakened grandiosity at first shyly and then rather imperatively to his therapist for confirmation. Small lapses or failures in his therapist's responses enabled Tom to deepen his capacity to soothe himself and to strive for and build in greater resourcefulness in regulating self-esteem. Along with a mirroring transference, there emerged an idealizing transference in which his therapist's calmness and understanding allowed Tom the "space" and time to experience and formulate his own needs and wishes. When these seemed amorphous and uncertain, he absorbed Tom's doubts and disappointments without censure, blame, or goading.

Goldberg (1978) describes the need of adolescents to come to grips with the boundaries of their capacities. This was difficult for Tom. Overstimulated by his mother's intrusion of her own expectations and goals for him but understimulated in the opportunity to reflect on and forge goals for himself, he retreated to his longing for an earlier state of wholeness. But through the space and time provided by the new selfobject therapist, Tom regained a sense of himself as the center of his own perceptions, an initiator in defining and elaborating skills that gave him mastery over his talents and enabled him to use these to work toward reliable goals.

It seemed clear from the manner in which Tom was able to engage in therapy that the parents of his earlier years had provided an empathic milieu for their small son. They had been joyous and proud of his attractiveness and intelligence. They were pleased by his performance and the response of others to him. A child's success does enhance parental self-esteem. It is only when the fragility and incompleteness of one or both parents intrude on the forming, reforming, and firming self of the child, when a parent desperately seeks to maintain an archaic merger with the child that self disorders ensue. The transformation and the vicissitudes of the self in adolescence require a concomitant transformation of the parental self. While remaining available according to the adolescent's need, parents gradually learn to accept a less central role in the life of their child. This Tom's mother could not undertake until she entered psychotherapy herself.

In considering Tom's self pathology, his therapist might have viewed his problems as stemming from fixation at a preoedipal level to avoid confronting his murderous rage at his father as rival. He may similarly have viewed Tom's reaction to his mother as a defense against, and retreat from, incestuous fantasies. But Tom's yearning for the mirroring archaic mother was a far cry from longing for incestuous union.

His therapist might have viewed Tom's fantasies about sitting in his lap and being closely held as an expression of homosexual longings. But a self psychological view permits us to understand his rage at his father's failure to perform the idealized assertive selfobject function of his earlier years, which then resulted in a too abrupt de-idealization, reactivating a longing to merge with the archaic selfobject father of his childhood. When these mirroring and idealizing needs met with failure to provide the nutrients by both parents, which the expanding and reforming self of adolescence required, he turned to self-medication to evoke a sense of wholeness and perfection. He chose as peers those whose similarly low self-esteem did not provoke a sense of discrepancy and fragmentation.

Viewing these transference needs as directed not to him as an incestuous object but to him as a new selfobject through whom interrupted self-development could continue, the therapist's response to Tom was to mirror and affirm his emerging pride in his physical and mental attributes. As new selfobject, Tom's therapist allowed himself to become the target of Tom's need to merge with and idealize his calmness and competence. It was not that the therapist was blind to or oblivious of oedipal issues, but that these could be resolved through his focus on Tom's mirroring, idealizing, and partnering needs. Through transmuting internalization Tom could acquire the self-function of regulating and shaping sexuality toward an effective relationship. Tom could become joyously alive to his maturing sexuality. His ability to form a responsive relationship with a young woman, his performance in school and other activities, his improved relationship with his parents and his sisters, and more important, his zest as he planned for college affirm the resiliency with which he could now respond to adolescent tasks.

The purpose of therapy was to reawaken the thrust to continue and complete development of an undernourished self. The therapeutic process enabled Tom to replace selfobject functions—missing functions—with self-functions. Through his therapist as new selfobject he could disentangle himself from the merger with his mother in order to define, savor, and claim his ambitions as his own. He could turn from his father's passive acceptance of the status quo to engage in a lively dialogue with selfobject mentors and peers, as he shaped his ambitions into his own realistic goals, both immediate and for the future.

This is a case of moderate adolescent disorder that yielded to twice-a-week psychotherapy over a three-year period. Anna Freud (1958) in a classic paper described adolescence as an interruption of peaceful growth. She noted that upholding a steady equilibrium during the adolescent process is in itself abnormal. Her description bears rereading:

> I take it that it is normal for an adolescent to behave for a considerable length of time in an inconsistent and unpredictable manner; to fight his impulses and to accept them; to ward them off successfully and to be overrun by them; to love his parents and to hate them; to be deeply ashamed to acknowledge his mother before others and, unexpectedly, to desire heart-to-heart talks with her; to thrive on imitation of and identification with others while searching unceasingly for his own identity; to be more idealistic, artistic, generous, and unselfish than he will ever be again, but also the opposite: self-centered, egotistic, calculating. Such fluctuations between extreme opposites would be deemed highly abnormal at any other time of life. At this time they may signify no more than that an adult structure of personality takes a long time to emerge, that the ego of the individual in question does not cease to experiment and is in no hurry to close down on possibilities. If the temporary solutions seem abnormal to the onlooker, they are less so, nevertheless, than the hasty decisions made in other cases for one-sided suppression, or revolt, or flight, or withdrawal, or regression, or asceticism which are responsible for the truly pathological developments. . . . [p. 275]

The crucial period of self organization that is necessary in adolescence may be accomplished with seeming ease (Offer and Offer 1975) or may become a turbulent period triggering destructive behavior, empty depression, or hypochondriacal preoccupation. Kohut (1971) differentiated between those adolescents who "look schizoid during a particular period because the life task is so great, and those in which there is such pervasive hollowness in their personality that only prolonged work will accomplish any healing for them" (p. 158).

Less dramatic is the loss of ambition, the failure to establish goals, and the toll of aimless drifting and waste, as in Tom's situation. Tom had been making futile efforts to overcome the threat of disintegration, to calm and soothe himself. The process of psychotherapy enabled him to regain initiative in undertaking adolescent tasks.

CONCLUSION

Psychopathology in adolescence extends from psychosis through borderline states to neurosis. Kohut described personality and/or behavior disorders expressed in severe substance abuse, delinquency, and suicidal depression as the attempts of an enfeebled, fragmented, chaotic self to overcome a sense of deadness, to recreate an illusion of wholeness (Kohut 1971, 1977, 1984). Goldberg (1978) described

> profound disturbances of catastrophic dimensions where self-fragmentation and deviant restitution challenge the therapist with the two-fold task of empathy with the suffering of the patient and the need to find a therapeutic intervention which may prove effective. . . . We allow ourselves to enter into a world of chaos and/or unreal resolution or restitution. We must let ourselves experience an alien and possibly hostile world which does not seem to offer sustenance or support to the patient or else to identify with a psychotic self which has managed to comprehend such a world via a delusional system or by way of a retreat from reality. . . . [T]here is an enormous range of pathology in this area but the methodology of empathic participation remains constant and, particularly with these individuals, profoundly difficult. An understanding of the self-fragmentation or disorganization or pathologic restitution allows a more rational choice of treatment. [p. 127]

Without being drawn into the chaotic disorganization of the adolescent, the therapist can then determine whether a controlled environment is necessary. He can determine whether the adolescent can tolerate an intensive psychoanalytic process, or whether psychotherapeutic intervention is indicated. "If the process of disorganization predominates, then our therapeutic activity devotes itself to putting things back together. If the new self is a damaged or injured one, then we work on the reparative aspect. If a total reorganization is called for, then analysis of an adolescent is prescribed" (p. 128). Essentially, Goldberg calls for a shift of emphasis from partial perspectives of personality, such as that of the Oedipus complex, to a total consideration of the epigenetic development of the self, as described by Kohut (1977, 1984).

6

Adults

Marion F. Solomon

The developmental task of the adult is achievement of intimacy, the ability to sustain affiliation and love. When the capacity for intimacy is disrupted, the danger, Erikson (1963) notes, is isolation. The role of the therapist in approaching an adult relationship is based upon an understanding of

1. how people develop capacities for self-other interaction,
2. the reasons why mates may misconstrue each other's signals,
3. the underlying, unresolved needs that reemerge in intimate relationships of adulthood.

Heinz Kohut (1971) reported success in the treatment of the narcissistically vulnerable through a process of empathic understanding and analysis of selfobject failures that occur in the relationships between patient and therapist. Although Kohut did not investigate the transference in intimate extratherapeutic relationships, those with self disorders have similar transferencelike reactions in other relationships (Solomon 1989).

Kohut (1984) recognized the importance of selfobjects in intimate relationships. "A good marriage is one in which one partner or other rises to the challenge of providing the selfobject function that the other's temporarily impaired sense of self needs at a particular moment" (p. 220). Despite his affirmation of the possibility for treating narcissistically impaired individuals within conjoint therapy, Kohut (1971) also conceded that individual psychoanalytic treatment of narcissistic disorders is a long and difficult process. One might question, he suggested, whether it would even be feasible to treat such disorders in marital therapy (personal communication).

Despite the difficulties, there are a number of reasons why development of a methodology for diagnosis and treatment of narcissistic disorders in conjoint therapy is necessary. Increasingly, adult patients seeking therapy do so because of problems in relationships. Sagar and colleagues (1968) found that 50 percent of patients identified problems with significant others as a primary issue in treatment, and an additional 25 percent listed difficulties related to marriage as one of their issues.

It is necessary to develop treatments for these problems. Most psychodynamic approaches focus on treatment of the individual, not the relationship. However, a psychodynamic self psychology model can be utilized with couples whose narcissistic vulnerability and proneness to chaotic or fragmented feelings, create pathological family relationships.

ADULT ISSUES OF INTIMACY

This chapter is concerned with adult issues of intimacy and with self psychological approaches to treating partners in conjoint therapy. Included is a description of narcissistic vulnerability within the context of a relationship. Using case examples, I illustrate that for those who have suffered early interactional failures, it is possible to achieve intimacy—the most important task of adulthood.

In conjoint therapy with adults, the therapist helps the adult discover and understand how the earliest models of relationships influence current interactions, and how, once identified, the person can begin to modify the internal representational structure and establish a lasting and intimate relationship.

All adults carry a world view colored by a representational model filled with internal images of self and others. In intimate relationships this internal model enables partners to anticipate, interpret, and respond according to the previous experiences of each.

DEVELOPMENT OF PERSONAL MODELS

The internal representational model is structured according to the earliest interactive experiences between infant and caretaker. An accumulation of interactions of a similar nature becomes the model upon which future interactions are anticipated and maintained. In normal development this relationship pattern is relatively stable and secure. The model provides the individual with an internal structure or means for assessing and relating to new and unfamiliar individuals, situations, and events.

Where the early relationships were unstable or where the caretaker response was inadequate to meet the needs of the developing child, a vulnerability to emotional injury may occur. For adults who continue to experience the aftereffects of early interactive failures there is an ongoing tendency to feel fragmented, constantly disappointed, misunderstood, or overly defensive against the possibility of getting hurt by another. The result is a narcissistic vulnerability, an expectation of injury in successive relationships. Often this expectation becomes a self-fulfilling prophecy.

In a relationship, not only do narcissistic individuals fail to perceive their partners as separate, they also suffer the return of old, deep, internal anxieties and defenses. These old "hurts" or injuries to the self are reactivated within the context of the present relationship. When there are interactions between such narcissistically vulnerable persons, each views the other through unreliable, distorted lenses. Attempts at intimacy usually result in failure.

The most profoundly disturbed are those who will never bond with another in *any* attempt at intimacy. Most adults enter into relationships with high hopes and expectations of an idealized love. Romantic love provides an illusion of perfect mirroring or twinship. The realities of living together too often result in disappointment, disillusionment, and the emergence of defenses. Once problems begin, they intensify and expand progressively.

By the time couples decide on therapy, the relationship may be described as too close or too distant, too chaotic or emotionally empty. Both see themselves as victims and often feel alone, empty, and depressed. The partner is identified as the problem, and yet each fears and expects to be blamed, and protects against further hurt. Both desire understanding and affirmation, yet neither has any idea of how to achieve it.

NARCISSISTIC VULNERABILITY

Kohut (1971) found that the diagnosis of a self disorder could best be made through careful observation of the transference. That is when the analyst is perceived as an idealized source of soothing, loving affirmation and approval or a perfect other who is capable of solving all problems, whose very presence is expected to heal all wounds, and who is often thought of as capable of reading minds.

After only a few sessions in individual psychotherapy, such a narcissistic transference becomes evident. In conjoint therapy it is not necessary to await development of the transference reaction to occur. A full-blown transference between the two walks in the door the moment a couple enters the office. By observing how they talk to each other, how they listen or do not listen to what is said by the other and by the therapist, how sensitive one or both appear to be, and how each defends against perceived hurts, the therapist gets important clues that aid in the understanding of the degree of narcissistic vulnerability of each partner.

We all tend to repeat aspects of early relationships. Those whose choices in their intimate relationships fit well together may find that marriage heals deficiencies through meeting some basic needs. As a relationship develops into one of mutual caring, the early passionate attachment and romantic love grow into a complementary enhancing quid pro quo. There are alternating times of nurturing and mirroring. Those whose early failures are greater than the capacity of their partner to overcome tend to be mated to others who have similar or complementary development failures (Dicks 1967). Each partner may find himself or herself in the position of endlessly attempting to achieve wholeness through fusion with the other.

There is a wide range of narcissistic needs from the relatively healthy to those with severe self disorders. Even with partners each of whom has a cohesive self, there is a wish that the mate will at times fulfill certain functions that affirm, mirror, and respond in ways that enhance self-esteem. In the more pathological form are those who exist in "an emotional wasteland surrounded by an aura of specialness" (Lansky 1989, unpublished speech). When people with severe narcissistic disorders enter into a relationship, there is often an insistent and demanding expectation that the mate be constantly available to fill selfobject functions.

Those who are narcissistically vulnerable depend upon the feedback of others to maintain a precarious balance of "wholeness." On reaching adulthood, such individuals are often involved in difficult, tumultuous love partnerships. Their relationships are characterized by excessive entitlement, and a fragility and brittleness.

As adults, these people are not prime candidates for intimate relationships. They believe that they are always giving to others and are constantly disappointed that others do not reciprocate. There is a failure to recognize that what they do for others is based on their own desires, not on what the other wants. They have great difficulty listening to their partners and responding empathically. Instead they are busy communicating their own wishes, and finding ways to make others accommodate them. Anxiety levels soar as soon as a need emerges and the mate is not immediately responsive to the need to be constantly available and present. The result is that the partner feels oppressed and enslaved by expectations and demands.

When an adult places a mate in the position of providing the mirroring, twinship, or idealizing function, the other is likely to find this oppressive. There is little room for empathy or awareness that the other may have separate needs or wishes. In fact, there is an incapacity, partially or fully, to see another person as separate from one's self. Confirmation of the grandiose fantasy of fusion requires control of a partner. The need for control is accompanied by fear that the partner will get angry and respond in ways that result in humiliation, rejection, or abandonment.

Since narcissistically vulnerable adults are unable to rely on a sense of their own separate existence, they need another's presence to maintain feelings of cohesiveness. There is always anxiety about the possible loss and abandonment accompanied by fear of fragmentation and disintegration.

COUPLES THERAPY

Couples in therapy for relationship difficulties range from relatively healthy to severely pathological. Virtually all, however, exhibit some degree of narcissistic injury. Most people initially feel that the goal of conjoint therapy is to change their partner in some significant way. They rarely recognize that their partner feels this same need. Each experiences the other as demanding and unreasonable. Often such conflict originates in simple but basic differences in values, attitudes, and belief systems. "You don't cook like my mother" is not just a complaint over lack of experience; it is a statement of conflicting tastes. This may extend to "You don't value money as I do," or even "You are crazy." Even when both partners can claim solid feelings of self-esteem and inner cohesion, such attacks inflict harm, cause narcissistic injury, and often elicit counterattacks.

Relationships in which one or both partners suffer from a narcissistic disorder are often based on the illusory premise that two people are joined together as one. In the minds of those with a narcissistic personality, there is no doubt about which identity should overwhelm the other, since all objects (including the partner) exist only to meet their principal emotional need—the never-ending quest to feel whole and safe. If the partner fails to meet this need, the response is often feelings of loss of self-cohesion, fragmentation, and narcissistic rage.

Stan and Ada

Stan's usual blustering rage at what he perceived as the failure of his wife, Ada, to manage the children and their home was interrupted during one fiery outburst. "I know it is upsetting to hear that her job will take her out of town on the day of your son's Little League championship game," I commented, "but you seem more than upset. You look as though you could kill. It's more than the game, more than the job. There's something about her not paying attention, not seeming to care. Can you help me to understand what it touches inside of you, what it reminds you of?"

Stan responded with a poignant account of his experience growing up during the Korean War years. With his father in the service and his mother preoccupied with work, he had learned not to expect anyone to come to special events in school, or to share the excitement of Little League games. It hurt to see the same thing happening to his children. As I encouraged Ada and Stan to discuss these issues, the intensity calmed down enough to consider some alternatives. However, the rage continued to seem disproportionate to the precipitating source.

I weighed the possibilities that the real problem was (1) Stan's overidentification with his son as a Little League star, (2) his jealousy of his wife's career success, or (3) his intolerance of being alone when Ada went on a business trip. Alternately, I considered that Ada, an adult child of alcoholics, who had experienced violent battles between her parents, might be provoking Stan's rage.

Recognizing that issues that arise and remain unresolved are likely to resurface at a later time, I waited to see how it would develop in the context of the session. Making an interpretation to either at this point might have been experienced as a threat or attack rather than an empathic understanding of the internal experience of each of them. I decided to stay attuned to both Stan's feelings of aloneness and Ada's fear of any anger on her husband's part.

Shortly afterward, Stan reported a similar instance of barely suppressed rage that had emerged during an argument over one of Ada's male co-workers. Stan felt that a man was paying too much attention to Ada when he had invited her to dance at an office party. Stan left the party in a rage. Ada cried as we talked together about it and Stan was still angry. I told him, "I can see how angry you are right now, but I need you to hold on to the feeling for a moment, so that I can also understand what Ada is feeling." I kept it short at this point because I knew that Stan could only hold his anger for a moment. Ada, still crying, explained how Stan shamed her in front of her co-workers. She was only trying to be pleasant to the new management trainee in the office. He had been there for a week and didn't know many people. I responded, "The embarrassment and anger that you felt has not gone away. You still seem very upset right now."

Ada's response was, "I'm terrified that he is going to hit someone again." I turned to Stan and said, "It sounds as though you have tried hard to control your anger, but have not always been successful. Whom did you hit?" Stan and Ada then proceeded to tell me of an incident shortly after their wedding when an old boyfriend of Ada's came over to their table in a restaurant and began talking. At one point he had put his arm around her shoulders and given her a hug. Stan could not contain himself, got up, and punched the man. In our session Stan said, "I told you it would never happen again, and it won't ever again."

Ada responded, "I don't know if I can believe you." Ada had her own reasons not to trust his temper. She had described in previous sessions her parents' marriage, full of emotional outbursts. She recalled now how she had spent many an evening locked in the bathroom while her father pounded on the door, threatening to beat her up.

For the moment, she had control of the situation with Stan, but from a lifetime of experience she believed that her role was either to calm things down, or to run fast and hide. "How do I know when you'll lose control—and maybe next time hit me?" she asked, turning to Stan. I turned to Ada and said that I did not know if Stan would ever hit someone again in a jealous rage, but the rage was still there and we had better understand what that was all about. I also told her that we needed to understand her old feelings and the threat of danger that seemed to be with her always.

Stan appeared vulnerable and emotionally fragile at this point. He seemed to alternate between feelings of shame and a proneness to anger. I asked, "Can either of you tell me what you know about your histories that would shed some light on this feeling of distrust between you; that you are not to be trusted, Ada, that you might want to be with another man? And Stan, that you cannot be trusted to control your temper?"

I silently noted that at this tense moment it was Stan, not Ada, who was willing to share his painful experience. With some hesitation, Stan related that his mother had a lover while his father was in Korea. The man had lived with the two of them in their small apartment. Stan, who was 6 at the time, knew that there was something wrong with the man's sleeping in his mother's bedroom. Then suddenly, after weeks or months (Stan could not recall), "Uncle Charlie" was gone. By Christmas his father was home. His mother had warned him never to mention Uncle Charlie's visit. When he asked why not, she had said that if Stan told, his father would leave and would never come back. "You don't want Daddy to leave forever, do you?"

Stan choked up and was unable to go on. I said, "There are many tears that go with that story. You have never had a chance to shed them. What you've done is put your memories in a box and locked them up. When something comes up in your life that pushes the combination to the lock, all the confused, hurt, angry, and frightened feelings that you couldn't feel then erupt at one time. And it all gets directed at Ada. I can see how the two of you have had so much trouble."

The fear of being "found out" is mixed with the wish to be understood at the deepest levels of one's being. When words are put to those things that are known deep within the self but had been kept out of the realm of consciousness, a feeling of relief is quickly recognized, both through body posture and because it enables the person to go on. When it becomes clear to both partners that their underlying messages will be heard, at least by the therapist if not initially by their mate, it is possible for them to learn different ways of responding. The initial anxiety that each had upon entering therapy quickly fades.

DECODING COMMUNICATIONS

The therapeutic role throughout this process is to make the sessions a place where feelings and fears can be identified and dangerous impulses explored. It is possible to examine how feelings arose in interactions in the past, what brought them up in the present, how they impact upon a current relationship, and how the feelings are contained, split off, or otherwise defended against.

The therapist begins by carefully listening to the problems presented by the couple and attempting to understand the underlying needs and fears related to love and loss, closeness and distance, dominance and control, danger and safety. As these are understood and shared with the mates, the focus is not on what either is doing wrong, but on how the behaviors and reactions of each may be a defense against narcissistic injury. Then each is given an opportunity to share how these defenses are experienced by the other.

During this process the therapist takes an active stance in establishing rules and boundaries to assure that old attack and defense patterns do not take over. Whatever the partners present at the beginning is translated with positive connotation as the best way that each knows to deal with the anxiety that has arisen in the immediate focus of discussion.

There are many opportunities to examine with the couple their individual and cumulative histories. How they present, who presents what, and how they hear each other provide insight into the transferential patterns, internalized object representations, needs, fears, and defenses.

Communications must be examined as messages about protection of a depressed or vulnerable self or about restoration of a fragmenting self. Symptoms are seen as messages about needs and vulnerabilities. Interpretations focus on the nature of disruptions of selfobject functions, threats of narcissistic injury, and the internal experiences of the self in the face of narcissistic wounds.

When anger and wrathful feelings erupt, the focus of the therapist is to understand how the person, feeling threatened, tries to restore a sense of vitality and self-cohesion. Similarly, an attempt is made to connect symptoms with the person's wish to restore cohesion and harmony of the self by using the symptom to regain a sense of power or reducing rage by projecting it elsewhere.

In this process psychological interpretations or instructions that suggest changes in actions or behavior toward each partner must be presented with care to avoid causing a narcissistic injury or damage to the vulnerable selves of either partner. This may at first seem difficult when, in the view of the therapist, one or both partners make overly demanding claims or expectations.

The "common-sense" response of the therapist may well be that such demands and unreasonable entitlements should be relinquished and reality-based limitations clarified. Unfortunately, such a response may be perceived as a negative intrusion and experienced as a narcissistic injury to an individual with a self disorder. Overblown demands are often a symptom of narcissistic pathology. Censure, deep psychological interpretations, or suggestions for new behavior that raise levels of anxiety may cause a defensive closing up, a burial or repression of narcissistic assertiveness, and an increase in the split in the personality. Often, a mobilization of the archaic grandiose self may occur on the principle that "the best defense is a good offense," thus escalating the destructive, attacking interactions of the couple.

Whether such interventions are done by the mate or the therapist, a series of narcissistic injuries will make treatment lose its value. This is why the use of paradox, while sometimes valuable in work with neurotics who have a more solid sense of self, should not be used in treatment with narcissistically vulnerable individuals. The defense against perceived attacks may increase resistance to treatment.

In conjoint therapy, couples are helped to formulate messages that accurately describe underlying needs and to receive messages from each other with fewer distortions. To this end, the therapist must translate or decode confusing messages and, in so doing, promote the safe environment in which anxiety-provoking or painful communications can be comprehended and tolerated. Successful decoding and empathic responses in conjoint therapy can result in the gradual disintegration of the rigid barriers that impede loving contact in a relationship, thus allowing the partners to give and receive growth-inducing functions in a more mature manner. As one sensitive young woman said to her husband after hearing his version of a fight they had had the night before, "Oh, you did that because you were hurt by what I said—I thought you were just purposely being mean."

Because the language of feelings and needs is rarely spoken directly but appears in encoded form, it is often difficult for partners to make themselves understood. One must have an understanding of the other's language as well as a willingness to hear it in order to decode it properly. It is at this level that a dynamically oriented psychotherapist who can examine current interactions between intimate partners in terms of historical patterns of relating as well as the here-and-now relationship can be of great assistance to individuals who are trying to improve their relationship.

The therapeutic stance in which there is a provision of safety allows partners to become closer in sharing material that previously had been considered embarrassing, shameful, or too distasteful to be accepted.

John and Ann

John, whose domineering attitude and endless list of complaints alienated his wife, Ann, was asked to stop and examine his reaction to her attempt to assert herself. He hesitatingly described his need to "puff myself up—make myself strong," because he believed that Ann needed him to be more powerful than she—strong enough to take care of her.

He told of his feeling throughout his early life that something within him was too weak, too feminine. He said that at the age of 13 while watching a movie he first heard the word "wimp" and felt he finally had a word to describe his lifelong feeling. He has behaved in his adult life in ways that could help him hide from this "weakness." He married his wife when she was going through an emotionally chaotic time. He took over the role of a father figure/mentor.

Ann responded, "What a relief. You have always told me you were a saint and I was the one with all the problems. I know I have problems. It is so good to know that I'm not the only one; you're not so perfect either." She too alternated between a wish to be taken care of by a powerful other and a wish to grow into her own strength. Each wished for the other to accept a role and each alternated by rejecting the roles played.

If either partner responds to the other's vulnerable area with an attack or provocative pattern encouraging old collusive battles, the therapist may then focus on that person—why the need to behave this way at this moment. Is there a fear that they will become too close, too weak, too vulnerable?

These interpretations are not confrontations. They are attempts to encourage self-disclosure toward a better understanding of the present in terms of the ways these individuals learned to be in the world and with each other. The goal is to foster collaboration between partners and between the couple and the therapist, increase their optimism about joint resolution of problems, and bring about the communication of underlying emotions during the problem-solving process.

Couples are relieved to learn what the behavior and statements of each really mean as selfobject fantasies are translated into individual needs and wishes. It helps to understand that the behavior is not meant as an attack but as a way of protecting against hurt. With this awareness, partners may be able to change patterns of defense and retaliation. As understanding increases and defenses are reduced over time, the partners may come to be remarkably responsive to each other.

From the start the therapist gives a message that conveys to the couple the goal of understanding as nearly as possible the needs of each partner, the things that bring on their emotional pain, and the way that each defends vulnerable areas. When needs, hurts, or defenses come up in the sessions, they will be viewed not as problems but as opportunities for exploration. The presenting problems, such as issues of money, work, sex, children, the difficulties of living, are all dealt with until an area of narcissistic need, injury, or defense arises. At that point, we temporarily put aside whatever is being discussed to make the therapeutic setting a container for the anxiety that inevitably emerges. We examine how a specific issue becomes part of the collaborative dance between the partners.

Conjoint treatment of self disorders requires an extremely slow pace. A repetitive pattern of interactions occurs among the partners and the therapist. Repeated expectations, demands, and questions place constant pressure on partners and on the therapist to react in a certain predetermined manner. Repeated hurts are inflicted, resulting in hurried withdrawal or scathing rage. Repeatedly, one partner turns to the other partner or to the therapist for approval or confirmation. If it is not immediately forthcoming, a deflation and lethargic disappointment occur in either verbal communication or body language.

Treatment focuses on the content and on the process of sending and receiving messages. It may include examining with the mates the minute details of feelings as they emerge at points where anger arises; it may involve asking about what they each expect during times when there are withdrawal, attack, and defense patterns; it may require asking how they protect themselves when they are feeling vulnerable.

Depending upon the issues for the couple, each of these may help to clarify the needs of the partner, and allow them to recognize areas that are being protected. It is the ability of the mates to overcome their need to hide shameful and embarrassing feelings from each other that allows them to relinquish repression of archaic narcissistic needs.

The therapist assists in this process by constantly reinterpreting content interactions to reflect underlying needs, for example, "You appear to be very upset and angry"; "You must have been very hurt by what was said." The goal is not only to change behavior. It is to reunite disavowed parts of the self and to aid in the reemergence of heretofore unacceptable narcissistic aspects so that emptiness, lethargy, and depressed feelings can be overcome. Consequently, each becomes a better mirroring selfobject for the other. Each acquires a new understanding that underlying needs may be very similar even when they present themselves differently. Where both are terrified of intimacy, one may seem overinvolved while the other withdraws. When both are hungry emotionally, one may appear to be a caretaker while the other seems to demand constant filling.

THERAPEUTIC CONSIDERATIONS

Within the atmosphere of a containing therapeutic environment, the therapist may stop the process when things begin to "warm up," tell the couple that they are getting to the heart of something that hurts them both a great deal, and suggest that they try to stay with what they feel as they speak and listen to each other. When there is an attempt to avoid or attack the other or change the subject, a comment such as, "I know what just happened must be very painful, what do you usually do when it feels too awful to tolerate?" is helpful. Responding to the pain with empathy, rather than responding to the issue precipitating the overwhelming affect, often reduces anxiety and allows the person to examine the cause of the burning feelings. The mate is then asked, "What feelings do you have that correspond with what you just heard?" "How do you defend against your too-painful feelings?" The discussion then focuses on the feelings themselves rather than on the issues that the mates usually fight about.

This then can lead into a discussion about how each perceives the other's feelings and behaviors, about how much they were aware of before this discussion, and about what they generally do when such feelings come up in their lives together. The therapist is in a position to show how each partner's usual defenses, which feel to the other as attacks or withdrawals, are meant to protect a vulnerable self.

As selfobject fantasies are translated into individual needs and wishes, couples are relieved to learn what the behavior and statements of each really mean. They begin to understand that the behavior is not meant as an attack but as a way of protecting against hurt. With this awareness, partners are able to change patterns of defense and retaliation. As understanding increases and defenses are reduced over time, they may come to be remarkably responsive to each other.

At first, the therapy sessions are a haven in which the mates come to interact with greater freedom. With the therapist's interventions, both partners are kept from destructive or injurious attacks. As they hear each other at a deeper level, they go home from sessions with increased ability to serve selfobject functions for each other. Receiving empathic understanding and a selfobject response to previously submerged frightening feelings makes communication with the partner easier. When it becomes less necessary to mobilize defenses against old needs and feelings there may be a transformation of the self. Narcissistic demandingness may be replaced by normal assertiveness. Timidity and withdrawal from the partner as a way to protect against childlike grandiose fantasies that cause shame and embarrassment may be replaced by a willingness to expose high aspirations and devotion to ideals, as well as a joyful acceptance of a healthy grandiosity.

CONCLUSION

An intimate partnership in which each adult provides good-enough (although at times imperfect) selfobject functions for the other helps to create the benign environment that makes it possible for emotional growth to take place. This, in fact, is the basis of all successful relationships. Where therapists can enhance the climate that promotes selfobject functioning for mates, we assist in the well-being of both individuals and couples.

The goal of treatment of self disorders is the development of a cohesive self through a process that Kohut (1971) calls transmuting internalization. Transmuting internalizations are the internal changes that occur as the individual increasingly develops the capacity to accept the hurts that are caused by failures of optimal responses by important others. During the treatment process there is an awareness that the other is trying to hear and understand in ways that differ from old patterns. There is a willingness to acknowledge wounded feelings as they occur rather than cutting off feelings and retaliating. There is an increasing ability to recognize messages to mean what the sender actually meant rather than distorting them. When there are provocations, attacks, or failures in empathy, they can increasingly be tolerated, through the facilitation of the therapist.

Through the building up of a tolerance to the feelings that had caused overwhelming shame or anxiety, the vulnerability decreases and there is less need to protect against overwhelming reactions. There is a restoration of a sense of vitality, cohesion, and harmony to the self.

Another goal of couples psychotherapy is to develop increasing tolerance of selfobject failures so that they no longer cause fears of loss of cohesion. Ideally, the structures of the self develop to the point where there is a gradual replacement of the need for selfobject functions with a firmed-up self and its functions. In the process of couples therapy, adults feel safe sharing heretofore cut-off aspects of themselves. They learn to relate to their spouses in an ongoing benign, nontraumatic environment with only occasional, usually manageable failures.

7

Elderly

Lawrence W. Lazarus

This chapter applies new theoretical insights regarding the psychology of the self as conceptualized by Kohut (1966, 1968, 1977) and others (Reich 1960, Goldberg 1973) to brief psychotherapy with elderly outpatients. A discussion of some developmental issues of aging from the perspective of self psychology and a brief review of the psychology of the self are followed by a description of elderly patients with disorders of the self. Some therapeutic strategies useful for working in a brief (time-limited) psychotherapeutic approach will be illustrated with clinical examples.

One of the basic developmental tasks facing the aging individual is to maintain self-esteem and a sense of bodily and emotional cohesiveness in the wake of the inevitable biological, psychological, and social stresses and losses in late life. Erikson (1968) characterized the last phase of the life cycle as the struggle to sustain ego integrity versus the failure to do so, which leads to despair and disgust. Meissner (1976) believes that the basic problem of aging is narcissistic loss and referred to Rochlin's (1965) discussion of this issue:

> The greatest test of narcissism is aging or old age. All that has come to represent value and with which narcissism has long been associated is jeopardized by growing old. The skills, mastery, and powers, all painfully acquired, which provided gratifications as they functioned to effect adaptation wane in the last phase of life. One's resources, energies, adaptability, and function, the intimacies of relationships upon which one depended, family and friends, are continually being depleted and lost. [pp. 377–378]

Cath (1976) describes the regression that can occur in an elderly person when attempts to find restitution or compensation for biopsychosocial losses are outweighed by depression and depletion. Should nothing relieve the depression-depletion-isolation cycle, further regression leads to gradual dissolution of the coalesced ego nuclei into more visible fragmented parts, along more narcissistic rather than object-related positions. As the cathexis of the superego and ego ideals is progressively abandoned, one no longer anticipates, hopes, dreams, or desires. Cath believes that the intervention of an empathic therapist can forestall this regression.

SELF PSYCHOLOGICAL ISSUES

The traditional Freudian (1914) view of psychosexual development conceptualized infantile narcissism as gradually maturing into object love. Kohut, based on the psychoanalysis of adult patients with narcissistic personality disorders (1966, 1968, 1971, 1977), departed from this Freudian view and proposed another major line of development of the self beginning with early precursors or way stations of the self (archaic nuclear self) that gradually undergo transformations into the cohesive self that, to varying degrees, attain higher forms (or developmental achievements) of the self. The self may be defined as a developmental psychological structure responsible for maintenance of one's self-esteem, self-image, feelings, and affects associated with bodily and psychological cohesiveness, and relative need for others to admire (or idealize) and to serve as selfobjects. The disturbances of narcissistic balance referred to as narcissistic injury are usually easily recognized by the painful affect of embarrassment or shame that accompanies them and by their ideational elaboration, which is known as inferiority feelings or hurt pride (Kohut 1966).

The development of a healthy self depends on the child's inherited biological abilities and the quality of his relationship with parental figures who serve as selfobjects, that is, objects experienced as part of the self that serve both mirroring and idealizing functions. At critical stages in the development of the self, the empathic responses of parental selfobjects provide the nourishing matrix that confirms the child's innate sense of vigor, vitality, and perfection (the function of the mirroring aspects of selfobjects) and that satisfies the child's need to admire and to feel merged with an infallible and omnipotent other (the function of the idealizing aspects of selfobjects).

During the normal development of the self (as schematically diagrammed in Figure 7-1), the infant's feelings of omnipotence and perfection as well as exhibitionistic displays (the grandiose self) inevitably meet with minor, nontraumatic failures on the part of the selfobjects to mirror empathically or respond appropriately to the child's grandiosity. In response to these normal, phase-specific empathic failures, the child's grandiosity and exhibitionism (the grandiose self) gradually become modified and transformed into realistic ambitions, confidence, and the wish to excel. In contrast, if the child's phase-appropriate exhibitionistic drives are not responded to empathically and appropriately by the selfobjects' approval, but instead are repeatedly and traumatically frustrated (for example, because of a parent's depression or narcissistic preoccupation), the exhibitionistic drives become repressed and thus inaccessible to the modifying influence of reality. They retain their primitive quality and drive for expression, rather than undergoing modification and transformation into healthy expressions of the self.

The other precursor of the child's cohesive self, the idealized parent imago, results from a projection of the child's original

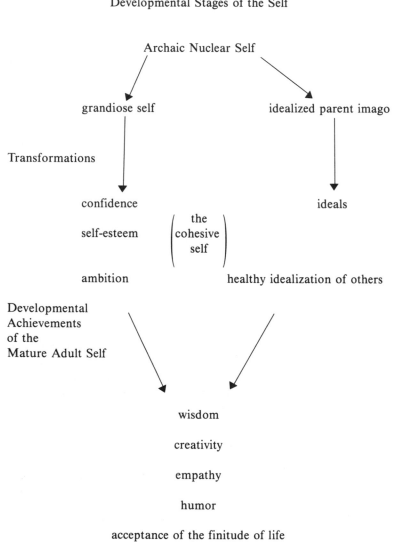

Figure 7–1
Developmental Stages of the Self

Archaic Nuclear Self

grandiose self   idealized parent imago

Transformations

confidence   ideals

self-esteem   (the
                 cohesive
                 self)

ambition   healthy idealization of others

Developmental
Achievements
of the
Mature Adult Self

wisdom

creativity

empathy

humor

acceptance of the finitude of life

feelings of omnipotence and perfection onto the selfobject (the parental figure), leading to an idealization of the selfobject. During the preoedipal and oedipal periods, there is a gradual phase-specific discovery by the child of the parents' real, as opposed to idealized, qualities. The child responds to this disappointment by internalizing the parents' idealized qualities, a process that contributes gradually to the formation of the ego ideal, the portion of the superego responsible for one's values and ideals. If the parent, because of self pathology, rejects the child's idealizations, such sudden traumatic disappointments may lead to a phase-inappropriate, massive internalization of the idealized qualities. A fixation at this stage of psychological development may lead to unrealistic demands for self-perfection and a continual need for reassurance from an omnipotent other to maintain a cohesive sense of self.

Normal, age-appropriate minor empathic failures on the part of the selfobjects lead to the gradual replacement of the selfobjects and their functions by an autonomous self and its functions—a specific process of psychological structure formation called transmuting internalization.

According to Kohut (1972):

the experiences during the formation of the self become the prototype of the specific forms of our later vulnerability and security in the narcissistic realm: of the ups and downs in our self-esteem, of our lesser or greater need for praise, for merger into idealized figures, and for other forms of narcissistic sustenance: and of the greater or lesser cohesion of self during periods of transition, whether in the transition to latency, to early or late adolescence, in maturity, or in old age. [pp. 368–369]

Kohut and Wolf (1978) state:

Depending on the quality of the interactions between the self and its selfobjects in childhood, the self will emerge either as a firm and healthy structure or as a more or less seriously damaged one. The adult self may thus exist in states of varying degrees of coherence from cohesion to fragmentation; in states of varying degrees of vitality; from vigor to enfeeblement; in states of varying degrees of functional harmony, from order to chaos. [p. 414]

Depending on one's innate biological abilities, interactions with nourishing parental selfobjects, and fortunate life experiences, each person attains, to varying degrees, such developmental achievements of the self as wisdom, creativity, empathy for others, humor, and acceptance of the finitude of life.

In his later writings, Kohut made a significant shift in conceptualizing the self not in isolation but as a lifelong sequence of changing self–selfobject relationships. Psychopathology in general, and self pathology in particular, are therefore defined in terms not of this or that defect in the self but in terms of a disturbance of the self–selfobject relationship during a particular stage of the curve of life. Applying these concepts to the psychopathology of the elderly, Kohut (1980, personal communication) suggests "focusing on the old and his environment as a unit rather than focusing only on the failures of the aged and on the defects of the self."

In his summarizing statement at the 1978 Chicago Conference on Self Psychology, Kohut explained:

> In the view of self psychology man lives in a matrix of self-objects from birth to death. He needs selfobjects for his psychological survival, just as he needs oxygen in his environment throughout his life for physiological survival. How accurately in tune with the small baby's various, specific needs were the responses of the selfobject at the beginning of extrauterine life, we will ask. Did the selfobject respond with proud mirroring to the first strivings for a move away, will be another question. And how, finally, does the selfobject milieu respond to a person's dying? With pride in him for being an example of courage in pain and decline? Or by withdrawing their mirroring from him at this ultimate point in the curve of life? [pp. 377–378]

Turning now to a conceptualization of self-esteem maintenance from a sociological perspective, Atchley (1982) believes that people who lose self-esteem in later life do so because (1) physical changes become so pronounced that the person is forced to accept a less desirable self-image, (2) self-esteem is too dependent on social or work roles, and (3) control over one's life and environment is diminished. It goes without saying that a fourth important factor that explains why some older people have difficulty sustaining self-esteem is problematic self-esteem regulation during the crucial formative (birth to latency) and subsequent developmental stages. Atchley believes that the elderly adaptively defend themselves against negative societal stereotypes of old age and the other potential eroders of self-esteem mentioned above (these adaptive defenses are familiar to psychotherapists) by (1) focusing on past successes, (2) discounting messages that do not fit with the older person's existing self-concept, (3) refusing to apply general myths and misconceptions about aging to themselves, (4) choosing to interact with people who provide an egosyntonic experience, or, in other words, make them feel good, and (5) perceiving selectively what they are told.

MANIFESTATIONS OF SELF PATHOLOGY IN LATER LIFE

In psychotherapeutic work with elderly patients, one observes the ebb and flow of self-esteem balance and imbalance. In response to stress and/or loss in the elderly person's selfobject milieu (that is, admission to a nursing home), one may observe a regression, in some ways adapative, to earlier developmental modes of preserving self-esteem and feelings of security. Hence, the physically impaired older person may become increasingly dependent on a health professional who is admired for healing powers. This idealization may be adaptive in that it enables the person to feel close to someone perceived as strong and beneficent. Another example is that of a demented older person living in a nursing home who misidentifies a young female nurse as her long-deceased mother. Although the misidentification could be attributable to neurological deficits, from the perspective of self psychology it may serve an adaptive, restitutive function by enabling the older person to feel reunited with a soothing selfobject of childhood.

Manifestations of self psychopathology in the elderly are seen not only in those with narcissistic personalities but also in varying ways (both quantitatively and qualitatively) in most personality types, and in patients with affective and anxiety disorders. Discussing brief psychotherapy of adult patients with stress-response syndromes, Horowitz (1976) noted: "Narcissistic considerations are present in every character type, not just the narcissistic personality, and some nuances of treatment (of the narcissistic personality) might be pertinent at any time" (p. 184).

Manifestations of self psychopathology in the elderly may include (1) exquisite sensitivity to perceived slights and insults; (2) reactive anger, rage (Kohut 1972), and withdrawal and/or depression in response to disappointment or rejection (experienced as a narcissistic injury); (3) wide vacillations in self-esteem; (4) a propensity to self-consciousness, shame, and embarrassment; (5) hypochondriasis (which may represent a hypercathexis of bodily parts and thus a temporary discohesiveness of the self); (6) overdependency on others for approval; (7) a tendency to view other persons not as objects separate from the self but as selfobjects or extensions of the self that serve to stabilize a precarious self; and (8) an overemphasis on physical attractiveness, possessions, and past accomplishments to cope with feelings of diminished self-esteem, emptiness, and depletion.

Clinical Example

Mrs. H., a 79-year-old housewife living with her partially blind husband in a small apartment, had always been controlling, self-centered, and perfectionistic. She described herself as a spoiled young girl, headstrong and self-absorbed. She had always been exquisitely sensitive to what she perceived to be slights and insults from others and reacted with indifference, arrogance, anger, and/or withdrawal. During her long marriage, her husband acquiesced to her wishes but his failing eyesight now limited his capacity to serve as an obedient selfobject. She became depressed and hypochondriacal in response to increasing physical incapacity from heart disease and arthritis. She visited many physicians whom she first idealized but then summarily dismissed when disappointed that they could not magically restore her health. She avoided former friends because she could not bear for them to see her in her present condition. As control over her selfobject world diminished, she became more controlling of her daughter, provoking guilt to increase her daughter's subservience. Attributing all her dysphoria to physical problems, she was very ambivalent about seeing a psychiatrist. She felt embarrassed and ashamed that others might think she was "crazy."

From the perspective of self psychology, her depression can be viewed as a reaction to narcissistic injuries caused by failing health, increasing sense of depletion, and lessening control over the selfobjects of her increasingly constricted world. She attempted to maintain a modicum of self-esteem and control over her self-object milieu by forcing the remaining selfobjects (the daughter) to fulfill her wishes. Her reactive anger was a response to the perceived failure of her selfobjects (for example, her husband and physicians) to soothe, heal, and provide other self-object functions she could not provide for herself. Her treatment will be discussed later in this paper.

Clinical investigators (Malan 1976, Mann 1973, Sifneos 1972, Wolberg 1965) who have studied the process and efficacy of brief, or time-limited, dynamic psychotherapy, all generally agree that this approach is best suited for patients with circumscribed and focal problems. A capacity for good interpersonal relationships, introspection and insight, and the development of a resolvable transference is in general correlated positively with clinical improvement. Examples of elderly patients who are suitable candidates for brief psychotherapy may include those with the following diagnoses (American Psychiatric Associaton 1980): (1) adjustment disorders, (2) post-traumatic stress disorders, (3) certain affective disorders, and (4) uncomplicated bereavement. Although patients with these psychiatric disorders may have the capacity for brief, insight-oriented psychotherapy where clarification and interpretation are among the principal psychotherapeutic techniques, many elderly outpatients require supportive approaches (e.g., suggestion, reassurance) as well.

Agreeing to a finite number of sessions, usually as few as eight or as many as twenty, may be especially suited to selected elderly outpatients because brief therapy (1) reinforces belief in the patient's ability to master current life stress just as the patient has mastered problems in the past, (2) reduces fear of protracted dependency on the therapist, (3) realistically considers not only the finitude of time but also the finitude of the patient's remaining life, (4) speeds up (or telescopes) the beginning, middle, and termination phases of therapy, (5) reduces the patient's financial burden, such as that imposed by the restricted number of outpatient visits reimbursable by Medicare and other insurance carriers, and (6) brings into focus early in treatment the inevitable termination phase.

THERAPEUTIC APPROACHES

Elderly patients with disorders of the self often enter therapy following a narcissistic injury (that is, forced retirement, the disruption of an important selfobject relationship). They want especially to feel understood and accepted by the therapist and are exquisitely sensitive to feeling misunderstood or rebuffed. The patients may even experience the need for psychotherapy as a narcissistic insult. Therefore, feelings of shame and embarrassment about being in treatment and sensitivity to the therapist's responses may call forth narcissistic defenses such as aloofness, withdrawal, and arrogance.

The Therapist as Selfobject

Since one of the major goals of brief psychotherapy with these patients is the restoration of self-esteem, the therapist serves as an empathic selfobject, that is, he or she empathizes with and clarifies from the perspective of self psychology the patient's understandable resistances to therapy, reflects empathically upon the stresses that led to therapy, and is cognizant of the patient's sensitivity to the therapist's inevitable empathic failures (that is, when the patient feels misunderstood). Functioning as a selfobject, the therapist understands the patient's tendency to vacillate between idealization and devaluation. The therapist's empathy helps to restore the patient's self-esteem. It is sometimes useful during the opening session to elicit how the patient has coped with past stresses in order to reaffirm the patient's capacity to cope with narcissistic injury.

> During the initial phase of psychotherapy with the physically impaired 79-year-old woman described earlier in this chapter, the therapist would occasionally try to interject a more hopeful view of her predicament, a view which did not reflect or mirror her inner sense of despair and depletion. She became sullen and angry at the therapist for misunderstanding her. When the therapist then empathized with her annoyance, her face brightened as she exclaimed a confirmatory "Yes! You understand." She needed to feel that the therapist understood her suffering and to feel in control of the therapist much the way she needed to control her increasingly constricted world. During a therapeutic session in her apartment, she excitedly explained to her therapist: "See! This is my little world. It extends from this telephone and table to the doorway." Pinned on the telephone, the agent of her communication with the outside world, were the telephone numbers of her psychiatrist, pharmacist, and other health professionals whom she perceived not as separate objects but as extensions of herself.

Restoration of Self-esteem

The therapist understands how patients with disorders of the self utilize the therapist to restore self-esteem. For example, the patient may reminisce about past accomplishments, recount innumerable past narcissistic injuries, and attribute responsibility and blame for current problems to someone or something else in order to bolster a diminished sense of self and self-esteem. The elderly narcissistic patient with lifelong perfectionistic strivings may have great difficulty accepting diminished abilities imposed by physical impairments. Feeling the same lifelong demands in the present to excel, the patient may be especially susceptible to depression. The therapist tries to help the patient modify self-expectations and to be more accepting of limitations. The relationship with an empathic therapist may help the patient to mourn the loss of selfobject relationships while serving as a bridge to reestablish a supportive selfobject milieu (that is, to reestablish old or develop new nourishing selfobject relationships).

Potential Countertransference Issues

The therapist may become bored and annoyed, and lose concentration because of the patient's continual need for mirroring and approval. Discussing the treatment of narcissistic personalities, Stolorow (1975) suggested that it is helpful "to recognize that their narcissism is literally in the service of the psychic survival of the self. . . . The therapist can endure his humble, and at times, thankless role in the narcissistic transference of being nothing more than the embodiment of a function which the patient's mental apparatus cannot yet perform itself" (p. 184). The therapist may feel uncomfortable with the patient's idealization and misidentify it as a defense against hostility or undermine the idealization under the guise of improving the patient's reality testing. Kohut (1968), discussing the psychoanalysis of patients with narcissistic personality disorders, pointed out that premature interpretation of the idealization may represent a defensive warding off of the therapist's own grandiosity. An appropriate therapeutic response for many elderly patients with disorders of the self is to calmly accept the idealization.

Termination Issues

As termination approaches, there is usually a recapitulation of the same issues that brought the patient to treatment. The patient may talk about the termination of other important relationships. For example, the patient may have entered therapy following the loss (through death or separation) of an important selfobject relationship. In therapy, the therapist may serve similar selfobject functions. Termination of therapy may stimulate feelings similar to those experienced during and after the loss that initially led to treatment, as the following case illustrates.

> Mr. T., a 72-year-old married, retired, depressed real estate salesman with dependent and narcissistic personality features entered brief therapy because of chronic feelings of depression, self-doubt, and marital disharmony. His retirement resulted in increased time with his wife, who had recently become active in the feminist

movement. She was critical of and impatient with his passivity and dependency. Mr. T. attributed his lifelong insecurity to the sudden death of his father when he was 10 years old and his mother's subsequent depression and emotional unavailability. He compensated for his lifelong insecurity and low self-esteem by becoming an intellectual, playing the part of the gracious host when entertaining, and succeeding in his career.

In therapy, he formed a dependent, eroticized, idealized transference to his 30-year-old female therapist, wishing that she would compensate for his wife's depreciation of him. Although his self-esteem and depression improved after twelve therapy sessions with his empathic therapist, as termination approached he became sullen and more impatient with his wife. He was unable to sustain the improvement without continued therapy. Six months after termination, some of his depressive symptoms returned and he entered treatment with a male therapist.

Some patients terminate therapy abruptly after only a few sessions because they feel that these few meetings were sufficient to reaffirm their self-esteem following a narcissistic injury, because they felt misunderstood by the therapist, and/or because being a patient in psychotherapy may be experienced as an affront to self-esteem. A flight from therapy may serve as external validation not only of the patient's sanity but also of one's mastery. It is important to help patients understand their resistances to therapy so that they do not interrupt treatment prematurely.

Termination can sometimes be facilitated by the reestablishment of an old, or the development of a new, selfobject relationship. The positive relationship with the therapist may enable the patient to establish other meaningful relationships.

Although brief (time-limited) psychotherapy with adult patients attempts to abide by a finite number of sessions, elderly patients are usually encouraged to return to therapy because of the possibility of subsequent narcissistic, as well as other, losses. It is often helpful to explore potential resistances the patient may have to returning to therapy, such as shame over disappointing the self or the therapist and the admission of vulnerability.

The 79-year-old depressed woman discussed previously improved in response to her therapist's mirroring and approval. After ten sessions she felt she no longer required regular appointments. With the therapist's encouragement, she reinstated her relationship with a supportive relative. Sensing the tenuous nature of her relationship with her family and her unstable health, the therapist asked if she might be reluctant to contact him in the future. She said she would feel ashamed at having to admit her need for further therapy. These and other resistances were discussed. Subsequent telephone sessions several times yearly over the ensuing years helped to maintain her improvement.

CONCLUSION

If one of the major developmental tasks of aging is the maintenance of self-esteem in the wake of narcissistic and object losses, then the psychology of the self provides an important theoretical framework that can complement traditional psychoanalytic and other models for understanding and treating many elderly patients. The elderly person's self-image and self-esteem are challenged at a period in the life cycle when the mental and physical apparatus may be less able to cope with, and to find restitution for, multiple stresses and losses. The therapist often observes adaptive, as well as maladaptive, attempts at maintaining and restoring self-esteem.

Brief, or time-limited, psychotherapy may be considered for some elderly patients with disorders of the self when a narcissistic injury, such as the loss of an important relation or failing health, may be the central issue that prompted entry into therapy. Functioning as a selfobject for such patients, the therapist is understanding of the patient's narcissistic defenses, need for positive mirroring, tendency to idealize the therapist, and exquisite sensitivity to empathic failures. Given the time restrictions of brief therapy, the goals are usually more limited than long-term psychoanalytically oriented psychotherapy. In addition to reestablishing or restoring self-esteem, other goals may include the patient's acceptance of his or her legitimate need for relationships that serve sustaining selfobject functions, the need to be more accepting of self-limitations (to modify the unrealistic demands of the ego ideal), and the learning of adaptive ways to cope with inevitable future narcissistic injuries. The patient may identify with the therapist's tolerant and accepting attitude, thus enabling a greater degree of self-acceptance. Many elderly patients enter treatment following a succession of disappointments and losses. Helping patients to sustain, master, and find restitution for these losses, and thus restore self-esteem, is a challenging and rewarding task for both therapist and patient.

PART III

APPLYING SELF PSYCHOLOGY IN DIFFERENT SITUATIONS

8

When the Patient Is Demanding

Anna Ornstein

SELFOBJECT TRANSFERENCES

Kohut developed the theory of the bipolar nuclear self (his highest level of abstraction or metapsychology) on the basis of transferences. Patients who failed to recreate the infantile neurosis in their analyses still developed transferences, but of a special kind. These were transferences in which the therapist was being used as part of the patient's self. Because of this particular quality, he first called these "narcissistic," later, "selfobject transferences." Once these selfobject transferences achieved a degree of cohesion, they lent themselves to systematic interpretations just as transferences that were based on the arrested Oedipus complex. Kohut (1971) described the various forms of selfobject transferences in his first major publication *The Analysis of the Self.*

In their effort to bring the theory of ego-psychology closer to the clinical moment, that is, the patient's experiences within the therapeutic dyad, Blanck and Blanck (1974) recognized "the need to describe the phenomena of developmental lags and organization levels where distinction of self and object images is so meagerly attained *that search is for an object with whom to interact in the immediacy of the experience*" (p. 88, italics added). However, these authors did not offer the description of transferences that would be characteristic for those clinical conditions in which there is a "search for an object with whom to interact in the immediacy of the experience." Instead, they retained the narrow definition of transference: "We are constrained by use to discuss transference (including transference neurosis) and transference—like phenomena within their generally understood meanings and definitions" (Moore and Fine quoted in Blanck and Blanck, p. 87). This was a definition that considered transference to be a displacement of patterns of feelings and behavior, originally experienced with significant types in one's childhood to individuals in one's current relationship.

But Kohut did not consider the transferences that arose in relationship to the non-neurotic conditions to be displacements from one's childhood to individuals in one's current relationships. Rather, he described them as selfobject transferences because he recognized that the essential feature was that the therapist was put to functional use by the core of the self. The question is: How do we know how the therapist is being "used" or experienced by the patient? And how do we know how the therapist's behavior, tone of voice, or choice of words affects the state of mind of the patient? Since our therapeutic attention is consistently riveted on the *meaning* that our manner and actions have for the patient—rather than on the "actuality" or "reality" of our manner and our actions—to grasp these meanings is the therapist's paramount task (Schwaber 1976). It is here that empathy, as a mode of observation—attuned to the patient's self-experiences—becomes intrinsically linked to the recognition of the selfobject transferences. In other words, there is an intrinsic, inseparable relationship between method of observation (empathy) and findings (selfobject transferences). My emphasis here is less on the various forms of selfobject transferences but rather on the empathic mode of listening which is the sine qua non both for the establishment of a therapeutic dialogue as well as for the establishment and recognition of one of the selfobject transferences. This requires, however, that communication occur in the interpretive mode (Ornstein and Ornstein 1977).

EMPATHIC INTERPRETATIONS

The stress on the central clinical and theoretical significance of empathy by self psychology has repeatedly been criticized. I believe self psychology has to take the blame for some of this criticism. By not making it clear that empathy means a particular listening position, a vantage point from within the patient's own point of view, self psychology has inadvertently encouraged an equation of empathy with kindness, tact, warmth, and other "positive aspects" of the therapist's behavior and personality. Some critics state that there is no need to stress empathy since analysts have always been empathic. However, when we consider how hard it is to achieve intuneness with another human being and how much harder it is still to maintain an empathic immersion into the patient's inner life over a prolonged period of time, I don't believe that this is a valid criticism. I believe that to maintain an empathic position, we constantly have to fight a natural tendency to pass judgment on what is "normal," "abnormal," "sick," or "healthy." This kind of judgment is unavoidable when the therapist is preoccupied with making a diagnosis. But as soon as we do that, we lose our empathic position; we are no longer focused on eliciting the meaning of a particular behavior for that particular individual but judge the degree to which the patient may deviate from a hypothetical norm. And who among us has not experienced the challenge of remaining within the empathic mode of listening and responding, when we become the targets of the patient's provocations, demands, and verbal assaults?

But the most important criticism related to empathy has to do with the mistaken assumptions that the emphasis on the central importance of the empathic mode of listening excludes the use of interpretations and that self psychology depends on empathy as a major curative factor.

To answer this particular criticism and elaborate on the technique of psychotherapy that uses the empathic mode of data gathering and is informed by psychoanalytic self psychology, I shall discuss (1) "empathic interpretations" and offer an explanation as to how I conceptualize the therapeutic process in which the therapist's primary attention is focused on the state of the patient's self, (2) a clinical example that illustrates these points, and finally, (3) the frequently raised question as to how psychoanalytic self psychology deals with the manifestations of hostility and aggression.

INTERRELATED ASPECTS OF EMPATHIC INTERPRETATIONS

Acceptance

Acceptance relates to the patient as he is, with his anxieties, defenses, the peculiarities of his character, and his symptoms. Acceptance means not losing sight of the fact that the roots of the affects and anxieties that had shaped the patient's personality and manifest symptoms are unconscious and overdetermined. While, in principle none of us questions the unconscious roots of defenses, symptoms, and characteristic personality features, in practice, therapists are not necessarily free of prejudices and judgments—prejudices and judgments that are based on conventional views related to health and illness—rather than on the understanding of that particular individual in terms of his or her uniqueness.

Understanding

Understanding is a therapeutic achievement that arises from therapeutic dialogue. I shall briefly describe the sequence of such a dialogue: listening from within the patient's perspective and without judging his behavior in terms of how it deviates from what the therapist considers "normal" or "healthy," the therapist begins to grasp the patient's subjective experiences, and offers her tentative understanding in the form of an open-ended statement. Such statements are not made categorically, nor are they put in the form of questions. The phrasing indicates the tentativeness. For example: "Tell me if I heard you right. . . ."

With the therapist making statements rather than posing repeated questions or remaining silent for long periods of time, until "everything" falls into place, she puts her own understanding "on the table." The patient may agree and further elaborate on these statements, or may disagree with the therapist's understanding of his subjective experiences. But in this form of a dialogue, the patient experiences himself as someone who has to help the therapist understand him, rather than experiencing the therapist (primarily through her indirect comments) as insisting, in subtle ways, that the patient "admit" what she, the therapist, in her superior wisdom, assumes to "know"; a "knowledge" that in most instances is based on theory rather than on the understanding of the patient's unique past and unique mode of dealing with life. This kind of interpretation, as I've indicated before, is an "explanation" of a particular piece of behavior or symptom complex that omits one of the most important aspects of the interpretive process, namely understanding.

In a dialogue in which the therapist aims at understanding in such a way that the patient can feel understood, the therapist is not trying to figure out what is being omitted, hidden, or concealed, but rather is attempting, jointly with the patient, to grasp what it is that the patient *is* experiencing. Feeling understood frequently results in the establishment of a silent merger–transference even in a once-weekly therapy. The resultant increase in self-cohesion permits a genuine exploration of those affects, wishes, fears, and fantasies that because of their threat to the cohesion of the self, had been until then repressed or disavowed. The joint exploration and increasing degrees of understanding deepen the therapeutic process. Once what had previously been unconscious becomes part of the therapeutic dialogue, the therapist is in the position to offer the patient an explanation in the form of a comprehensive interpretation.

Explanation

Explanation is an interpretation that is only complete when it includes the understanding of the explanation. Understanding, the crucial first step in the interpretive process, is complete only when it is expanded into explanation, through which the patient can develop increasing insight into the deeper roots of the nature of his difficulties. Explanation raises what has been empathically understood to a level of cognition that facilitates insight.

Ms. Clark

Ms. Clark, a 28-year-old single woman, had lived a marginal existence since dropping out of her first year of college. At that time she had to be hospitalized, after which her family rented an apartment for her where she lived with her dog, to which she was deeply attached. She worked for a few years and was married briefly. After the birth of her second child, she was hospitalized again and was diagnosed as having a borderline condition. Because of her extremely poor housekeeping that seemed to endanger the children's health, she was given a housekeeper by the Welfare Department. However, she still couldn't "keep it together" and eventually the children were removed from her home with the intent of having them adopted. The patient responded to this with anger and indignation, and she desperately tried to enlist the therapist's help to *do* something in her behalf. The therapist refrained from intervening in an active way. She understood her task to be to help the patient accept the reality of her situation, namely that as long as she could not keep her house relatively clean, her children would be placed in a foster home where their meals and bedtimes would be regular. The therapist, an advanced female resident in psychiatry,* always combined the "pointing out of reality" with what she thought were empathic comments, such as that she understood how terrible it must have been for the patient to have had to accept the fact that she had to give up the children. These pseudo-empathic comments regularly resulted in the patient's increasing sense of indignation

---

*I am grateful for Dr. Sheila Wall's permission to use this clinical vignette.

and anger at the therapist and the threat that should she be denied custody, she would kill herself.

I shall select a segment of the treatment in which it was possible to recognize a change in the therapist's approach and the effect that this change had on the process of treatment. The therapist, after having "battled" with the patient in trying to affect a change in her attitude regarding the reality of her situation, shifted to an empathic–interpretive approach. The segment began with Ms. Clark telling the therapist that the welfare worker, after visiting her home, had told her that in order for her to get her children back, she would have to get rid of her dog; the dog was shedding heavily and the apartment was in a terrible state. This was an impossible choice for her to make and again Ms. Clark appealed to the therapist to do something. The therapist felt resentful and resisted what she felt was a demand for action, but not wanting to express her anger, she remained silent. This increased the patient's rage; she became more demanding and asked that the therapist at least give her some advice. The therapist, with irritation in her voice, "explained" to the patient once more that she could not intervene in her behalf, nor was she prepared to give her advice. She offered her nothing instead. A few days later Ms. Clark's mother called to say that the patient had made a suicide attempt. The therapist then arranged for a family meeting, which, however, did not materialize, and the next time the therapist saw the patient was at her regular appointment. Ms. Clark entered the office angrily and again demanded that the therapist intervene in her behalf. The therapist, expectedly, experienced irritation but this time she made her reality oriented comment in a way that more closely reflected on the patient's internal state. She said that the intensity of Ms. Clark's wish to have the children back in the home did not yet assure that in reality she would be able to care for them, and she added that she understood why Ms. Clark found it impossible to make a choice between the dog and her children. After all, the dog had been with her for a very long time, and had been a faithful companion to her during some of the most difficult times in her life. Also the dog was easier to please and possibly rewarded her more readily than did her children. The patient relaxed visibly and it was at this point in the hour that she told the therapist about her suicide attempt the week before. Feeling understood increased her self-cohesion and expectedly promoted a more open, less defensive mode of communication. Therapist and patient were then able to process the previous hour and what had led up to the suicide attempt, namely, the feeling that her therapist did not understand what she was going through and this made her feel utterly hopeless about the future.

The therapist's comments regarding the patient's difficulty in making a choice between the dog and her children represented a change from the position of an external observer to that of an empathic one. Earlier, she felt disgust that a mother who so badly wanted to have her children back was unable to part from a dog. I believe, however, that the therapist's changed attitude did not simply represent the overcoming of undesirable countertransference reactions; her empathic position was conveyed in her comments indicating both acceptance and understanding.

During the next two hours, the treatment took on an added dimension: the patient began to remember significant childhood experiences that enabled the therapist—and the patient—to recognize some of the genetic sources of the patient's current difficulty, especially those she referred to as her "laziness" and tendency to procrastinate. As the patient was describing, in some detail, the sense of frustration when she did her laundry with an outmoded, cumbersome washing machine, she recalled having experienced the same sense of futility when, as a child, she was asked by her mother to cleanse the rug of lint. But she could never do a good enough job of that; mother always found more lint on the rug. The emergence of these memories, corresponding as they did with the patient's current experiences, made it possible for the therapist to *explain* the source of Ms. Clark's problems; these explanations were offered in the form of comprehensive genetic interpretations. For example, the therapist could say that she could now see why Ms. Clark, not having grown up with feeling joy and pride in what she did, had a hard time motivating herself to do anything. She could appreciate that Ms. Clark would now make every effort to avoid the feeling of frustration and futility that accompanied her activities around the house. Tracing her "laziness" and tendency to procrastinate to its genetic source had also helped to illuminate the nature of her relationship with the therapist and other important people in her life, including her parents. The periodic outbursts of angry demandingness toward her therapist appeared to be desperate appeals to be saved from reexperiencing the frustration and disappointment that, once again, she could not live up to the expectation of others, this time to the expectations of the Welfare Department and her therapist. She had begged the therapist to explain to the welfare workers that they were asking of her the impossible, just as she wished as a little girl that her mother had known that she could not get rid of the lint on the carpet. When the therapist refused to intervene in her behalf, Ms. Clark had felt that nobody understood what she was experiencing, and it was then that she either threatened or actually attempted suicide.

However, once the level of understanding between therapist and patient was optimal, Ms. Clark could describe poignantly how she experienced herself in relationship to the therapist. In most social situations, she said, she felt as if she were "a square peg in a round hole"; only with the therapist did she feel that she fitted comfortably into her surroundings.

As the therapist became more attuned to the presence of an idealizing (merger) transference and the effect that the disruption of the transference (primarily due to her failure to understand the meaning of the patient's request to her) had on the patient's overall functioning, she could also appreciate better the effect that her responses—and her silences—had on the patient's mental state. The increase in the therapist's capacity to be in tune with the patient solidified Ms. Clark's confidence in the therapist's emotional presence and she began, with some resistance, to express the wish that the therapist recognize the small but significant improvements she was making in therapy. These were the tentative, rather cautious signs of an early mirror transference. However, here too, the therapist was at first at a loss as to how to respond to such expectations. She recognized the patient's wish to be praised, she knew that praise was not what was called for, but she did not know what else to do, so she remained silent. Ideally, the process of treatment is best served—for psychotherapy as well as psychoanalysis—when the response to such expectations is stated in the interpretive mode. In this instance, it would have been helpful if the therapist had said that she could understand that at this time in her life Ms. Clark did not want her efforts to be dismissed; she wanted to be recognized for working hard to overcome her inhibitions (her "laziness") that had been part of her life for so long. A comment such as this would have validated the legitimacy of the wish to be praised, a response that can have long-term therapeutic benefits, while praising only increases the patient's dependency and attachment to the therapist. Recognizing and interpreting the legitimacy of the wish to be praised—especially when this can be linked to genetically significant childhood experiences—has to be differentiated from offering praise that, more often than not, is patronizing and does not promote self-awareness.

The empathic mode of listening, the use of interpretations as a primary mode of communication, and the recognition of selfobject transferences deepened the therapeutic process and was accompanied by considerable symptomatic improvement. Ms. Clark began to be on time for her therapy hours, she looked a great deal neater than previously, and began to look at her adult life anew. Most surprising to the therapist, however, was Ms. Clark's statement that she actually enjoyed the absence of her children, and that it would be best if they did not return to her until she felt differently about herself and about them.

This segment of a treatment process answers several questions regarding psychoanalytic psychotherapy that is guided by psychoanalytic self psychology. One of the questions that is most frequently raised regarding self psychology has to do with the method self psychology employs, the method of empathy. The establishment of a therapeutic dialogue in which the therapist formulates her comments in such a way that the patient *feels understood* (that is, the patient can resonate with what the therapist says) could be misunderstood to mean that the therapist does not say anything that is not already conscious for the patient. What about unconscious wishes, hopes, and fantasies and the resistances related to them? Without bringing these into the treatment process we would be maintaining the artificial demarcation between "uncovering" and "supportive" forms of treatments that I consider artificial and unwarranted. But how is one to reach the deeper layers of the psyche with the empathic mode, without confrontations, without increasing the patient's resistances? I am suggesting that when attention is paid to the state of the self (its vigor, aliveness, capacity to regulate self-esteem) above all considerations, then repressed and disavowed affects, needs, and wishes will be experienced—and reported—as soon as the self becomes sufficiently consolidated in the therapeutic process. The consolidation of the self, in turn, is directly related to the experience of feeling understood. Under these circumstances, affects (anger, love, shame, exhibitionistic wishes, and grandiose and sexual fantasies) can be experienced and eventually explored in their genetic origin, whereas before, because of their threat to the cohesion of the self, they had to be repressed or disavowed.

When the therapeutic dialogue is conducted in such a way that the patient feels understood, an idealizing (merger) transference may become established. Under these circumstances, the therapist can make use of disruptions that inevitably occur in such transferences. Once these transferences are recognized and interpreted, not only does the treatment reach new levels of understanding but the patient—pari passu—consolidates an otherwise fragmentation-prone self. In other words, the increase in the consolidation of the self enables the patient to experience—and to express—those affects that, because of their intensity and/or particular content, could not be tolerated previously. The exploration of these affects, and their gradual acceptance by patients as their own, constitutes the integration of the repressed and split-off part of the psyche. In this approach to psychotherapy, introspection and increasing self-awareness are not antithetical to treatment that aims at "the strengthening of the ego" nor is the strengthening of the ego an accidental "by-product" of treatment in which improvements are explained (retrospectively) as having occurred because of identification with the therapist or by other, nonspecific features of the treatment. Rather, they are directly related to the specific content of the interpretations that meaningfully link the present with the past.

An additional comment regarding the therapeutic dialogue and how it helps to initiate the therapeutic process has to be made: the dialogue helps a person become a patient. Since the therapist's clarifying comments are not directed primarily toward events in the patient's life but rather toward the patient's subjective experiences of these events, the patient "learns" to direct his attention inwardly; he learns to become introspective.

Where does anger fit into the process of treatment that is informed by psychoanalytic self psychology? Since the patient's experiences have to be understood within the context of the therapeutic relationship, anger, too, is best understood when its emergence is not considered to be simply (or solely) the expression of the patient's psychopathology. When viewed within the context of the therapeutic relationship (and certainly once selfobject transferences have become established), the appearance of anger that does not disrupt the transference would have to be welcomed, since it indicates that the childhood defensive solution in which the fear of retaliation or the fear of being overwhelmed by anger played a major role is now being overcome. Anger that is expressed and the source of which is jointly explored with the therapist has to be differentiated from narcissistic rage experiences that temporarily disrupt the transference and may lead to temporary fragmentation. However, once the rage subsides, the source of the rage can be traced and interpreted within the transference and genetically, which usually proves to be one of the most productive experiences in the treatment process.

This view of anger in psychotherapy is different from one in which the therapist interprets anger as a *displacement* from important people in the patient's past onto the figure of the therapist (see definition by Moore and Fine as quoted by Blanck and Blanck 1974). In this (classical) definition of the transference, the therapist is considered to be the target of the patient's instinctual drives (sexual and aggressive), as were the primary objects of his childhood. As a displacement from the past, the therapist, with her interpretations, attempts "to correct" the patient's misperceptions. She may say in essence: "Express your anger, after all, I am not your mother and/or father, *I* can take it."

In contrast, when interpretations are directed toward the patient's subjective experiences (what it feels like to be angry), they are not correcting a misperception or displacement but are responsive to the patient's subjective experience of dreading a potentially disruptive and destructive affect. In other words, the problem is seen in the capacity of the patient's self to contain and regulate the affect of anger and not in the patient's capacity to differentiate past from present. This is in keeping with Eissler's (1953) frequently quoted statement that what is of importance is the structure of the ego in which the symptom is embedded, rather than the structure of the symptom itself.

We are now left with the question of whether or not self-cohesion would have to be given primary consideration on all levels of psychological organization or only on the "low level" ones as was exemplified by Ms. Clark? To elaborate on the impact of self psychology on the treatment of patients with "higher level" ego organization, I would have to discuss the manner in which self psychology views the Oedipus complex; its contribution to normal and pathological development (Kohut 1977, Ornstein 1983a). What is important to say in this regard is that we no longer distinguish between preoedipal and oedipal conditions in which only the latter are supposed to give rise to transferences but not the former. Rather, we now recognize preoedipal as well as oedipal forms of selfobject transferences. We are also suggesting that in terms of psychopathology, structural defects and deficits may occur at any point in the course of development, including the oedipal one, and that conflicts and compromise formations are best considered as secondary to these structural deficits. It is the supraordinate position of the self relative to the mental apparatus that puts the cohesion of the self (its vigor, aliveness, capacity to contain and regulate affects) into the forefront of the therapist's considerations (Kohut 1977). And this is why I maintain that considerations relative to the state of the self ought not be restricted to the treatment of severely impaired and sick patients but that this be considered as primary in the treatment of all patients, regardless of the nature of the psychopathology. Pathogenic conflicts, in this particular theoretical orientation, are viewed as secondary, that is, as the breakdown products of an enfeebled and/or fragmentation-prone self.

CONCLUSION

Self psychology and the systematic use of empathy as a mode of listening and responding have affected the conduct of psychoanalytic psychotherapy. A clinical example taken from the treatment of a patient who was diagnosed as having a borderline condition was used to demonstrate that feeling understood firms up the self in a way that enhances introspection and permits the use of interpretations as the therapist's primary mode of communication. The clinical example also demonstrated that when the therapist maintains an empathic position, the patient, even in once-weekly therapy, is likely to develop one of the selfobject transferences. Further, that when empathic interpretations are used as the therapist's primary interventions, structural changes are likely to occur in such a way that treatment results in "true healing" rather than in the fostering of a lifelong dependency on the therapist.

9

When the Patient
Is Psychotic

Lawrence Josephs

THE PSYCHOTIC PATIENT AS "TRAGIC MAN"

Patients who suffer from schizophrenia may be thought of as examples of what Kohut (1977) called "Tragic Man" (p. 133). Tragic Man seeks to express creatively the pattern of his nuclear self, even though his failures overshadow his successes. The nuclear self consists of nuclear ambitions and nuclear ideals. In their healthy actualization, these ambitions and ideals result in a mature form of self-respect and admiration for others (Kohut 1971). In psychosis, nuclear ambitions are actualized through a delusional reconstitution of the cold, paranoid, grandiose self, and nuclear ideals are actualized through the delusional reconstitution of the powerful, persecutory, omnipotent parental imago. Kohut (1984) believed that only an "etiologically decisive organic element" can account for the oscillation between periods of gross psychotic disorganization and periods of organized functioning of stable compensatory structures (p. 212). In terms of prognosis, Kohut believed that psychoanalytic psychotherapy could help to reestablish, support, and strengthen the patient's defensive and compensatory structures, but that a cohesive nuclear self could not be established anew through psychotherapy and that there would be a persistent hollowness in the center of the patient's self. Kohut (1984) believed that to create a nuclear self anew, the therapeutic process would need to penetrate beneath the defensive structures and permit the prolonged reexperiencing of "oscillations between prepsychological chaos and the security provided by primitive merger with an archaic selfobject" (p. 8).

An individual with schizophrenia can be viewed as a tragic hero who, like Shakespeare's Prince Hamlet, has suffered "the slings and arrows of outrageous fortune" in being born into a traumatically unempathic familial milieu, perhaps with a "broken brain" (Andreasen 1984) as well. When, as an adult, such an individual finally resorts to some extreme measures in the struggle for psychic survival, and society responds with institutionalization—be it in a state hospital or a boarding home—a bitter fate is often sealed for life. It is not the schizophrenic patients' victimization that makes them tragic heroes, but rather their private and rarely understood "victory in defeat," whereby they assert the inviolability of the self in the face of its complete fragility.

Looking at schizophrenia through the lens of tragic heroism leads to a distinctive interpretation of schizophrenia that proves quite useful in an empathic approach to psychotherapy. Josephs and Josephs (1986) described how paranoid delusions can be understood as concrete symbolizations of actual experiences in which patients felt traumatically misunderstood and mistreated by those on whom they hoped to depend. This interpretation focuses on the so-called "kernel of truth" in a delusion (Freud 1937).

PARANOID DELUSIONS

Paranoid delusions reflect desperate attempts to communicate feelings of violation, indignation, and outrage that such traumatic experiences engender. Grandiose delusions of specialness may symbolize the affirmation of a sense of one's ultimate uniqueness and self-worth in a world in which one feels utterly ignored and neglected. Grandiose delusions of power reflect an attempt to restore a sense of control to a world gone madly out of control. The detachment and flat affect of the residual phase of schizophrenia may reflect an effort to preserve some remaining sense of safety, security, and privacy among people who are viewed as essentially intrusive, if not hostile. A chronic patient's dependency on others for care can be understood as a last-ditch attempt to preserve a tenuous bond to an all-protective and nurturing idealized parental imago. A chronic patient's passivity and detached compliance can be construed as a false self designed to keep domineering and overcontrolling people at bay, thereby retaining some inner sense of autonomy. A deteriorated patient's poor grooming and hygiene as well as near-total apathy can be construed as a poignant enactment of the utter wretchedness of life in a world in which one is essentially abandoned and homeless. Recourse to primary process language in schizophrenia can be construed as an expression of the futility of being unable to convey personal experiences in everyday language and an attempt to make oneself understood at a gut level through the language of dreams (Josephs and Josephs 1986).

In a sense, schizophrenic patients find surrealism more convincing than realism as a mode of self-expression. From an empathic point of view, the issue is not so much whether these strategics of adaptation arc effective or not, but whether they reflect a hope for a "new beginning" (Balint 1979) regardless of the low probability that such a hope is realistic.

The obvious critique of such an interpretation is that even when real opportunities for a better life are presented to schizophrenic patients, they may repeatedly prove incapable of using these opportunities effectively and consistently. In some respects, these patients construct their own downfall through withdrawal and apathy. In this sense, such patients are not heroes, nor do they feel like heroes in their shameful sense of themselves as defective outcasts, barely human at all. From the vantage point of unconscious conflict, one could suggest that any fantasy of existential heroism is purely a compensatory defense against abysmally low self-esteem, as well as a rationalization of a sense of victimization that justifies hatred and vindictiveness while denying sadism, envy, and greed. The paradox of schizophrenia is that it is truly a "victory in defeat." Those who suffer from schizophrenia have certainly been defeated in adapting to the demands of a harsh—if not insane—social reality and by the frightening nature of their self-created demons. Nevertheless we can still discern that in some manner these people have remained noble. Perhaps in our respect for that inviolate core of selfhood there is some hope for the emergence of an authentic self that will be more than a bolstering of a compensatory false self surrounding a central hollowness.

THERAPEUTIC TECHNIQUE

The crux of therapeutic technique from a self psychological perspective is consistently to empathize with the patient's subjective experiences and to interpret the adaptive import of the patient's actions in terms of the individual's unique perspective, regardless of how distorted and maladaptive that viewpoint may seem to an observer. This technique differs from an ego psychological approach, which emphasizes correction of the patient's faulty reality testing. It also differs from a conflict/defense approach, which emphasizes interpretation of defensively disowned aspects of self and external reality.

A common criticism of a self psychological approach is that the patient may construe the therapist's consistent empathy as confirmation of a grossly maladaptive paranoid/psychotic orientation, which is then left unchallenged and unmodified. Such criticism may be refuted with the self psychological hypothesis that consistent empathy allows the patient to use the therapist as a selfobject; such a relationship provides the patient with an increased sense of self-cohesion, enabling an advance from regressive and pathological states to a more reality-oriented and mature level of functioning. The potential danger of even the most tactful reality testing or interpretation of defense with schizophrenic patients is that they will experience the challenge to their subjective view of reality as an attack on the sense of self. Feeling thus threatened, these patients will simply repair the damage to their self experience with characteristic compensatory mechanisms— whether paranoid attack, schizoid retreat, or passive compliance— without ever digesting and integrating the therapist's interventions. In the long run, many patients may never move beyond subtle, or not so subtle, negative transference to the therapist as an invalidating and impinging presence who must be neutralized.

Mr. N.

Mr. N. grew up in a working-class family in which he was the second youngest of ten children. He described his mother as simultaneously infantilizing and neglectful, and his father as domineering, belittling, and neglectful toward both the patient and his mother. His father served a seven-year prison term beginning when Mr. N. was 3 years old. At age 10, Mr. N. initiated what was to become a life of petty thievery and mixed substance abuse. As an adolescent he frequented female prostitutes and became a homosexual prostitute himself, although he never accepted the passive role in anal intercourse.

As a young adult Mr. N. rarely worked. His father died when the patient was 19, and Mr. N. was the only family member remaining at home with his mother. His thievery escalated into armed robbery, and he was often both perpetrator and victim of violent acts. His mother died when he was 28, immediately after he had entered a residential drug and alcohol rehabilitation program, in which he continued for a year. After leaving the program, he worked for a year as a parking lot attendant, remaining drug free until he suffered his first acute psychotic decompensation. During this episode, he believed that the FBI and the Mafia intended to murder him. After a brief hospitalization, he reconstituted and then returned to a life of petty thievery and substance abuse. He was arrested for possession of illegal drugs and given a six-month prison term. In prison he was terrorized and raped by other inmates. When he again decompensated at the age of 32, he was transferred to a public psychiatric hospital, where I saw him for three years in twice-weekly psychotherapy sessions. Mr. N.'s response to group psychotherapy (of which I was a co-leader) is described in Josephs and Juman (1985).

The False Self

During the first six months of treatment, Mr. N. attempted to present himself as a problem-free person. Although he acknowledged his history of thievery, substance abuse, and psychotic decompensation, he claimed that these activities were all behind him because he was cured. His stated goal was to get a job in the community, buy a car, and get married. Mr. N. entered the hospital's community-oriented program, which would help him find a job prior to discharge. In therapy sessions, Mr. N. typically discussed the progress he felt he was making in the hospital and criticized other patients whose apathy or incoherence he found incomprehensible. Mr. N. claimed that he had never felt depressed in his life, and he could not understand why other patients did not make more of an effort to better themselves. Rather than interpret his denial and minimization of the severity of his problems or suggest that perhaps he was criticizing in other patients what he disliked in himself, I simply reflected Mr. N.'s sense of himself as being a self-sufficient person who had raised himself in the streets, needing to rely solely on himself—qualities that he viewed as a mark of distinction in comparison with the open dependency of other patients.

Although Mr. N. initially evidenced no inner life at all, he gradually began to talk about his ongoing conflicts with ward staff members, whom he keenly resented. Mr. N. had one problem on the ward—he usually took a nap when he was supposed to socialize with other residents. As a result, he failed to earn enough token economy points to obtain weekend passes or to move into an advanced phase of the program. Mr. N. described the ward staff as patronizing and insulting, and admitted that he often wanted to give up on the community-oriented program and simply be discharged. I interpreted the injury to Mr. N.'s pride in his autonomy when his opinions were not taken seriously, when his imperfections rather than his assets were selectively focused on, and when he was not given the recognition and rewards that he felt were his rightful due:

Patient: I let little things upset me. I don't say how I feel when they insult me. Mr. D. said, "Here's Mr. Sleeper, he's a lazy bum." I don't say nothing. I hold it in.

Therapist: Even though you feel put down, you hold it in like you don't want to be brought down to his level.

Patient: They don't understand that it triggers off emotions. I can think of slick answers. I want to curse him out and beat him up, but I just keep my mouth shut.

Mr. N. began to take pride in not letting the ward staff get the best of him and in not giving them the satisfaction of his failure. After a year and a half, he entered the final phase of the program and began a job in the community loading trucks.

The Idealized Parental Imago

Mr. N. quit his job in the community after one week, stating that the work was beneath him and that he wanted to be discharged so he could learn a trade. Several months later he admitted to me that he felt somewhat inadequate in relation to the men he had worked with, who were married and had cars and homes. He believed that once they came to know him they would have a low opinion of him, so he thought he might as well quit before openly failing to fit in. After quitting, Mr. N. became depressed and psychotic, with suicidal ideation, and he initiated a series of transfers to an acute care ward. He described how, behind the facade he presented to the world, he had been privately dealing with a devastating sense of loss in response to his mother's death. He spoke of his efforts to somehow reunite with her:

Patient: Before I go to bed at night, I close my eyes and say, "Ma." I get a picture of her in a white dress. I picture her face. She's just floating around. I don't know if she's in the sky or in the air or in my mind. I call out, "Ma, Ma, Ma," but I don't want to say it loud because I might find out that I was alone. I think about my mother every day.
Therapist: Like you couldn't go on without her.

Mr. N. described the connection between feeling like a failure in the hospital, suicidal ideation, and reunion fantasies:

Therapist: How do you imagine you would kill yourself?
Patient: I'd get a razor blade after shaving and I'd go back into the woods. I'd cut my wrists deep, right through the vein. It wouldn't

hurt. The blood would drip out and I would be drained. I'd be thinking about my mother and father wherever they are. My soul leaves my body from loss of blood. Maybe I can get an image of her soul. She's trying to communicate with me that there's life after death. Sometimes I'm looking in a mirror at myself and I'm waiting for her to appear. She starts to appear. I see her face and then it goes away.

Therapist: You miss her very much. Like nothing in the world is more important than to be with her.

During this phase of therapy, when Mr. N. was both delusional and suicidal, I neither questioned the validity of his delusions nor challenged the assumptions underlying his suicidal despair. He was impervious to such interventions, which were frequently made by staff members on the acute care unit. Instead, I attempted to empathize with his exquisite sense of loss and his attempts to reunite somehow with his mother in whatever way imaginable and at any cost.

At this point, the therapeutic experience was unique for Mr. N. As a "macho" antisocial character, he had never before confided to anyone his sense of personal failure and humiliation, his longings for maternal love, and the reunion fantasies that constituted such a vital aspect of his inner life. The technique that allowed for this unfolding was my willingness to empathize with the legitimacy of the patient's prior devaluation of the community-oriented program and the people who ran it. Consequently, Mr. N. was gradually able to distinguish me from a sadistic authority and to accept me as a safe person to whom he could admit his vulnerabilities. If I had sided with so-called objective reality and social adaptation, Mr. N. would probably have decompensated nonetheless after attempting to work in the community and would have viewed me as just one more of the many insensitive, coercive people who had set him up for a humiliating and public defeat.

The Grandiose Self

As Mr. N. emerged from his depression during the third year of treatment, he had no interest in reassuming a false self, at least in therapy. He gradually began to reveal various aspects of his antisocial grandiose self:

Patient: My lazy daisy childhood. I thought I was the best cool dude, smoking and stealing money. It was my turf. I was king of the playground, king of the kids, leader of the pack, ace boom cadoom, the main kazane, the master, el superior, the supreme being, the boss. . . . In front of the judge when I was 13, I acted scared, innocent, like a little baby. I got home, nobody said a word. The next day I did a B&E and got $150. I ripped off that motherfucker. I don't know why I call everybody I ripped off a motherfucker. I guess I'm rubbing it in. I was king of the motherfuckers.

Therapist: You seem to feel most alive when you're king of the motherfuckers.

Patient: Put a gun in my hand and say, "Give it up, motherfucker." I could get $10 or $15 for your fan. And then there was the old mamaroonie. I'd rip off Mama, take 10s, 20s from her pocketbook. I don't mean that, Dr. Josephs. My mother was a good mother. I shouldn't talk like that.

Therapist: So you'd even rip off your own mother.

Patient: A few times. That's the way it goes. It was easy. She never accused me. Now I've got to get out of this hospital and live a clean, constructive life. I'll work and collect S.S.D. I'll make money the old-fashioned way, earn it. No more ripping people off. No more king of the motherfuckers. I'm not a hardened criminal, just a petty thief. I'm too old and I can't afford to go to jail anymore. I've overcome it with age. I grew out of it—too bad.

During this phase, Mr. N. described his antisocial exploits, drug experiences, and macho sexual conquests with an unbridled enthusiasm and robustness that stood in stark contrast to his prior cool, problem-free façade and his psychotic, suicidal despair. Mr. N. seemed to be saying, "This is the real me; as despicable as I am, at least I'm alive and kicking." Rather than drawing his attention to the self-defeating consequences of his actions or to the numerous victims he left behind—all of which he knew without being reminded—I instead reflected the heightened sense of phallic pride, potency, and mastery that such experiences engendered, as sadistic as his intentions were.

Mr. N. began to discuss situations that had led to the diminution of his grandiose self. In bits and pieces he confided the details of how he had been assaulted and sexually abused in prison and how he felt ashamed of what he had been forced to do. In addition, he began to perceive some connections between the diminution of his grandiose self, his relationship with his father, and his persecutory auditory hallucinations:

Patient: I had a dream. A guy is whipping me. He's got food in a bag. I'm starving, thirsty, and hungry. He says, "Say 'I'm a monkey's uncle.'" I say, "I'm not." He says, "If you don't say it, I'll whip you." I pull the whip out of his hand and start to lash at him. I grab the bag and throw the whip away. When I was 10 and 11, my father used to get me in a scissors' lock around my waist and I had to say "I'm a monkey's uncle" for him to let go. When I go to sleep, I hear voices. My father calling me "my little chicken." I tell him in my head, "Don't call me chicken. Leave me alone. I'm not a chicken. A chicken is a coward." He called me and my younger brother his two little chickens and my mother the hen. She called him the rooster. I'm a rooster just like him. I don't like voices in my head tormenting me. What right does he have to call me a chicken? He smacked me in the face when I was 3 and wouldn't get off a tricycle, and then he left me high and dry for seven years when he went to prison.
Therapist: You'd really like to get even.

Mr. N. explained that although he sometimes felt defeated, he never gave up deep inside:

It's like I'm going into the ring to fight for my life. I'm fighting the champion who's better than me. He's punching me. I fall down bleeding. I swing back. He kicks me when I'm on the ground. I'm still swinging. I fight till death. I separate from myself, leave my physical body, and go into the spiritual world. I'm a ghost. My spirit won. Victory in defeat. If it weren't for you and C [*his best friend, another patient*], I'd get drugs. I just need somebody to listen to me.

Most likely, it was my empathy with Mr. N's. experience of his grandiose self that allowed him to acknowledge the humiliating life experiences for which his grandiose self compensated. Concurrently with revealing these different aspects of his struggle to actualize his grandiose self, Mr. N. began to take the initiative to arrange for his discharge. He decided that it was time to get on with his life and to see what he could make of it.

Treatment Issues

Mr. N. remained dependent on maintaining a fantasy of merger with an idealized image of his mother to preserve some basic sense of belonging and security. Drug abuse, suicidal ideation, and hallucinations of her image appeared derivative of oneness fantasies in which he merged with her. Mr. N. was able to merge with an idealized paternal imago and appropriate its phallic power through identifying with his father's devaluatory and sadistic attitude toward both Mr. N. and his mother. Symbolic and sadistic conquests of both men and women in sexual relations, acts of violence, and stealing expressed the affirmation of his exaggeratedly macho, antisocial grandiose self. His rage, sense of shame, and occasional paranoia when his grandiose self was enfeebled reflected the reexperiencing of his sense of humiliating emasculation in response to his mother's infantilization and his father's sadistic belittlement. For Mr. N., submission to anal penetration by a sadistic male rival reflected the concrete symbolization of his sense of enfeeblement.

Mr. N. had never overtly rebelled or asserted himself in response to his mother's infantilization or his father's belittlement. Instead he asserted himself by seducing them into believing that he was an obedient and dutiful son while secretly making fools of them by stealing from them and being delinquent. In this sense, Mr. N.'s false self was a disguised expression of his antisocial grandiose self whereby he proved his superiority to others by cleverly becoming top dog in a dog-eat-dog world. Yet his false self fooled not only others but also deceived himself. By pretending that his overt compliance was simply a pretense, he could deny to himself his humiliating dependency on his mother and disavow that he would indeed infantilize himself to remain involved with her.

The therapeutic relationship could easily have been undermined by the potential negative transference of viewing the therapist as the sadistic, domineering father bent on forcing Mr. N. into submission through anal rape. In a sense, Mr. N.'s attitude toward the demands of coping with objective reality reflected his belief that accepting reality was equivalent to a humiliating defeat in which both his manhood and his sense of identity would be lost. To the extent that the patient did not see me as a representative of that despised reality but instead as willing to enter his world and stand with him in his struggle against degradation, Mr. N. could draw strength from me as a selfobject and begin to acknowledge some of the deep narcissistic injuries from which his pathology derived. Through this process, Mr. N. was able to relinquish to some degree an unrelentingly paranoid orientation and to view himself, his life, and others from a somewhat more humanistic perspective. As the therapist, I conceived of my selfobject function as a "witness to tragedy" whose role was not to undo emotional trauma by providing a corrective emotional experience, but rather to validate the reality of shattering emotional trauma, thus enabling the patient to accept the possibility of a permanently enfeebled self that must be endured for life. For Mr. N., the end result of this interaction was neither the revival of a defensive false self nor the establishment of a cohesive nuclear self impervious to future psychotic decompensation; instead it led to the articulation of some inchoate sense of the tragic and the ironic in life. On that basis, the patient was able to develop some degree of genuine self-respect and empathy for others.

CONCLUSION

In terms of technique, this case illustrates how an empathic approach helped to improve the patient's reality testing by repairing damage to his self-esteem so that it became unnecessary to explicitly correct paranoid distortions in his thinking. In addition, without explicitly interpreting defenses, I was able to use empathy to allow the patient's formerly disavowed experiences to unfold, such as fantasies of merger with his mother, fears and memories of being emasculated and humiliated, and wishes and memories of exacting a sadistic revenge.

Chronically disturbed patients experience many aspects of psychopharmacological treatment, psychiatric hospitalization, and psychosocial rehabilitation as grievous narcissistic injuries.

Although mental health workers are well aware that schizophrenic patients require tremendous amounts of support, encouragement, and guidance, many of the more subtle empathic failures to which these patients are extremely vulnerable remain largely unrecognized by workers in the field. The crux of psychotherapy in this particular case centered on forming a relationship in which Mr. N. felt free to discuss openly the daily insults to his self-esteem. My empathy with these injuries helped Mr. N. to repair the damage. Perhaps when treatment providers set themselves up as experts on how best to adapt to reality and encourage patients to follow that vision, many patients, in merging with an idealized authority figure, can reconstitute themselves. Unfortunately, that tie is often broken as the patients are encouraged to become increasingly independent once their more troublesome symptoms are in remission. They may feel that they have been cut adrift in a lonely world in which they are quite vulnerable. In addition, having conformed to a vision of reality essentially not their own (that is, remaining on medication for life), they eventually reassert their previously sacrificed sense of autonomy by refusing to comply with treatment recommendations. Perhaps an empathic self psychological approach to psychotherapy minimizes the hazards inherent in the reconstitution of the false self by providing patients with a way to reconstitute themselves in a more authentic manner.

10

When the Patient Exhibits Narcissistic Rage

Jayne Patrick

KERNBERG'S APPROACH

To date, treatment issues involving the more primitive narcissistic personality disorders have received only limited attention, compared with, for example, the vast literature on the treatment of borderline pathology. This relative neglect may be a function of the fact that patients with severe narcissistic pathology present chronic and intense rage reactions, and this is usually seen as a significant obstacle to their involvement in an ongoing therapeutic relationship. Kernberg (1975) refers to these patients as narcissistic personalities who function at an overt borderline level. He indicates that they show "non-specific manifestations of ego weakness," for example, "severe lack of anxiety tolerance, generalized lack of impulse control, striking absence of subliminatory channeling, primary process thinking clearly noticeable on psychological tests, and proneness to the development of transference psychosis" (p. 265). Kernberg sees patients with severely disturbed narcissistic personality disorders as differing from those with borderline personality disorders in that the former possess a grandiose self, which, however, is lacking in sufficient integration to enable these individuals to function socially at the level of the majority of narcissistic personality disorders.

Until now, only Kernberg has addressed the need for a treatment paradigm specific to this population. His approach emphasizes the elaboration of the negative transference; it seems to differ from the modified approach he utilizes with borderline patients only in that he leaves certain aspects of the grandiose self untouched. Kernberg attributes the origins of these patients' intense rage reactions to constitutional factors and to early deprivation of oral needs. His approach to treatment emphasizes "consistent interpretation (not only of the origins of the narcissistic rage but of the secondary gains derived from its expression in the transference) and limit-setting when such gains cannot be avoided by interpretation alone" (p. 268). Kernberg stresses that the prognosis for severely disturbed narcissistic personality disorders is often unfavorable, owing to the unmanageability of their rage reactions and their propensity for early termination.

KOHUT'S APPROACH

I would like to suggest that in fact these patients can be treated more successfully, if we are willing to adopt an alternative stance with regard to their expressions of narcissistic rage. If we insist upon viewing the phenomena of rage reactions as a source of secondary gain, their origins to be interpreted through the elaboration of the negative transference, then, as Kohut (1977) states, the therapy inevitably serves as a rage-inciting function. This is because the patient experiences the therapist's insistence of the presence of a primary envy–hostility complex in his archaic core as a repetition of the unempathic approach of his parents in early life. Owing to severe deficits in these patients' self structure, such an approach only serves to overwhelm their fragile defenses and drives them from treatment. I believe that more empathic under-standing of these patients' rage reactions is the key to a more successful treatment approach; I would like to suggest that in severe narcissistic personality disorders, rage reactions can serve several interrelated functions. These are (1) communication of selfobject needs, (2) narcissistic repair, (3) revenge upon a disem-pathic selfobject, (4) restitution of selfobject bonds, (5) creation of a more responsive selfobject, and (6) working through a reevoked experience of loss and deprivation.

The very fact of being in treatment, as well as the experience of relating to even the most empathic therapist, acts to provoke chronic and intense rage in the more severely disturbed narcissistic personality disorders. Involvement in the treatment process per se signifies the abandonment of their position of self-sufficiency and produces intense anxiety as well as rage. Furthermore, these pa-tients tend to be particularly fearful that the therapist will use them to satisfy his own narcissistic needs; thus, they are predisposed to seek revenge from the very onset of treatment.

TWO FORMS OF RAGE

I would like to describe briefly two forms in which these patients' rage reactions frequently find expression: criticism and intimida-tion. When severely disturbed narcissistic personality disorders do not attempt narcissistic repair by simply abandoning the therapist, they direct their efforts in the therapy to this purpose, often through intense, unremitting criticism of the therapist. To some authors, notably Rosenfeld (1971), this sort of unrelenting criti-cism of the therapist, in the context of a significant aggressive shift, basically represents a transference psychosis (the projection of the infantile sadistic superego into the therapist). However, I would like to suggest that such an onslaught of criticism repre-sents, in this population, what Epstein (1979) refers to as the patient's efforts to "establish a more tolerable balance of goodness, badness, and power" (p. 265). I have come to believe that for severely disturbed narcissistic personality disorders the experience of helplessness (i.e., lack of power) is the most intolerable aspect of the inequities in the therapeutic relationship. In addition to criticizing the therapist, these patients are particularly given to intimidation. This often takes the form of anecdotes designed to impress the therapist with the patient's propensity for violent acting out. While such communication may be designed to test the therapist's capacity for acceptance of the patient's bad self, or to convince the therapist that he runs a serious risk in frustrating the patient, they can also serve to signal the patient's need to demonstrate his superiority over the therapist, and thus to disavow his helplessness and repair his damaged self-esteem.

Of particular importance to our understanding of the dynamics of rage reactions in severely disturbed narcissistic personality disorders is the distinction between verbal and nonverbal aggressive outbursts. With regard to the latter, Epstein (1979), in his examination of this phenomenon in borderline patients, attributes it to the "intensity and virulence of the unconscious envy and hate" aroused by the therapist's interpretive activity. Rosenman (1981) relates the failure of interpretation to deter the release of aggression by the patient seeking revenge for injury to the fact that the patient regards the therapist (akin to his mother) as having knowingly injured him. In the case of severely disturbed narcissistic personality disorders, however, I am inclined to feel that Gedo's (1981) discussion of archaic states activated in the therapeutic relationship is more germane. He comments that in these states the patient's condition of regressed helplessness involves "(a temporary) loss of the capacity to use verbal symbols" (p. 80).

I believe that this type of regressive phenomena is highly characteristic of severely disturbed narcissistic personality disorders, and may arise, as Meissner (1979) suggests, from their wish to experience symbiotic relatedness in the therapy. However, the regression also reevokes the patient's traumatic early experience of disempathic mothering. Under these circumstances, these patients' difficulty in finding words adequate to communicate their affective state reinforces the experience of intolerable helplessness, which appears to be a core feature of their rage. In that the therapy acts to reevoke a (partially) verbal experience of narcissistic injury and helplessness, such patients are inclined to seek nonverbal means of redressing the balance of power in the therapy relationship.

I would like to suggest, then, that at the height of a regressive crisis, nonverbal aggressive outbursts (particularly intimidation) are sometimes to be expected in the treatment of severely disturbed narcissistic personality disorders. However, contrary to Epstein's view, I do not believe such behaviors reflect the patient's unconscious wish to destroy the therapist and the therapy itself. Rather, it is my opinion that such behaviors can act to preserve the therapy, by providing sufficient narcissistic repair in the only form assimilable by certain of these patients, thus permitting them to continue in the relationship. In these patients' regression to a preverbal archaic state of helplessness, the therapist continues to serve needed selfobject functions. Thus, these patients' efforts at narcissistic repair, which also embody their desire to restore the selfobject bond with the therapist, are dependent for their efficacy on the therapist's capacity to recognize their intimidating behavior for what it is, and to respond empathically.

Mrs. D.

> I would like to present a clinical vignette to illustrate this perspective. The patient, whom I shall call Mrs. D., is a woman in her late thirties, whose presenting complaint was that life was not worth living. She related that for the past two years she had been spending up to 80 percent of her waking hours in bed and often neglected to bathe herself or perform basic housekeeping tasks. Meal preparation and what housekeeping chores did get done were performed by her mother and three children, ages 10, 13, and 15. Mrs. D. was approximately 100 pounds overweight; she was an avid reader, whose vocabulary attested to an above-average intelligence. In the vast majority of our sessions during the first fifteen months of treatment Mrs. D.'s mood state reflected a brooding resentment. Our exploration of her past relationships with significant others often seemed only to fuel her sense of injustice. Mrs. D.'s smouldering resentment sometimes took a more active form, as when she drove her car onto the sidewalk in pursuit of some teenagers who had mocked her. She habitually drove her car, which was not road

safe, twenty miles over the speed limit. Mrs. D. also perceived herself as having a rather intimidating presence and knowingly exploited this in her interactions with strangers.

Although I had originally diagnosed Mrs. D. as a borderline personality disorder, I came to recognize that she did not exhibit symptoms of identity diffusion or clinging dependency, nor did she seem to have any conscious or unconscious fears that a more adult level of functioning would result in abandonment or rejection. Rather, it was her belief that she was owed the kind of physical care her mother provided because her parents had not allowed her to develop the qualities needed to lead a well-adjusted productive existence. Her earliest memories were of her mother exhibiting impatience with her "babiness" and of making her the unwilling confidant of marital complaints and unremitting criticism of the patient's father.

Following Mrs. D.'s divorce, after ten years of marriage to a man who she described as alternatively ignoring her and beating her, Mrs. D.'s parents actively encouraged her behavioral regression. She came to view herself as unable and unwilling to cope with life and elected to take advantage of her mother's willingness to feed and clean up after her, in the hope that this form of nurturing behavior would, in the course of time, help to repair her narcissistic hurts and to correct deficiencies in her self structure. After two years of bed rest, Mrs. D. was willing to admit that it was not enough.

I would like to describe the focus of the period of therapy immediately preceding a further regressive shift (which was characterized by Mrs. D.'s efforts at omnipotent control and demands for affirmation, alternating with expressions of rage and frustration at my failure to provide same and to intuit perfectly her needs). After approximately fifteen months in therapy (twice-weekly sessions), during which time Mrs. D. had been hospitalized twice, she announced that she did not intend to be hospitalized again. Her two previous hospitalizations, to which she had consented, were in response to her expressing suicidal ideation and fearing loss of impulse control. I sought to explore the meaning of this position with her, which greatly surprised Mrs. D. as she assumed that I would automatically endorse such a goal. She complained that the hospitalizations had been humiliating experiences and had not really helped her. She went on to say that when her self-destructive feelings intensified, she would have to cope with them outside of hospital. She seemed to be looking for approval from me at this point. I commented on this and added that it was not clear to me what would be in her best interests in any given instance. This made Mrs. D. angry, and she would only repeat that she would not allow herself to be hospitalized again. I wondered whether she thought that I was withholding a vote of confidence or was seeming to infantilize her, or whether I seemed to be abandoning her by not affirming my commitment to join with her in this goal. Mrs. D. found some truth in all of these possibilities, and said that my lack of enthusiasm made her feel confused and defeated. I saw myself in this instance as failing to provide a wished-for mirroring function, but my desire to do so was overridden by my concern that the patient might find herself in need of the protection and external structure afforded by hospitalization and unable to alter her position because of my endorsement. Communicating these thoughts, however, had little impact.

As is readily apparent, the interpretations I made during this period fell short of communicating an adequate awareness of Mrs. D.'s intrapsychic reality as she experienced it. In addition, I failed sufficiently to conceptualize the nature of the selfobject transference she was exhibiting and to relate it to her disappointment in early nurturing experiences. In retrospect, I believe Mrs. D.'s relating to me during this period constituted a form of pseudo-idealizing transference. That is, I see in her responses an attempt to take on goals, behaviors, and attitudes that she believed I espoused and would desire her to acquire. Meissner (1979) describes this phenomenon in severely disturbed narcissistic personality disorders, stating that their objectives "are much more directed toward drawing others into the position of giving, supporting, taking care of, or otherwise filling up the intense neediness and deprived emptiness that characterize their narcissistic vulnerability" (p. 179). He comments further that "the assumption of impotence, need and dependence, thereby induc[es] the therapist (he hopes) to use his omnipotence on his behalf. Such patients tend to set unrealistic and grandiose goals so that change or progress in the therapy cannot approach the fantasy and therefore gives little satisfaction" (p. 190).

In her transference responses, Mrs. D. was re-creating the ambiance of a mother–child dyad in which the child is able to gain the mother's acceptance only through premature autonomy strivings and sensitivity to the mother's need for narcissistic validation. Thus Mrs. D.'s expressed intent to remain out of the hospital was designed primarily to serve a seductive purpose. By my failing to recognize and communicate my understanding of this motivation to her, she was first led to experience me as encouraging her to strive for a level of functioning that exceeded her capacities (in the service of meeting my narcissistic needs), and then as not recognizing in her failure to perform a desire for symbiotic relatedness in our relationship.

It would seem that the purpose of the pseudo-idealizing transference in severely disturbed narcissistic personality disorders is to reevoke the quality and conditions of the original mother–child relationship as a prestage to experiencing the therapist reparatively as new object, as Rothstein (1980) states, in the metamorphosis of his psychic structure. Seen in this light, the patient's seductive behavior affords him a means of determining the degree to which the therapist is likely to use him for narcissistic gratification; it also serves the purpose of demonstrating to the therapist that the patient is owed the merger experience he desires, because he is obviously unable to live up to the therapist's expectations (which, like those of the original maternal object, are demonstratively unreasonable).

Within a few weeks of voicing her goal, Mrs. D. found herself becoming increasingly tense at home and in her outpatient programs. While her suicidal ideation had never completely disappeared, it now intruded into her consciousness with greater intensity and frequency. I drew her attention to a possible connection between these phenomena and her decision never to be hospitalized again. This seemed to have no meaning for her. At this point Mrs. D. requested and received additional psychotropic medication, which temporarily gave her a feeling of greater control. I noted, however, that there now appeared to be a provocative quality to the manner in which she voiced her self-destructive impulses. She spoke of wanting to make gashes on her arms and to burn her hair as a means of relieving tension. I readily acknowledged my grave concern and indicated that she now seemed to be putting me in the position of urging hospitalization on her while she herself refused to consider it. Mrs. D.'s tension and self-destructive impulses abated, only to escalate again.

I came to realize that I had been cast in the role of persecutor, either seen as demanding that she remain out of hospital, or (when I affirmed that this was not my position) as demanding that she subjugate herself to humiliation by consenting to be admitted. At this juncture Mrs. D. also began to speak of my inability to understand her needs and of my standing aloof from her troubles. She saw me as despising her for staying in bed and neglecting herself and her children. She indicated that more than anything else she needed to feel good about herself and that forcing herself to function at a higher level was not giving her any good feelings, only making her feel worse. It was obvious that Mrs. D. held me responsible for this state of affairs, as I had undoubtedly provided support and admiration in the past when she had related her efforts to clean house, make meals, etc. Thus I came to recognize that she now wished me to make no implicit demands on her and to convince her that I accepted and admired her for merely existing. Mrs. D. acknowledged that this was in fact the case. She went on to say that she believed that she had not had this experience with her mother as long as she needed it, and may not have ever had it; she believed that her mother provided physical care now only because it allowed her to feel like a martyr and because it made the patient more readily available to hear complaints about her husband (Mrs. D.'s father).

Although I believe I had shown an empathic understanding of Mrs. D.'s desires for acceptance and admiration for simply existing, I had failed to address adequately her feelings of frustration at being unable to experience this form of gratification with me, or to acknowledge her wish to merge with me as an omnipotent other who would be perfectly responsive to her needs, nor did I fully explore the genetic antecedents of her frustration. As a result, Mrs. D. was not able to continue working through these feelings, and instead was derailed into restoring narcissistic equilibrium herself by altering the balance of power between us.

At this time Mrs. D. came to view me as deliberately withholding concern and relief from her. She became increasingly belittling and preoccupied with the injustice of the inequities between us. This led to her expressing fantasies, such as bringing in a can of soda and flinging the contents at me and around my office. I recall making the comment to her that abandoning controls to that extent would not only make her feel bad about herself, it would damage me in her eyes, and thus make me less able to be of help to her. Furthermore, I indicated that while I could accept her need and desire to express her anger and frustration in this fashion, unless she stopped at the level of fantasy, it would be extremely difficult for me to continue treatment with her.

Although I felt that Mrs. D.'s controls were slipping, I hesitated to make a unilateral decision to hospitalize her, hoping either to assist her to resist her destructive impulses by verbalizing her fantasies or to persuade her to agree to hospitalization. Mrs. D. presented as depressed and very withdrawn over the next few sessions. This was followed by a dramatic mood change; although inaccessible, she now appeared lively, sarcastic, and fairly cheerful. I found myself totally unable to make any meaningful contact with her. As our time in the session drew to a close, she suddenly looked rather frightened yet resolute. She reached down into her handbag and drew from it a large kitchen knife and began to raise it over her head. Needless to say, I was startled and quite frightened. After some moments I was able to persuade her to give it to me and to agree to immediate hospitalization. Mrs. D. appeared at that point to be in a disassociative state, but recovered quite quickly. When questioned by ward staff, she would only say that she was "fed up" with me and with herself, but insisted that she had never really intended to harm me.

I next saw Mrs. D. three days after this incident. She appeared embarrassed and uncomfortable, but also far more relaxed than I had seen her in some months. She was concerned only that I might decide to discontinue the therapy. She wished to assure me that she would never behave in a similar fashion in the future. Mrs. D. also apologized for frightening me. Nonetheless, it was altogether apparent how much satisfaction she had derived from this incident. After much exploration it became clear to both of us that Mrs. D. had wished me to experience her frightened, helpless, and frustrated feelings; by arousing these affects in me she also felt less alone. Furthermore, she acknowledged that she had found the physical expression of her aggressive feelings far more satisfying than putting them into words. Mrs. D. felt that she had had no words for her feelings, that she had no impact on me or my words on her. She was thus also attempting to reestablish contact. Mrs. D. wished to test my acceptance of her and to use my acceptance to increase her own. She hoped that if I were to experience intense feelings of fear and anger, I could better help her to understand and cope with such feelings in herself. Finally, she wanted to have the experience of power over me, however temporarily. Thus it was essential to her that she succeed in frightening me, not merely in making me angry (as, for example, by carrying through with throwing soda at me). Therefore, Mrs. D. was willing to risk terminating the therapy, if by doing so she stood a chance of transforming me into a more responsive selfobject.

I elected to continue therapy with Mrs. D., feeling certain that she would not seek to intimidate me physically again, as I was convinced that her extreme behavior had served its purpose as a threat. Over the course of the past two years, Mrs. D. has shown some signs of emerging from her regressed state. The most striking evidence of change has been her exercise of initiative and a new-found enjoyment in her relationship with her children. Correspondingly, Mrs. D.'s involvement with her parents has been greatly reduced, and she is more skillful and persistent in negotiating with others. During this period Mrs. D. set a few goals for herself, which required a modicum of perseverance and optimism and the capacity to cope with disappointment. Her relative success in these endeavors was due, in no small part, to her carefully choosing objectives that would benefit her alone, and that did not, in her view, lend themselves to being taken over by me for my narcissistic gratification. As I continue to work with her, I anticipate that her feelings of being exploited and forced into premature autonomy will undergo further elaboration in the transference when Mrs. D. is at the point of seeking employment or vocational training. To date she has not made any significant moves in this direction, owing, I believe, to the intensity of her unresolved feelings of anger and fear connected with performing and producing.

I have attempted in this clinical example to illustrate the central role that I believe balance of power issues hold for severely disturbed narcissistic personality disorders. It may not always be possible to avoid acting-out behavior that takes the form of physical intimidation. Not only do these patients regress into (transient) archaic preverbal states in which their accessibility is quite limited, they are also prone (during these periods) to develop punitive, self-restitutional fantasies that admit only nonverbal forms of expression. However, as I have also sought to demonstrate, a more complete understanding of the nature of the narcissistic injuries experienced by these patients in the context of the therapeutic relationship could conceivably restore their narcissistic balance sufficiently to enable them to continue working through their archaic merger fantasies. Particularly when such an empathic understanding is inadequate, the patient is forced to take on this selfobject function himself. While he may initially approach this task through verbal attacks upon the therapist, he is at this point vulnerable to further regression to a preverbal state in which his experience of helplessness is intensified. In this state the patient's remaining controls tend to be abandoned and physical intimidation becomes probable.

CONCLUSION

The purpose of this chapter has been to draw attention to the various interrelated functions that the expression of rage serves in severely disturbed narcissistic personality disorders and to identify these functions in the context of these patients' selfobject transference responses. In addition, I have tried to show how, given the combination of these patients' self-structural deficits and their internalized, intensely negatively charged self and other representations, a self psychological approach to treatment is likely to prove more effective than one that emphasizes the elaboration of the negative transference.

11

When the Patient Is Depressed

Jeffrey Deitz

Self psychology, with its different approach to transference and aggression, provides alternate guidelines for the treatment of patients who are depressed.[1] In the traditional psychoanalytic approach to depression, the main dynamic is unconscious rage that, having been withdrawn from a lost object, is re-directed toward the patient's ego. The classical analytic approach to depression discourages the development of the idealized transference, which it views as the patient's defensive strategy to avoid overt expressions of rage. Consistent with this formulation, psychodynamic therapy is designed to mobilize the patient's rage and encourage its expression.

---

[1]The author thanks Frank Lachmann for his supervisory efforts and scholarly advice, and Arnold Goldberg for his comments and encouragement.

In contrast, Kohut viewed rage as a reflection of a fragmented self, the unwelcomed consequence of a rupture in the idealizing transference. He believed that the development of the idealized transference was a necessary and major aspect of treatment that serves to activate internalized self representations associated with the patient's internal sense of cohesion and integration. Consequently, he advocated the reestablishment of the idealizing transference through the therapist's empathic responses to the patient's sense of inner disappointment and hurt (Hall 1985, Goldberg 1978). The term "selfobject transference" conveys this functional aspect of transference.

NARCISSISTIC INJURY IN DEPRESSION

Narcissistic injury is a blow to one's sense of self. Coping with life's disappointments requires (1) activation of soothing contact with positive self representations, (2) deactivation of unobtainable expectancies, and (3) modification of unrealistic expectations. In psychotherapy, the therapist is in a position to observe (1) the depressive affect following the narcissistic injury, (2) the conscious and unconscious processes by which intense disappointment is reversed, and (3) the consequences of a failure to deactivate and transform negative or unrealistic expectancies.

Disappointment and loss occur throughout development. According to self psychology, differential responses to these experiences depend on the level of maturation when disappointment occurs, the degree of distress that is experienced, and the quality of relationships with others. During development, reversal of intense and distressing reactions take place in interaction between a disappointed child and his or her parent or surrogate. Ideally, the parent senses the distress of the child. Empathic responses attenuate painful affect and assist in reactivating the preexisting cohesive state (Bacal 1985, Stern 1985).

From the first weeks of the child's life, mother and child influence each other (Beebe and Lachmann 1987). Studies of maternal–infant regulation patterns in the sleep–wake cycle (Chappell and Sander 1979) and regulation of gaze and vocalizations during maternal-infant face to face play at 3 to 4 months (Stern 1974, Stern et al. 1975, Stern 1985) clearly demonstrates the capacity of each to respond to cues in the other. Without this basic attunement, an infant cannot develop adequately (Sander 1977, 1983).

The development of the child's capacities and sense of self influences and is influenced by others. Mother does more than respond to her child's needs. Parent and child influence each other in ways that activate different states within each other. With feeding, for example, mother's behavior may activate a state of pleasurable satiety in her child while at the same time the child's behavioral response influences mother's feeding behavior. During the normal course of development, children learn to activate their own states of satiety in their mother's absence. They gradually assume activating functions, while at the same time decreasing dependency on the parent as an activator.

A child must also learn to activate the soothing states originally engendered when the parent ministered to losses and disappointments. If the parent empathically resonates with the child's distress, there will be multiple opportunities for reparative/restorative interactions. These come naturally during development. It is the ability to activate the affective tone of these experiences, to self-soothe, that is so important later in life.

The need for self-soothing in the face of narcissistic injury is ongoing and basic: there is a continued need to learn how to generate affective contact with positively toned self representations (Kohut 1984). What is activated, therefore, is termed a good selfobject. Good selfobjects are generated through relationships, activities, and pursuits that activate dimensions of internalized self representations linked to positive affects. In psychotherapy, those aspects of the therapeutic relationship that activate selfobject functioning are considered selfobject transferences.

Coping with disappointment is assisted immeasurably by one's capacity for selfobject activation. Individuals whose development lacked reparative/restorative interactions with their parents, or whose state of depression precludes contact with them, do not have memories of being soothed and comforted from which to draw when attempting to initiate good selfobject functioning. Consequently, they are more vulnerable to the depressive affects generated by inevitable narcissistic injuries (Hall 1985).

SELF PSYCHOLOGY AND DEPRESSION

As they occur throughout development, there are multiple opportunities for reparative/restorative interactions between therapist and patient. In his work with depressed patients whose development lacked empathic responses from parents, Kohut sensed the importance of permitting selfobject transferences to emerge.

Self psychological therapists find that disturbances in the sense of self come alive in treatment whenever ruptures of the selfobject transference arise (when the patient is disappointed in the therapist or in the therapy). The narcissistic rage that emerges results from the patient's inability to restore his or her positive self representation alone. The concept of the aggressive drive does not explain this phenomenon. The therapist's empathic responses reestablish the selfobject transference, restore the patient's sense of cohesion and integration, and reactivate contact with positively toned self representations (Hall 1985, Goldberg 1978). Just as the goal in the parent–child relationship is for the child to internalize the various selfobject functions in the absence of the parent, the goal of psychotherapy is to develop the patient's capacity to activate good selfobjects without the actual presence of the psychotherapist, that is, to function with relative autonomy.

It is possible to formulate a psychodynamic theory of depression using the concepts of self representation, selfobject activation, and selfobject transference to describe the depressive process with its difficulties in the regulation of mood and self-esteem. No matter that a depressive process begins in response to an exogenous event (either object loss or narcissistic injury), or in response to a loss of endogenous capacities to activate functioning that influences mood in a positive direction. In a self psychological formulation, many depressive processes, from decompensation to resolution, can be explained by an acquired, inherited, or developmental deficit or dysfunction in the ability to activate and/or maintain contact with self representations that are linked to positive affects.

Working with depressed patients, self psychologists investigate how and when such deficits/dysfunctions arise. Not limiting their review of the patient's history to one period, they learn what mechanisms and strategies have been used in the past and are used currently to attain and maintain contact with self representations linked to positive emotions. They are interested in how the relationships, attachments, and pursuits in the person's external world activate positive self representations in the person's internal world.

The self psychologist addresses the current-day presentation and functioning of the depressed patient while maintaining interest in the patient's past. Classical analytic theory emphasizes the pathogenic reactivation of the patient's unresolved conflicts from childhood. While the self psychologist also notes past unconscious conflict, focus is on the patient's history of self representation. Emphasis is on relationships and pursuits where positive feelings, such as pride, joy, and cohesion have previously emerged, if only temporarily. It then becomes possible to ask "What forces are at work now that keep the person from activating aspects of the self that would allow him or her to feel better?"

Mr. R.

> Mr. R. was a 73-year-old man who deteriorated into an unconsolable depression with psychosomatic preoccupation, profound anergy, and suicidal despair in the eighteen months following the death of his wife of forty-three years. Eight months after she died, he had a mild heart attack, which he experienced as completely disabling. He withdrew from every relationship and activity that was previously enjoyable. Weight loss, and an angry insistence that nothing could be done to influence his dysphoric mood, completed the clinical picture.
>
> A traditional psychoanalytic approach would posit the persistence of unconscious rage (at the dead wife or other figure[s] from Mr. R.'s present or past) that had been withdrawn from the object and directed against Mr. R.'s ego. The therapeutic task would be to mobilize his rage and its associated unconscious fanta-

sies. However, in this case, interventions that directed Mr. R.'s attention to his anger provoked episodes of more rage, chest pain, defensive denials of anger, and withdrawal. Antidepressants afforded little, if any, symptom relief. Mr. R.'s belief that nothing could be done to change his depression was reinforced.

Using a self psychological approach, Mr. R.'s therapist focused on those aspects of Mr. R.'s relationship with his wife that activated dimensions of his self representation linked to his feelings of cohesion. Treatment also included contact with Mr. R.'s children. They revealed that their mother had a special way of "getting through to father" when he was moody and depressed. She would lovingly "needle" him in a way that made him feel challenged and activated in a positive way. It became clear that Mr. R. had become dependent on the mood-altering aspects of the needling interactions with his wife. They had served an organizing and cohesion-engendering selfobject function for him. He had naturally turned to her for this particular kind of comfort when he felt disheartened. In her absence, he had no one to whom he could turn. Thus, the narcissistic injury involved more than object loss, it involved losing dimensions of himself that were activated within him through his interactions with his wife.

Mr. R.'s depressive symptoms attenuated when, after repeated empathic attunement and mirroring, a merger transference developed in which Mr. R. believed that his therapist knew precisely what it felt to be like him. Basic cognitive techniques initiated this feeling. For example, when Mr. R. overstated that he was totally disabled from working due to his heart condition, his therapist noted that it was understandable that he felt that way when he compared himself with his former, tireless self. Seeing himself as disabled was a consequence of a comparison with an unconscious, but still operative, preexisting self representation of the tireless worker.

Empathic reflections on his tendency to see himself as the only one who could feel what he was feeling were key to the development of the merger selfobject transference. On one occasion, Mr. R. bitterly asserted that his therapist was too young to understand how powerfully he had been affected by the loss of his wife. His therapist, addressing Mr. R.'s feeling of being totally alone in his misery, responded, "You feel alone and can't believe that I can understand." This conviction that his psychotherapist understood and could "get through to him" activated a dimension of his self representation by re-creating the emotional climate that existed in his relationship with his wife. Thereafter, his energy level, somatic preoccupation, and dysphoria improved noticeably. He began to resume activities that were previously enjoyable, leaving the hospital on brief passes to be with his children, grandchildren, and friends whom he had not visited since his wife's death.

In therapy, feelings of merger reactivated dimensions of his self representation with which he had lost contact. They re-created aspects of the feeling tone he had experienced in his relationship with his wife. The cohesion engendered by the selfobject transference enabled Mr. R. to begin to mourn this fundamental, devastating loss. It was not only that he missed Mrs. R. and was angry about it. *He missed the sense of self that had been activated within him by her doting ways.* He called it the "kingly feeling," and tearfully told of the royal way in which she had catered to his needs. No matter how hard he had tried after her death, he had been bitterly frustrated in his efforts to resurrect that dimension of his self representation in her absence.

Once his attempts to revive a previously active self representation had been identified, he began the painful but necessary process of consoling himself in his grief, just as his wife would have when she was alive. Thereafter, he regained his sense of pride in being a grandfather, a part-time worker, and a friend. The vegetative depressive symptoms improved further.

Mr. R. poignantly revealed how deeply his pride in his former sense of self had been shattered by the dual loss of his wife and his health. The depression remitted completely and he required little psychotherapy to maintain his gains. Follow-up revealed that he resumed part-time work in his former occupation, and recommenced an active social life. Importantly, he reestablished close and loving relationships with his children and grandchildren. Depression did not recur in the final years of his life.

To encourage the emergence of merger feelings, it was important to address Mr. R.'s wishes (his "id") in terms of the self representation that he was trying to revive. True enough, Mr. R. wanted to be cared for, but id interpretations of that aspect of his behavior would imply that Mr. R. was behaving childishly, wishing for something he could not have. An id interpretation would miss the point that he was really yearning to be cared for in a particular way that would serve to reactivate the kingly feeling he had enjoyed only when being cared for by his wife. Similarly, he *still* wanted to work those ten-hour shifts that would serve to preserve his self representation as a tireless worker.

The technique of self psychological theory includes interpreting how Mr. R.'s present self representation (seeing himself as disabled) contains an unconscious reference to his former sense of self (seeing himself as tireless). Such interpretations affirmed and validated Mr. R.'s pride in himself. The soothing contact with positive dimensions of his self allowed him to deactivate his expectation that he work tirelessly regardless of his age. Once deactivated, the wish could be transformed into one more consistent with reality.

Interpretation that his wish for royal treatment included an unconscious reference to his wife (he wanted to be her king) allowed him to come to terms with the loss of his kingdom (and its one subject, his wife, the queen). Consequently, the wish for kingly treatment from his children could be deactivated and transformed into a meaningful and appropriate relationship with his grandchildren. He came to sense that his therapist truly understood how profoundly the loss of his wife and health had injured his sense of self.

The processes that activated Mr. R.'s positive feeling states were at issue, not his rage at the lost object. *The rage in Mr. R.'s depression was a by-product of the condition, not a causal factor.* It is narcissistic rage (Kohut 1984) and can be understood as Mr. R.'s intense frustration with his inability to activate a desired internal state or self representation, not as rage at an object per se. Mr. R. was angry with his children because of the frustrating recognition that he could not make them function in a way that would activate his former sense of himself, the feelings of royalty he had once experienced with his wife.

CONCLUSION

During life, disappointment and object loss are inevitable. Self psychology provides a useful framework for understanding and treating the patient who is depressed. Empathic attunement to the emergence of the selfobject transference and an appreciation of its potential to influence mood and self-esteem facilitates the alleviation of symptoms, the restoration of the patient's integration, and a sense of cohesion.

12

When the Patient Abuses Alcohol

Jerome Levin

Heinz Kohut's (1971, 1977a) insights into the psychodynamics of addiction are directly relevant to our understanding and treatment of the alcoholic. Kohut sees narcissistic disturbance as central to the psychopathology of the addict. The core difficulty of these narcissistic personalities is the absence of internal structure; explicitly, there are deficits in the self's capacities for tension regulation, self-soothing, and self-esteem regulation. The alcoholic's pathological drinking is an attempt to make up for this "missing structure," that is, the alcoholism serves to reduce tension and regulate self-esteem in the absence of adequate intrapsychic resources to achieve such regulation. Thus, in early sobriety these deficits in the structure of the self, with their concomitant psychological dysfunctions, will continue to disable the alcoholic until psychic structure can be built.

Kohut's view of narcissism differs from both Freud's and Kernberg's. In contradistinction to Freud's view of narcissistic libido as the precursor of object libido, Kohut believes that narcissistic and object-libidinal strivings develop along independent lines. That is, narcissism is seen not as a stage in the development of object love, but rather as an aspect of human life that has its own developmental history in which the self and its libidinal investments evolve from a fragmentary stage into a cohesive, archaic form (the nuclear self) and finally into a mature form. The development of mature object and idealized selfobject love are parallel, but independent, processes.

Kohut differs from Kernberg in believing that the grandiose self (a term he coined) is a normal, albeit archaic, rather than pathological, structure. Kohut is particularly interested in early self structures: the grandiose self, twinship selfobject, and the idealized selfobject (or idealized parent imago). These structures constitute the nuclear self, which Kohut views as tripolar.

SELF PSYCHOLOGICAL ISSUES

Let us attempt to elucidate these concepts. Kohut defines the self as a unit cohesive in space and enduring in time, which is a center of initiative and a recipient of impressions. It can be regarded either as a mental structure superordinate to the agencies of the mind (id, ego, and superego) or as a content of those agencies. Although Kohut believed that these conceptualizations were complementary rather than mutually exclusive, he emphasized the self as a central or superordinate principle in his later theories. It is, so to speak, the organized and organizing center of human experience, which is itself experienced as cohesive and enduring. How does this sense of an I (self), which coheres in space and endures in time, develop? According to Kohut, the infant develops a primitive (fragmented) sense of self very early. That is, each body part, each sensation, each mental content is experienced as belonging to a self, to a me, as mine; however, there is no synthesis of these experiences as yet. There are selves, but no unitary self. Nor are there clear boundaries between self and world. Kohut designates this stage as the stage of the *fragmented self*; it is the developmental stage at which psychotic persons are fixated or to which they regress. Although there are important differences, Kohut's stage of the fragmented self corresponds to Freud's stage of autoeroticism; it is another way of understanding the stage of human development that precedes the integration of the infant's experienced world.

At the next stage of development, an *archaic, nuclear self* arises from the infant's experience of being related to as a self, rather than as a collection of parts and sensations, by empathic caretakers. This self is cohesive and enduring, but it is not yet securely established. Hence, it is prone to regressive fragmentation. It is nuclear in the sense of having a center, or nucleus, and it is archaic in the sense of being a primitive (that is, grandiose and undifferentiated) precursor of the mature self. The archaic nuclear self is tripolar in that it comprises three structures: the grandiose self, the idealized selfobject, and twinship. That is, in this stage there is a differentiated self, which is experienced as omnipotent, but there are no truly differentiated objects. Objects are still experienced as extensions of the self, as selfobjects. At this stage, the child's grandiose self attempts to exercise omnipotent control over his selfobjects. In healthy maturity, all loved objects have a selfobject aspect. However, here the experience of the object as a selfobject is a reversible "regression in the service of the ego," which lacks the rigidity that characterizes the experience of objects as selfobjects in pathological narcissism.

The internalization of psychic structure (albeit in rudimentary form) is co-determinous with the formation of the nuclear self. As Kohut (1977a) puts it, "The rudiments of the nuclear self are laid down by simultaneously or consecutively occurring processes of selective inclusion and exclusion of psychological structure" (p. 183). Failure to adequately internalize functions originally performed for the child by selfobjects results in deficits in the self. Addiction is a futile attempt to compensate for this failure in internalization.

To paraphrase Kohut: it is the inner emptiness, the missing parts of the self experienced as a void, that addicts try to fill with food, with alcohol, with drugs, or with compulsive sexuality. It cannot be done. Whatever is compulsively taken in goes right through and no psychic structure is built; that can only be done by transmuting internalization of self–selfobject relationships. It is abysmally low self-esteem, doubts about being real or of existing at all, and terror of fragmentation that addicts, including alcohol addicts, try to remediate by their addictions. They always fail.

Of crucial importance are the internalization of tension regulation, self-soothing, and self-esteem regulation, as well as the selfobject's function as stimulus barrier. Kohut's stage of the archaic self corresponds, in some ways, to Freud's stage of (primary) narcissism. It does not develop into object love, however, but into mature narcissism, which is characterized by realistic ambitions, enduring ideals, and secure self-esteem.

Pathological narcissism is the regression/fixation to the stage of the archaic self. It is characterized by the presence of a cohesive, but insecure, self that is threatened by regressive fragmentation; grandiosity of less than psychotic proportions, which manifests itself in the form of arrogance, isolation, and unrealistic goals; feelings of entitlement; the need for omnipotent control; poor differentiation of self and object; and deficits in the self-regulating capacities of the ego (self). Further, affect tolerance is poor. The tenuousness of the cohesion of the self makes the narcissistically regressed individual subject to massive anxiety, which is, in reality, fear of annihilation (that is, fear of fragmentation of the self). Narcissistic personality disorders are also subject to "empty" depression, reflecting the relative emptiness of the self, or the paucity of psychic structure and good internal objects. In the condition of pathological narcissism, these manifestations of the grandiose self and/or the idealized selfobject may be either blatantly apparent or deeply repressed and/or denied, with a resulting façade of pseudo-selfsufficiency, but they are never smoothly integrated into a mature self, as in the case of healthy narcissism.

In Kohut's formulation, the overtly grandiose self is the result of merger with (or lack of differentiation from) a mother who used the child to gratify her own narcissistic needs. It is a "false self" in the terminology of Winnicott (1960). Kohut envisions this false self as insulated from the modifying influence of the reality ego by a vertical split in the personality. The reality ego is in turn impoverished by the repression of the unfulfilled archaic narcissistic demands by a horizontal split (repression barrier) in the personality. For our purposes, the salient point to be derived from Kohut's and Winnicott's theories is an understanding of the overt grandiosity of the alcoholic as a manifestation of a "false self," which is isolated, both affectively and cognitively, from the more mature reality ego, which is itself enfeebled by its inability to integrate the archaic self. Hence, some sense can be made of the coexistence of haughty arrogance and near-zero self-esteem so frequently seen in alcoholics.

The therapist's first task with the recovering alcoholic (and all other patients) is *building a relationship*. Because the treatment will end unless the therapist succeeds in establishing a meaningful relationship with the alcoholic, the building and preserving of bonds between therapist and alcoholic *always* take precedence in the therapeutic interview. Bonds are built by empathic listening, supplemented by the clearing of resistances.

It is the *attitude* of the therapist that is crucial, especially with patients who are as sensitive as alcoholics are in early sobriety. What is required is active listening, the projection of interest and concern, and nonjudgmental positive regard for the patient. However, the situation with the newly sober alcoholic requires some modifications of Freud's excellent advice on conducting the early stages of treatment. The modification essentially consists of greater overt activity on the part of the therapist. Although empathic listening and clearing of treatment-threatening resistances remain paramount, the therapist must also serve as an expert on the disease of alcoholism; he or she has an educative function to perform.

The therapist is also dealing with an impulse disorder that may be acted out at any time, possibly ending the treatment. Insofar as possible, this acting out must be anticipated and circumvented. It is intolerable affects that lead to the drink. Unconscious and/or disavowed affects are particularly dangerous. Any intense feelings, "positive" or "negative," conscious or unconscious, that remain unverbalized are a threat to sobriety. The therapist must therefore actively encourage the expression of feelings and must appropriately interpret some of the emotional discomfort as a symptom of recovery. In other words, the acting out of the resistance by drinking must be anticipated and dealt with before it occurs. Of course, this is not always possible; it is a goal, not a demand on the therapist. Therapy at this stage of recovery is so very difficult because the therapist has little time in which to deal with the patient's conflicts since those conflicts may be acted out by drinking and terminating the treatment. We do not have the luxury of waiting the patient out, however desirable this may be. Thus, what is required is a sort of bob and weave on the part of the therapist. Empathic listening, imparting of information, and the elicitation of feelings must be integrated into a coherent style. It requires a great deal of "therapeutic tact" for the therapist to sense when to do what in order to maintain the relationship. However, the growing attachment of the patient to the therapist provides the cement which holds both the patient and the therapeutic relationship together. Thus, Freud's recommendations for beginning the treatment remain pure gold that we must, however, necessarily alloy in order to successfully treat early-sobriety alcoholics.

INTERNALIZATION OF SOBRIETY

Virtually no chronic alcoholic wants to get sober. The pain is too great. The regressive pull is too great. That is why either actual external events—such as the loss or threat of loss of a job, or the loss or threat of loss of a mate—or events experienced as external—such as the loss or threat of loss of health—are so often the precipitants of the emotional crisis that results in the alcoholic's becoming sober. These external events furnish the apparent motives for sobriety. At this point the alcoholic is "doing it for them." Such motivation is often not sufficient, and external controls such as those provided by hospitalization are necessary to achieve sobriety of any duration. After leaving the hospital, the alcoholic may remain sober out of fear of losing something valued. It is still being done for "them." This is the stage of "I can't drink" (Zimberg 1978). The hope is that a gradual process is initiated at this point by which remaining sober comes to be something that the alcoholic wants to do rather than something that must be done.

If this process is successful, the stage of "I won't drink" is reached. The controls that were originally external or experienced as external are now internal. Now, no asylum walls or chemical barriers are necessary. Internalized controls maintain sobriety, and the stage of "I don't have to drink" has been reached.

It is not known exactly how this control becomes internalized. Identification helps; in fact it may be the key. This is one reason that AA and peer counseling can be so effective in establishing stable sobriety. The alcoholic is provided with figures with whom to identify. They too are alcoholic, but they are no longer active; they are recovering. It is not with Bob or Jane or John or Sally that the alcoholic must identify, but with Bob's or Jane's or John's or Sally's sobriety. The alcoholic may also identify with his nonalcoholic therapist's sobriety, although here the identification is less direct. At first the identification is with the sobriety of the other, but slowly that sobriety is drawn within. It is as if the sobriety of the other is mentally ingested, digested, metabolized, and assimilated until it becomes part of the mental world of the newly recovering alcoholic. Although this is only a simile, it comes as close as we can get to an understanding of the process of internalization. Through this process the controls that allow others to remain sober become the controls of the newly sober one.

With time, sobriety becomes more rewarding. The pain of early sobriety recedes, the residual pain is endurable, and the alcoholic wants to remain sober. Sobriety becomes part of the recovering alcoholic's ego-ideal—of the ideal self. Living up to one's ego-ideal increases self-esteem and that feels good; hence, it is a behavior one tries to maintain. This is the case with the recovering alcoholic's sobriety. Remaining sober is no longer a struggle; it is an increasingly comfortable decision.

Sally

Sally came to me for the treatment of a post-traumatic stress reaction. She had been in an automobile accident and was badly shaken. Her face had been scarred and she was deeply depressed. Plastic surgery later restored her face, leaving little evidence of the accident, but she didn't know that was going to happen when she first came to my office. Sally was young and very appealing. She had been referred by her attorney, who had not mentioned alcohol, so I was surprised when she told me that she was an alcoholic. She said that she had been alcoholic since the age of 12 and had "hit bottom" four years ago. I asked her how old she was. She said, "Twenty-five." My next question was, "How did you get sober?" She replied, "The part about getting sober wouldn't make sense unless I told you about my drinking too: should I do that?" I said, "Sure." This is her testimony:

> Well, I don't know where to start. I come from an alcoholic family. Both my parents died of alcoholism. Well, I think my father died of alcoholism; he deserted us when I was 4. I remember the last time I saw him. We were eating in a diner and I was spilling my food. He screamed at me and said I was disgusting. I always felt that he left because I was so disgusting. I feel like a pig; I'm a compulsive overeater, too. I know in my head that he didn't leave because of the way I eat, but I don't know it in my heart. I think I still believe it. Things got worse then. My mother drank more and more and we had very little money. Sometimes there was no toilet paper in the house, but there was always beer. Later we moved to my grandfather's. He was rich, but he grabbed my pussy sometimes and I didn't know what to do. I think he was senile, but he drank too so maybe that was it. After I grew up, my mother told me she knew what he did to me, but she was afraid to do anything about it because he might have thrown us out. She was drunk when she told me that. Why did she have to tell me? I hate her for letting it happen, and I hate her for telling me that she let it happen. How could a mother do that? I have a daughter. I'd cut off his balls, if a man did that to my daughter. How could she? My grandfather got more senile and I don't know exactly what happened after that. My mother was like two people. When she was sober she was wonderful—beautiful and interested in me. But very snobby and uptight. Then I didn't think she was a snob, I thought that she was a great lady—perfectly dressed and so elegant. I loved her so much. Then there was mother when she was drunk. Sloppy and falling down, she'd sit with her legs spread with no panties and you could see everything. She'd curse and then try to play the great lady again, "Oh, my dear" and all that shit. I hated her then.

I was around 10 when I started having sex play with my cousins and some of the neighborhood kids. Mostly with the boys, but sometimes with the girls too. Do you think I'm a lesbian? I loved sex—it felt so good and it made me feel good about myself. Somebody wanted me. Maybe I felt guilty underneath. Later I hated myself and maybe all that sex play had something to do with it. I was raised a strict Catholic—sort of—once I was naked—I had just gotten out of the tub and I did an imitation of the Virgin Mary—I was about 6—and my mother really whaled my ass with a ruler. When I was about 10 my mother met my stepfather. Eddy was a complete asshole. He drank all the time, too. Can you imagine marrying a fucking drunk like him? Then mother really dropped me. She was more interested in drinking with Eddy. I started getting in trouble in school—at 11 I got fucked for the first time. And I mean got fucked, not made love to, by some 20-year-old pervert. Can you imagine an 11-year-old getting fucked? I loved it or thought that I did. I hung out with all the older boys. They had cars and liquor. I can't tell you how many cocks I had in me. Big ones, small ones, white ones, black ones. And you know I was never sober once. Every one of those guys had something to get high on— beer, pot, hard stuff. I loved booze from the first time I tasted it. It was even better than sex. I drank a lot. Any boy or man who gave me something to drink could have me. Sometimes I really liked it, but I liked fooling around with other girls even more. I think I was really turned on by myself—when I played with the other girls. My mother and stepfather raised hell when they weren't too drunk to care and finally my mother had me put away. Can you imagine that? What kind of fucking mother would put a kid in the places she put me? For God's sake, one place had bars and I was locked in. I hate her for doing that. Mental hospitals, homes for delinquent girls, the House of the Good Shepherd, the whole ball of wax. Finally I got out—I wasn't actually in any of those places for very long, its just the idea—how could you do that to a kid—and I met Calvin.

What a bastard he was. Oh, I forgot to tell you that when I was 15 I was team banged—raped—by a gang who pulled me into an alley and fucked me until my thing was raw and bloody. They beat me real hard too, but not so hard as Calvin did later. Oh yeah, Calvin beat me all the time. I must have been crazy but I loved him. He took me away from my hometown and my mother didn't bother me anymore. He sort of made a prisoner out of me—if I even went to the grocery store without his permission he beat me. He had a big one, the biggest I ever saw and I had seen plenty, so I thought he was a great lover. He always had beer and weed and other stuff and I stayed high most of the time. He's the father of my child. When I went into labor he was stoned. He slapped me and called me a rotten whore. He wouldn't go to the hospital with me. Do you know what it's like for a 16-year-old kid to have a baby alone? Forget it.

I never cheated on Calvin but he never stopped accusing me of being with other men and hitting me. Sometimes he hit me with a wooden plank. I think I thought I deserved it—that I needed to be punished for all the things I had done. I needed Calvin to beat me. As long as he supplied drugs and alcohol and beat me I would have stayed. It was the way he acted around the baby that made me leave. One day when he wasn't home and the baby was about 2 I ran away. I couldn't stand his insane jealousy anymore; he was even jealous of the baby. A guy crazy enough to be jealous of his own kid, that's sick. He was real sick; sick in his head. I couldn't stand any more so I ran away and went to a town in the mountains where my older sisters and brother lived. Something in me said *enough*, you've been punished enough. Of course I kept on drinking. There wasn't any more sex, not then, just falling down drunk every day. I went on welfare and sometimes I worked off the books. I was sort of dead, no, not *sort of*, just plain *dead*. That went on for a few years and I hated myself more and more. I tried to be a good mother through it all and I don't think I did too badly, but God, was I depressed!

My stepfather was dead by then and my mother was far gone. I think I saw it in her before I saw it in me. My brother was in the program—A.A. that is. I thought he was a jerk, a real ass, an uptight loser. Who else would join those holy rollers? What I couldn't figure out was how such a raving asshole could be happy, and the damn jerk *was* happy. Even I could see that. He did something really smart; he didn't lecture me. In fact, he never even mentioned my drinking. Damn good thing he didn't, because the way I rebelled against everything and everybody I would never have listened. What he did do was tell me what had happened to him— ran his story as they say in A.A. I didn't want to hear that shit and I told him so, but I did hear it in spite of myself. I was getting worse; I was more and more terrified that Calvin would come back and kill me—I guess I thought that he should because of the way I was living, but I didn't know that then, I was just scared. I was getting sicker and sicker from all the drinking and I never had any money; it got to the point where I couldn't stand any more. If it wasn't for my daughter I would have killed myself, but I couldn't get out of it that way. I don't know why, but one day I asked my brother to take me to a meeting. An A.A. meeting that is. I think it was the guilt— once I didn't have Calvin to beat me I couldn't stand the guilt—I *knew*—I mean I really knew what it's like to have alcoholic parents. I loved my daughter—she has such a sick fuck for a father, so I wanted her to have at least one parent with her head screwed on straight. So I went to that fucking meeting. I loved it—I mean I *loved* it—like I never loved anything. For Christ's sake, I even identified with the coffee cups. When I do something I *do* it—I went all the way—the whole nine yards. I was sick—sick, sick, sick from my crotch to my toes, not to mention my head. I was so scared; I hadn't had a sober day in years, but I've made it a day at a time. I haven't made it any too swiftly. I still can't stand the guilt and the rage; you wouldn't believe how angry I get, and the crying. I cry all the fucking time, but I don't drink, I don't drug, and I don't care if my ass falls off, I'm not going to. At least not today.

I didn't want to be like my mother. I *won't* be like her. She's dead now. I couldn't stand it when she died—she died from her drinking—she had an accident while drunk, it was kind of a suicide. I knew she was dead, but I didn't know it. I couldn't let her go—not the awful way it was—if she was sober and I was sober I could have let her die, but she wasn't, so I knew but I didn't know she was dead. I never accepted it; she couldn't forgive me dead, nor I her. Then one day I went to the cemetery. I looked at her grave for a long time. I couldn't believe she was dead; I started screaming, "Move the fucking grass, move the fucking grass, Mother." I screamed and screamed but she didn't move the fucking grass and I finally knew she was gone. I went to my home group meeting hysterical. All I said was she couldn't move the fucking grass and I cried the rest of the meeting. Nobody said a word, they just let me be me; they didn't try to take away my pain and I didn't want or need anybody to take it away. What I needed was somebody to be with me in that pain, and they were.

I love the fucking program and all the crazy screwed-up people there. They're like me; I'm crazy too, but I'm sober. For God's sake, can you imagine what it would have been like if I was

drinking when she died? Thank God I wasn't. I hate her—I love
her—I still can't let go of her although I know she's dead. I hate
alcohol. I hate drinking; look what it did to her, to my father, to
me. How did I get sober—I don't really know—I sort of had two
bottoms—a beaten bottom and an alcohol bottom. In that first
bottom I sort of saw myself and saw I couldn't go on exposing my
daughter to that stuff; the second was luck or something. No, not
exactly luck or not only luck. It had something to do with willingness—I became willing to go to that meeting. Maybe I had just had
enough; I didn't want any more pain for me or for the baby; she's
not a baby anymore. They say, "Why me?" in the program. When
you're drinking you have the "poor mees," so you're always asking,
"Why me?" If you recover, you say it differently. I don't know why
me. The way I lived, I should be dead but I'm not. I don't know if I
deserve it or not, but I'll take it.

MAJOR TASKS IN WORKING
WITH ALCOHOL ABUSE

Sally is a very clear example of an attempted self cure of narcissistic deficit and narcissistic injury by substance abuse. All such
attempts at self cure are futile, eventually leading to further narcissistic injury. This was so for Sally. Although alcohol and drugs
turned out to be the wrong medicine, Sally had found another way
to heal herself or start to heal herself before she came for therapy,
and the therapist largely stayed out of her way and was nonimpinging as she continued to heal herself. His relative "inactivity"
allowed identification and transmuting internalization to take
place. This led to structure building, firmer self cohesion, and
greater ego strength. Most alcoholics and substance abusers do
not have Sally's powerful drive for health and they require more
active interventions on the part of the therapist. Self psychology
has a number of powerful interventions to suggest for use in
working with these patients. In their respective ways they address
what theory understands as narcissistic deficit and narcissistic
injury and their attempted self cure through the substance abuse;
the attempt to fill inner emptiness due to failures in transmuting
internalization; the acting out of and turning against the self of

narcissistic rage; idealizing, mirror, and twinship transferences to alcohol and other drugs; attempts at omnipotent control through substance use and abuse; attempts to boost abysmally low self-esteem through the use of alcohol; and shame experiences both antecedent to and consequent upon alcohol and drug abuse. The following eleven suggested ways to translate theory into concrete interventions need to be modified so a particular patient can hear them, but they are models of great utility in working with alcoholics and substance abusers.

1. This intervention addresses the narcissistic wound inflicted by not being able to drink "like other people." The admission that one is powerless over alcohol, as A.A. puts it, or that one can't drink without the possibility of losing control, as I would put it, is extremely painful. It is experienced as a defect in the self, which is intolerable for those who are as perfectionistic as alcoholics usually are. The self must not be so damaged and deficient. Additionally, to be able to "drink like a man" or "like a lady" may be a central component of the alcoholic's self image—his or her identity. This is particularly so for "macho" men, but is by no means restricted to them. The therapist must recognize and articulate the conflict between the patient's wish to stop drinking and the patient's feeling that to do so entails admitting that he or she is flawed in a fundamental way. The therapist does this by saying, "You don't so much want to drink as not want not to be able to drink." This makes the patient conscious of the conflict in an empathic way and allows him or her to struggle with this issue. This often opens the way for the patient to achieve stable sobriety.

2. All addictions, including alcoholism, are one long experience of narcissistic injury. Failure usually stalks the alcoholic like a shadow. As one of my patients put it, "When I drink, everything turns to shit." It sure does when an alcoholic drinks. Career setbacks, job losses, rejection by loved ones, humiliations of various sorts, ill health, economic decline, accidental injury, and enduring "bad luck" are all too frequent concomitants of alcoholism. Each is a narcissistic insult. Cumulatively they constitute a massive narcissistic wound. Even if outward blows have not yet come, the inner blows—self-hatred and low self-regard—are al-

ways there. The alcoholic has all too frequently heard "it's all your fault" in one guise or another. The therapist must empathize with the alcoholic's suffering. "Your disease has cost you so much," "You have lost so much," and "Your self-respect is gone" are some ways the therapist can make contact with the alcoholic's pain and facilitate the alcoholic's experiencing this pain instead of denying, acting out, and/or anesthetizing it.

3. Alcoholics feel empty. Either they have never had much good stuff inside or they have long since flushed the good stuff out with alcohol. "You drink so much because you feel empty" makes the connection as well as brings into awareness the horrible experience of an inner void. After sobriety has been achieved, the genetic determinants of the paucity of psychic structure experienced as emptiness can also be interpreted.

4. Alcoholics frequently lack a firm sense of identity. How can you know who you are if your experience of self is tenuous, and its inner representation lacks consistent cohesion? The therapist can comment on this and point out that being an alcoholic is at least something definite—having an identity of sorts. When an A.A. member says, "My name is _____ and I am an alcoholic," he or she is affirming that he or she exists and has at least one attribute. With sobriety many more attributes will accrue—the self will enrich and cohere. Saying, "You are confused and not quite sure who you are. That is partly because of your drinking. Acknowledging your alcoholism will lessen your confusion as to who you are and give you a base on which to build a firm and positive identity" is a way of conveying this to the patient.

5. Many people drink because they cannot stand to be alone. They drink to enjoy someone's companionship. They have not developed what Winnicott (1958) calls the "capacity to be alone." Winnicott thinks that this comes from the experience of being alone in the presence of another—from having been a small child in the presence of an empathic, nonimpinging other who has become internalized so that one is not really alone when one is by oneself. Being alone in this sense is very different from defensive isolation driven by fear. Presumably, those who drink for companionship have never acquired the capacity to be alone. This, too,

should be interpreted, "You drink so much because you can't bear to be alone and alcohol gives you the illusion of having company, of being with a friend. After you stop drinking it will be important for us to discover why it is so painful for you to be alone."

6. Alcoholics form selfobject (narcissistic) transferences to alcohol, as do other drug abusers to their drug of choice. Relating to alcohol as a friend can be regarded as forming a twinship transference to alcohol. Alcoholics also form idealizing and mirror transferences to alcohol. The imago of the archaic idealized parent is projected onto alcohol and it is regarded as an all-powerful, all-good object with which alcoholic drinkers merge in order to participate in this omnipotence. "Alcohol will deliver the goods and give me love, power, and whatever else I desire" is the drinker's unconscious fantasy. The therapist should interpret this thus: "Alcohol has felt like a good, wise, and powerful parent who protected you and made you feel wonderful, and that is why you have loved it so much. In reality it is a depressant drug, not all the things you thought it was." The therapist can go on to say, "Now that drinking isn't working for you anymore, you are disillusioned, furious, and afraid. Let's talk about those feelings."

7. One of the reasons that alcoholics are so devoted to the consumption of alcohol is that it confirms their grandiosity. Another way to say this is alcoholics form a mirror transference to alcohol. I once had an alcoholic patient who told me that he felt thrilled when he read that a sixth Nobel prize was to be added to the original five. He read this while drinking in a bar at 8 A.M. His not-so-unconscious fantasy was winning all six.

The therapist should make the mirror transference conscious by interpreting it. "When you drink you feel that you can do anything, be anything, achieve anything and that feels wonderful. No wonder you don't want to give it up."

8. Alcoholics, without exception, like others with narcissistic behavior disorders, have abysmally low self-esteem no matter how well covered over by bluster and bravo it may be. Self psychology understands this as an impoverishment of the reality ego consequent upon failure to integrate archaic grandiosity, which is instead split off by what Kohut calls the "vertical split" and which

manifests itself as unrealistic reactive grandiosity. At some point the therapist needs to say, "You feel like shit and that you are shit and all your claims to greatness are ways to avoid knowing that you feel that way. You don't know it, but way down somewhere inside you feel genuinely special. We need to put you in touch with the real stuff so you don't need alcohol to help you believe that the phony stuff is real." The particular reasons, antecedent to and consequent upon the alcoholism, that the patient values himself/ herself so little need to be elucidated and worked through.

9. Sometimes the patient's crazy grandiosity is simultaneously a defense against and an acting out of the narcissistic cathexis of the patient by a parent. That is, the patient is attempting to fulfill the parent's dreams in fantasy while making sure not to fulfill them in reality. This is especially likely to be the case if the patient is an adult child of an alcoholic. Heavy drinking makes such a defense/acting out easy. If the alcoholic patient's grandiosity does seem to be a response to being treated as an extension of themselves by either parent, the therapist can say, "One reason you feel so rotten about yourself is that you're always doing it for Mom or Dad and not for yourself. You resent this and spite them by undermining yourself by drinking."

10. Many alcoholics have a pathological need for omnipotent control. Alcohol is simultaneously experienced as an object they believe they can totally control and coerce into doing their will, and an object which they believe gives them total control of their subjective states and of the environment. This can be seen as a manifestation of their mirror/idealizing transferences to alcohol. Alcoholics frequently treat people, including the therapist, as extensions of themselves. The A.A. slogans, "Get out of the driver's seat" and "Let God and let go," are cognitive behavioral ways of loosening the need to control. Therapists interpret this need to control in the patient's relationship with alcohol, in the patient's relationship with other people, and in the patient's relationship with the therapist. For example, "You think that when you drink you can feel any way you wish," "You go into a rage and drink whenever your wife doesn't do as you wish," or "You thought of drinking because you were upset with me when I didn't respond as you thought I would."

11. Alcoholics and their children suffer greatly from shame experiences. Alcoholic patients are ashamed of having been shamed and often drink to obliterate feelings of shame. Therapists need to help alcoholic patients experience rather than anesthetize their feelings of shame. One way to do this is to identify such feelings of shame that are not recognized as such. For example, "You felt so much shame when you realized that you were alcoholic that you kept on drinking so you wouldn't feel your shame."

Sally amply exemplifies the relationship between narcissistic deficit, narcissistic injury, and the futile attempt to remediate the former and heal the latter through the addictive use of substances—alcohol and food—and compulsive actions—sex and excitement. Sally suffered massive failures of internalization, leaving her with gaping structural deficits. She also felt dead, doubting both her aliveness and her existence, and sought out stimulation of any kind, even beatings, to feel alive. Lacking idealizable parents she found Calvin; having had little phase appropriate mirroring of her archaic grandiosity, she found alcohol. In addition to mirroring her, alcohol gave her the illusion of cohesiveness. The amazing strength she did display may have been possible because her mother very early on was "good enough." Sally's capacity for splitting also helped her preserve a good mother from whom she could draw some sustenance in face of all the "badness" of her later, and by then overtly alcoholic, mother. Sally never integrated the two mothers, which in her case worked for her, at least in some ways. Her "bad" mother became Sally's split-off grandiosity and denial. So split off from any kind of reality testing was this side of Sally's vertical split that her unassimilated grandiosity came very close to killing her. The mother's grandiosity did kill her. On the other side of the vertical split, Sally's reality ego was impoverished, depressed, empty, fragile, and never far from fragmentation. The phase-appropriate grandiosity of the stage of the archaic nuclear self had never been integrated into her reality ego—it couldn't be because it had never been adequately mirrored. In Winnicott's terms, her true self was buried for safekeeping in a dangerous, treacherous environment. Whether we understand this in Kohutian or in Winnicottian terms, it is clear that this defensive system made survival possible *and* that a major aim of treatment must be its modification.

The child of an alcoholic carries a special kind of narcissistic injury. Humiliation and shame are recurrent and the wounds go deep. Sally's narcissistic injuries were denied, repressed, and/or acted out as was the narcissistic rage as a natural reaction to these injuries. Sally's delinquency was an attempt at self cure. As Winnicott says, when there is an antisocial tendency there is hope. Sally found some kind of solace, responsiveness, and, in however distorted a form, mirroring in her acting out. It also allowed her to externalize her rage. However, what saved Sally was her ability to love and to seek love. She never gave up her search for good objects that she could idealize and internalize. Alcohol was one such object—one that traumatically failed her, but she didn't give up. Abandonment depression and abandonment rage were central to Sally's psychopathology, but they could be worked through in the transference because she transferred, because she was still searching for relationship. Her love for her baby, probably an identification with the early good mother, got her away from Calvin, and her ability to enter into a twinship with her brother allowed her to identify with him and join A.A. The A.A. Program then became an idealized object. She formed the same kind of transference with me, and the working through of her predominately idealizing transference, which also had aspects of mirror and twinship in it, enabled her to build psychic structure. Of course, she was sober by then or this would not have been possible.

The scene in the cemetery was crucial to Sally's recovery. As long as she couldn't let go of the bad mother or of just plain *mother*, there was no way that she could internalize a good object. Bad mother was a pathological introject, the content of the vertical split. Only by letting her die and then mourning her could Sally recover the energy to cathect a new object and by transmuting internalization acquire the psychic structure she lacked. Mourning is not possible during active addiction to alcohol or to other substances. I have found in case after case that facilitating mourning must take priority in the therapy of stable sober alcoholics Only then can the work proceed as one hopes it will.

CONCLUSION

Self psychological psychoanalysis is not the treatment of choice for most recovering alcoholics. Rather, what is indicated is once- or twice-weekly intensive, insight-oriented psychodynamic psychotherapy that is informed by Kohut's insights into the viscissitudes of narcissism. These patients have an intense need for mirroring, or approving confirmation, as well as a need to idealize the therapist. They are also particularly narcissistically vulnerable. The treatment should therefore focus on blows to the alcoholic's low self-esteem (alcoholism inflicts such terrible narcissistic wounds), failures of the childhood environment to supply sufficient phase-appropriate mirroring and opportunities for idealization, and the alcoholic's experience of much of the world as an extension of self. Anxiety is usually understood and interpreted as panic fear of psychic death, rather than as a manifestation of intrapsychic conflict, and rage is usually understood and interpreted as narcissistic rage, fury at the failure of the selfobject to perfectly mirror or protect, rather than as a manifestation of mature aggression.

Much seemingly irrational behavior can be understood in terms of both the alcoholic's need for omnipotent control and the rage that follows failure to so control. The grandiosity and primitive idealization of the archaic, nuclear self also explains the perfectionism of alcoholics and the unrealistic standards that they set for themselves. Most alcoholics have not developed realistic ambitions or livable ideals—these are characteristics of the mature self. The alcoholic's depression can be understood in terms of the paucity of psychic structure, which was never built up through the normal process of transmuting internalization. This empty depression also reflects the repression, rather than the integration, of the archaic, nuclear self and the failure to integrate the split-off grandiosity of the vertical split. The emptiness does not abate with sobriety. Further, the narcissistic rage to which the alcoholic is so prone can be turned against the self, resulting in intensely angry depression, sometimes of suicidal proportions. Failure to internalize the stimulus barrier and poor resources for self-soothing render the alcoholic especially vulnerable to psychic injury. Therefore, events in daily life threaten the alcoholic's already tenuous self-esteem.

The insights of self psychology into the dynamics of pathological narcissism are relevant and helpful in working with stably sober alcoholics. Further, Kohut's technique can be used in a modified form in which the narcissistic transferences (attenuated in psychotherapy) are allowed to unfold, the patient's need to control and to participate in greatness is accepted, and a slow working through is used to help integrate components of the archaic, nuclear self into the reality ego.

13

When the Patient Abuses Food

Diane Barth

With the prevalence of eating disorders in the female population today, it has become more important than ever to understand the dynamics of this syndrome and the types of interventions that are most useful in their treatment. Although much has been written about their etiology, there is no definitive answer to the question of why people develop this condition. Theorists have cited various possible causes, such as difficulty separating from mother (Chernin 1985) and other pathological family dynamics (Jones 1985, Minuchin et al. 1978, and Wilson 1983), sociocultural factors (Orbach 1978), and diverse intrapsychic issues (Wilson 1983).

Working with patients who have eating disorders, I have found that many of their experiences involve "self" issues, such as attempts to maintain self-esteem and self-cohesion.

In this chapter I utilize a broad definition of eating disorders to include the disorders of bulimia, anorexia nervosa, and compulsive overeating.

BULIMIA

Bulimia, or bulimia nervosa as it is called in the DSM-III-R, is defined as a disorder involving "recurrent episodes of binge eating (rapid consumption of a large amount of food in a discrete period of time); . . . a feeling of lack of control over eating behavior during the eating binges"; use of "either self-induced vomiting, . . laxatives or diuretics, strict dieting or fasting, or vigorous exercise in order to prevent weight gain." There is also "persistent concern with body shape and weight" (p. 64).

In my experience, individuals who have this disorder often have inaccurate perceptions of body shape and weight, accompanied by self-criticism and the fantasy that weight loss will alleviate all of the things they dislike about themselves. In the broad use of the term, I also include those individuals who do not binge on large amounts of food but who regularly purge after eating what feels to them an excessive amount, even if it is only a whole bran muffin instead of half a bran muffin.

ANOREXIA NERVOSA

The DSM-III-R defines anorexia nervosa as a disorder with a weight loss or maintenance of weight "15 percent below that expected" for the individual's height, bone structure, and age; "intense fear of gaining weight or becoming fat, even though underweight"; disturbance in body image, "e.g., the person claims to 'feel fat' even when emaciated"; and, in females, primary or secondary amenorrhea (absence of three consecutive menstrual cycles) (pp. 63–64). I would add that many people with anorexia and bulimia often become compulsively involved in excessive exercise regimes.

COMPULSIVE OVEREATING

The DSM-III-R does not have a diagnostic category for compulsive overeating, but this disorder is so widespread that it would be negligent to leave it out of this discussion. Compulsive overeating may include a history of dieting alternating with overeating. Often but not always it involves the kinds of binge eating described as a component of bulimia. Many individuals with this disorder experience uncontrolled patterns of significant, regular weight loss and gain (of at least ten pounds, and usually more than that). They often maintain wardrobes in different sizes (what several of my patients have called their "fat clothes" and their "thin clothes"). Along with the distorted body image that accompanies the other disorders, the compulsive overeater must cope with significant physical changes in appearance, often within very short periods of time, which have significant impact on self-image and self-esteem.

There are four major areas from self psychology that I believe can contribute significantly to a therapist's work with this population. These are (1) the focus on self-esteem and self-cohesion as basic needs of all human beings, (2) the view of symptoms as attempts to restore and/or maintain self-esteem and self-cohesion, (3) the use of empathy as a primary therapeutic tool, and (4) the concept of the selfobject.

1. Stolorow and Lachmann (1980) tell us that it is human nature to strive for self-esteem and for a cohesive, stable sense of self over time and across stressful situations. Many individuals with eating disorders have neither a stable sense of self nor a sense of self-esteem. The symptoms help to alleviate feelings of fragmentation, disorganization, confusion, and self-hatred, while at the same time confirming a stable, if negative, sense of self. As one woman poignantly put it, "It's better to hate yourself than not to have a self at all."

2. It is a logical next step to think of symptoms as part of an effort to organize the self and/or maintain self-esteem (Kohut 1971, Ornstein and Ornstein 1980, Tolpin 1983). The symptoms of an eating disorder, for example, may be a way of soothing painful and unacceptable feelings or of adapting to an environment in

which the self is constantly subjected to painful and/or damaging experiences. As Hartmann (1958) has described, symptoms are not simply evidence of psychopathology but are also often evidence of an adaptive response to a maladaptive environment. While eating disorders may seem maladaptive to an outside observer and may indeed cause the individual pain, they can also be highly successful methods for protecting a damaged self in a frightening world.

This approach is helpful with a form of behavior that is frequently encountered in the individual with an eating disorder and that has often been labeled as resistance to the therapeutic process. Many people with eating disorders have difficulty articulating their feelings, even though they may be intelligent and highly verbal in other areas. From a self psychological perspective, this difficulty can be viewed as both a developmental deficit that will be corrected as a natural response to the therapeutic process and also as an adaptation to some aspect of the individual's experience.

From this point of view, no matter how much an individual may hope that therapy will help her, she will also fear (either consciously or unconsciously) that it will disrupt the very sense of herself that her symptoms help her maintain. Furthermore, if earlier experiences have led to what Ornstein (1974) has called "the dread to repeat" painful disruptions in self-cohesion and self-esteem, it may be more adaptive to "resist" the therapy than not to do so.

3. Kohut and his followers did not invent the concept of empathy as a psychotherapeutic tool. They were preceded by Freud (1916–1917), Jacobson (1964), and Winnicott (1965), to name only a few. But they have emphasized the importance of the therapist's ability to understand the patient's experience from the patient's point of view. The therapist's empathy is often a novel experience for many individuals with eating disorders, who have never before felt that someone else was actively attempting to understand their perspective. They are often highly critical of their own feelings and thoughts and therefore unable to empathize with themselves. The capacity to empathize with themselves is also hindered by an inability to formulate their own thoughts and feelings. Thus an important part of the therapeutic work involves

an identification with the therapist's stance, and the subsequent development of empathy for their own feelings and needs. Such "self" empathy is necessary for the feelings to be articulated, recognized, and integrated into an individual's overall sense of self. Patients' abilities to utilize the therapist's attitude toward themselves is part of a selfobject transference. Kohut (1971) defines a selfobject as a person or an object that fulfills certain needs for an individual that the individual cannot provide for himself or herself. These needs may be in the realm of self-esteem regulation, that is, those actions or behaviors that increase or decrease a person's self-esteem, or they may be in the more general realm of self-regulation—for example, helping the person to place limits on his or her feelings and/or actions. For many people with eating disorders, unable to soothe themselves in other ways and unable to trust others to provide selfobject functions (Ornstein 1974), the symptoms, rather than another person, provide some of these functions.

Waelder (1936) pointed out that most symptoms have multiple meanings or functions. Following this idea, it is important for a therapist to try to understand the meanings a symptom has for a specific individual without imposing an "experience-distant" theoretical stance on the client's experience. Eating disorders are complex and require the therapist's patience and willingness to explore many possible dynamics before they even begin to respond to therapy. Understanding the importance of the symptoms in the maintenance of self-esteem and self-cohesion can help the therapist to have patience with stubborn, recalcitrant symptoms and to understand why simply making unconscious fears and fantasies conscious is not enough to lead to change.

I will discuss the implications of the concept for therapy with individuals with eating disorders in the context of three clinical vignettes. While I have chosen to present examples of each of the disorders discussed in this chapter, these illustrations are not intended to suggest general explanations for the specific syndromes. They are offered as examples of the way a self psychological perspective can help therapist and patient explore together what Palombo (1985) calls "the nature of the [individual's] experience" without making experience-distant "generalizations about the intrapsychic states" based on the symptoms (p. 33).

The following clinical examples will illustrate some ways this approach affects the therapeutic process.

Denise

One component of what appears to be resistance in some individuals with eating disorders is their difficulty paying attention to and describing their inner experiences. Thus, what may seem to be resistance to discussing certain feelings may actually be an inability to differentiate one feeling from another or to put feelings into words. In these cases, the therapist must be sensitive to the possibility that to ask for a deeper discussion of feelings will be experienced as a criticism and may cause someone already feeling inadequate to withdraw from the therapeutic relationship. A self psychological approach is helpful in these cases, as it focuses on an aspect of the patient's experience that she *can* talk about rather than one that theory indicates she *should* talk about.

> Denise was one of these people. Thirty years old when she began therapy, she had suffered from compulsive overeating for as long as she could remember. A chubby child, she had been put on a diet by the time she was 4 years old, and she could remember sneaking candy and cookies from that time on. Her weight, which was at a high of nearly 200 pounds when she began therapy, had fluctuated between 140 and 180 pounds since high school. She had been "on every diet in the book" and had been in a variety of forms of therapy, always with an initial success (loss of weight) and subsequent failure (regain of the weight).
>
> She began therapy by telling me of all her disappointments with previous therapies and diets. Then she told me that she had been binging for the past six weeks and could not stop herself. "If there's food within half a mile of me, I *have* to eat it." She had been considering having her jaw wired, but had decided to try therapy once more before resorting to such a drastic measure. In response to my question, she could not tell me of any incidents or experiences that might have triggered the compulsive eating six weeks earlier. As far as she could tell, "It just happened. Like it always does."

Although Denise was an intelligent, articulate young woman, she had little awareness of or capacity to describe her inner experience. She could not tell me what she was thinking or feeling before she began to eat, nor could she tell what she *wanted* to eat most of the time. "I just shove anything into my mouth." She could tell me what she *had* eaten—often taking up a significant part of the session with this information, then demanding to know what she could do about "the way I eat."

I felt that Denise was talking about what was most important to her and what she *could* talk about. I told her that I needed to hear more about her eating and asked her to tell me as much about it as she could. Not just what she ate, but when, where, and how. How did it feel in her mouth? in her stomach? in between?

Initially Denise had difficulty talking about anything other than quantity, which she wanted me to help her control, but when I gently but firmly insisted that she could not control the amount until she knew much more about her eating, she became interested in talking about other elements of her eating—not the feelings or events which triggered a binge, but the eating itself—when she ate, what she ate, what she was doing, and what she was thinking about when she started to eat, even what show she was watching on television or what commercial had just played. Gradually, so gradually that neither of us actually noticed when it first occurred, she began paying attention to other inner experiences. For example, she noticed one day that she was thinking about dinner on her way home from work. "And then I thought, 'I don't want to eat all by myself.'" So she stuffed some bread and butter into her mouth—"it was all I had in the house"—and went out and bought a gallon of ice cream, which she ate in front of the television. "I guess ice cream doesn't feel like dinner. It's okay to eat ice cream alone."

We also learned that she often binged after a difficult day at work. "I've just realized that I can go for a whole day at work eating 'normally,' and then I get on the bus to go home and start thinking about what I'm going to eat. And nothing seems right. So I go to a deli and just get something easy—usually ice cream." As we talked more about what she might *want* to eat, we learned that Denise seemed to eat ice cream more on the days when she felt criticized or potentially criticized. "I can't stand to make a mistake. No, that's not right, I can't stand for anyone to *catch* me making a mistake." Her self-esteem was badly damaged when someone caught her

making a mistake, and she utilized food to fill herself back up—
unfortunately, also simultaneously reinforcing negative feelings
about herself.

Other information about Denise's inner experience gradually
became available. We learned, for example, that she often felt
emotionally empty. "I don't feel like I have anything inside. Nothing interests me. I don't read, I don't think. All I do is go to work,
eat, watch TV, and go to sleep. And not necessarily in that order."

She was ashamed that she had no interests. "I do things that
other people want to do, because I want to be with those people."
Much later in our work together, she came to the conclusion that
what interested her most was people, and she changed careers,
moving into a field in which she could put her interest in people to
work. But at this point, she had just begun to recognize that her
self-esteem was very much tied to what she believed people thought
about her.

This was most obvious in her feelings about her weight. "People look at me and see a fat woman with no willpower. It's humiliating. I wish I could wear a sign that said, 'This is a psychological
problem and I'm working on it.'" By this time, Denise was taking it
for granted that her eating was a psychological problem, and she
had almost stopped looking for a "magical answer" to her weight
problem. She was working hard to know her own inner experience
for the first time in her life.

Jenny

The dynamics I described in the previous case, and which I will
describe in the two following cases, can apply to individuals with
any of the three types of eating disorders discussed in this chapter.
Many people with both anorexia and bulimia come into therapy
with the same focus on their eating and the same difficulty talking
about their inner experience that Denise displayed. Jenny was
another of those people. Jenny, however, had much more difficulty
forming a therapeutic alliance than did either Denise or Patricia,
who will be described next. Since one often learns a great deal more
from one's failures than from one's successes, I am going to present
an empathic failure that unfortunately disrupted Jenny's therapy
and which graphically illustrates the difference between an em-

pathic stance and a therapist's sympathy (which in this case was not empathic).

Jenny was 20 years old and anorexic when she began therapy. Excruciatingly thin, she did not think that she had a problem but came to see me because her boyfriend insisted that she get help. "It bothers him that I don't eat more," was her response when I asked why he was so insistent. She did not know why it bothered him.

Did she think it was a problem?

No.

I worked with Jenny to some extent in the same way I worked with Denise, looking for a topic that might interest her, but her overt resistance was far greater than was Denise's. However, she continued to come to her sessions, always arriving on time, so I assumed she was getting something from it and did not press her to work "my way."

A little bit at a time, I learned about Jenny. Since Jenny was most interested in her eating and her concern about gaining weight, I learned first about the very restricted diet she allowed herself and the rituals that accompanied each bite she took—for example, two spoonfuls of cottage cheese and half an apple for breakfast, eaten in alternating bites, starting and ending with cottage cheese. I learned that one of the reasons her boyfriend had pushed her to seek help was that her eating interfered with their social life, since she ate such a limited variety of foods and did not enjoy being in social situations where food was a central part of the activity. I also learned that she hated to go out to dinner with friends, because she "had" to split the bill with them even though she had eaten far less and therefore should have spent far less than the others. "I don't like to make a big deal about it," was her answer when I asked if it would be possible to suggest she only pay for what she ate.

I also learned about Jenny's lifelong dream of being a ballet dancer. She had been dancing since she was 7, and although she had professional training, she had never danced professionally. She felt inadequate and humiliated, and she hated her body. She could tell me everything that was wrong with her body. She was too broad here, too narrow there, not turned out enough, not flexible enough, and so on. She spent hours in dance classes examining herself in minute detail in the mirrored walls of the dance studio.

While we were working together, Jenny began performing with a small dance troupe. Although she was ashamed of the fact that the group danced only in tiny performance spaces, and to recorded music rather than to a live orchestra, she allowed herself a brief expression of pleasure over the fact that she was performing.

She had only participated in a few performances when she broke her foot. She came to her therapy session the day after that happened and proceeded to ignore the fact that her leg was in a cast and she was on crutches.

I waited for about ten minutes before I brought it up by gesturing to her leg and asking what had happened.

"I stepped off a curb and broke my leg. I can't believe it. How stupid could anyone be?"

I expressed my sympathy, commenting that it was bad luck, but that I did not understand why she was blaming herself for it. Angrily, she told me that she did not want to talk about it.

I nodded. There was a long silence—not unusual with Jenny, but harder than usual for me to tolerate because of my concern about what this physical injury must mean to her and my belief that if she could talk about it, it might ease some of her painful feelings about it.

When she did speak, it was to tell me about feeling victimized by her boyfriend, because he wanted to eat at an Italian restaurant even though he knew she "could not get anything" to eat there. This was another subject she had discussed repetitively in previous sessions, without any change in her capacity to deal with the situation.

I wondered aloud if she was focusing on this situation as a way of avoiding something that might have been more upsetting to her. She did not know what I meant. I said that she seemed pretty disturbed by what had happened to her ankle, but that she also seemed to want to avoid talking about it. I added that I imagined that it must be very upsetting coming at this time, when she had just begun dancing professionally.

She burst into tears and told me again that she did not want to talk about it. "You're pushing me and pushing me!" she shouted, "and it's not working for me at all!" She told me that this therapy was not for her and left my office, despite my suggestion that she remain and try to work this out with me.

Jenny did not return my phone calls and never returned to therapy with me. In retrospect I was aware that, although I was probably on target with my interpretation, I was not hearing her when she told me that she was not ready to explore the feelings that accompanied the narcissistic injury that the physical injury caused her. From a self psychological perspective, my need to "help" her to feel her repressed feelings was unempathic and unhelpful. If I had been comfortable exploring the topic she had introduced, I would have been technically empathic and perhaps might have helped her remain in therapy long enough eventually to feel safe experiencing some of those more painful, less available feelings. This is, in fact, one of the most difficult aspects of doing therapy with individuals with eating disorders—accepting that their defenses (symptoms) are also adaptive, and that when the therapist becomes a successful selfobject, they slowly become less necessary.

Kohut (1971) discussed this phenomeon in relation to people who have "hypochondriacal" concerns. Instead of regarding the somatic complaints as resistance, Kohut saw them as communications and listened to them with interest. His interest and his understanding of the messages communicated helped his patients develop a sense of safety in the therapeutic relationship, as well as a greater self-awareness. With this, they were able to achieve a greater sense of continuity and self-cohesion over time.

Patricia

Patricia entered therapy with me shortly after she graduated from college. She was living at home and working part-time at a job her father had helped her to find and that she wanted desperately to leave. She also wanted to move out of her parents' home, to find a career direction, and to improve her relationships with men.

She had never had a long-term relationship, but had always had a boyfriend when she wanted one. She had several women friends to whom she turned for "support and sustenance." As she described her women friends and her current and past boyfriends, it seemed to me that the men were interchangeable with one another, as were the women. Although she needed each sex for very specific functions, Patricia did not seem to differentiate between one woman and another, or one man and another.

What she required was women who "understood" her, by which she meant had the same feelings about things as she did, and men who found her attractive, liked her sexually, and enhanced her self-esteem in ways her women friends could not. It was also neces-

sary that she admire the men, something she did not need or expect
to feel for women friends.

In her descriptions of an almost compulsive need for sex that
paralleled her compulsive need for huge amounts of food, I heard a
panicky sense of not knowing who she was or where she began or
ended, either physically or psychologically. It would have been easy
to hear both behaviors as derivatives of unconscious and unacceptable drives, as some theorists do. I chose instead to follow a self
psychological approach in which I explored with Patricia the
meaning of the apparent drives. From this perspective, the symptoms appeared to be attempts to soothe hurt and angry feelings
resulting from damage to self-esteem. The compulsive binging,
purging, and sexual activity seemed to me to be an attempt on
Patricia's part to restore her self-esteem and sense of continuity
rather than a defense against instinctual drives. At any rate, looking
at the bulimia as a drive derivative would not have helped Patricia
to understand the purpose the behaviors served for her. And there
was no question in my mind that for Patricia, as for other women
with bulimia, they did serve a purpose.

Patricia did not know that I worked with people with eating
disorders when she began therapy with me. It was several weeks
before she shared the information that she had bulimia, although I
was not surprised when she did tell me. At that point I asked her, as
I do with most individuals with bulimia, to begin to pay attention to
what she was doing, where she was, and what she was thinking
about at the moment she began to plan her next binge.

We soon began to notice that her compulsive binges and
purges (Patricia was a vomiting bulimic) and her nearly overwhelming sexual desires were often triggered by a feeling that someone
upon whom she counted for understanding and support had let her
down, disappointed her somehow. This was true in her relationships with friends, co-workers, her parents, her boyfriends, and, we
soon found, with me. As individuals we all seemed interchangeable,
noticeable to Patricia only in terms of whether or not we met
certain needs that she could not meet for herself. The need for
understanding and support from others was central for Patricia.
The people to whom she turned for this understanding functioned
as selfobjects for her.

For Patricia, "understanding" her meant actually experiencing what she experienced, because, as she explained to me, unless
her selfobject felt what she felt, she could not feel it herself.

Kohut initially described two forms of selfobject transference—the idealizing transference and the grandiose or mirror transference. Later (1984) he described a third, the twinship or alter-ego transference. Stolorow (1986) and Basch (1986) have suggested that there are other forms of selfobject transferences. Patricia's selfobjects were in part mirroring selfobjects, in part twinship or alterego selfobjects, and in part something else, something perhaps a little more primitive, in that it was a little less separate from her sense of self than an idealized, mirroring, or twinship selfobject.

Stolorow (1986) points out that the selfobject experience is an intrapsychic rather than interpersonal one. The selfobject may be experienced as a separate object, but the function provided by the selfobject is experienced intrapsychically. This means that a selfobject failure may not necessarily be an objective failure. Yet the therapist who points out the "reality" of the experience will lose the opportunity to deepen the process of understanding that is a major component of psychotherapy.

It gradually became apparent that Patricia's craving for food and sex, her binging and vomiting cycles, and her almost delusional bodily sensations of growing and shrinking were often directly related to episodes of feeling misunderstood or not understood by her selfobjects. This became evident in the transference when we began to explore what she experienced as my empathic failure—that is, my failure to function as a validating and confirming selfobject.

As do many people with bulimia, Patricia had an almost physical response when she felt disappointed by me. Although she could not articulate her feelings at the moment, I had immediate cues that something had gone wrong. Her face, usually open in an almost childlike way, became closed and stony, and her speech, usually organized, although dramatic, became rambling and disorganized.

The first few times this occurred, I asked Patricia what had happened. She was unaware that anything had changed in either her manner or her feeling state. I pointed out the changes in her facial expression and her speech, but I did not press the matter, since she was clearly not ready to make such differentiations. I hypothesized that she was either afraid to do so, perhaps because to do so would threaten our relationship in some way, or else because she was actually unable to recognize such changes in her self-state—both of which are frequent dynamics in this population.

I watched for the next opportunity to observe the behavior with the hope of beginning to understand—at least for myself— what triggered it. It appeared to be the kind of loss of cohesion described by Kohut (1971, 1977, 1984) as a response to an empathic failure on the part of a selfobject. I was therefore on the lookout for this reaction in response to some of my interventions.

One day Patricia began to speak of feeling as though she lived in a glass house. She could see other people, and they could see her, but she could not touch them or be touched by them. I said that I understood (which I did, as it seemed to describe perfectly what occurred in the therapy). I asked her if she thought this ever happened in our sessions. She looked surprised and thoughtful, then nodded. "Is that what you meant when you said I seemed to pull away the other day?"

She now seemed ready to look at this subject. I thought I would risk adding to the experience with my own imagery, although I was aware that at times patients can experience such additional input from the therapist as an empathic failure (Kohut 1971). I told her that yes, it was what I had meant, but that my experience of it at those times was as though she was behind a mattress rather than a glass wall. I could hear her, but not clearly, and I could not see her, metaphorically speaking, at all.

She loved the metaphor, felt deeply understood by me, and actually began to have some awareness of the way she pulled away from me when she felt I did not understand her. This seemed to pave the way for us to look at moments when she did pull away, which in turn led to an exploration of what she felt when I failed her. There were many moments of failure, but now we had a metaphor with which to describe her reaction, and she began to recognize it herself when it happened. We now had the necessary base of noncritical self-awareness that allowed us to begin to explore what triggered her withdrawal from me.

Only if the therapist can accept that the patient *must* resist in order to protect the integrity of a fragile and vulnerable self can the patient eventually enter into the therapeutic alliance and make use of the therapist as a selfobject. This is a divergence from classical theory, in which resistance is seen as maladaptive, to be analyzed and overcome. From a self psychological point of view, the resistance, what A. Ornstein (1974) calls the dread to repeat, is perhaps the only method the individual has at his or her command to protect self-esteem and self-cohesion.

Patricia could not ally herself with me enough to explore her feelings with me until she repeatedly experienced my noncritical acceptance of her need to withdraw from me. I encouraged her to look for inner clues that would signal that she was withdrawing. She was very tuned into her own physical responses—feeling big, small, fat, growing, disappearing. I asked her to tell me as much as she could about her physical experiences at the moment that I sensed her withdrawal. As she did so, she began to realize that she felt criticized by me. We soon learned that each time my perspective was different from hers, she felt criticized, diminished, and lost a sense of who she was. Recognition of this chain of events and of her fear that I wanted her to be just like me, not a person in her own right, was generally enough to help her reorganize.

As Gedo (1979) suggests, it is sometimes important to help patients set limits on their feelings when they cannot do it themselves. For people with eating disorders, this may mean helping them to "close doors," to recognize when their anxiety is escalating to what may become intolerable dimensions, and to help them calm down and even temporarily suppress certain thoughts and feelings so that they do not need to binge and overeat, purge, or resort to starvation to soothe themselves.

Patricia was unable to utilize the explaining, or interpreting, component of therapy for some time. She was struggling simply to allow herself to know what she felt. It was confusing to her to try to understand it in the context of earlier experiences, which she remembered only as also muddled or confused.

Each time we explored something she experienced as an empathic failure on my part, Patricia became more comfortable recognizing her own needs and feelings and modulating them by talking about them and asking for what she needed from me rather than by bringing on food and/or sex and then feeling worse than before about herself. As she found herself able to discuss her needs with me, and to find ways of getting those needs met (sometimes simply *discussing* her needs met them), her self-esteem increased, her ability to tolerate not always getting her needs met increased, and her binging and purging decreased gradually.

After nine months in therapy, Patricia moved out of her parents' home and began a job she found herself. Although she hated it, it was the first full-time job she had ever held for longer than a month. She also began a relationship with a man who, for the first time in her experience, "actually meets my needs!"

Healing the Rupture

When things began to deteriorate between Patricia and this man, I made a comment in an attempt to help her maintain the relationship. I realized later that this was out of my countertransferential need, not out of a response to her needs.

I was concerned that she was about to sabotage the best relationship she had ever been in, and I was eager to make an interpretation that would keep her from repeating destructive patterns of relating to men. As a result of the work we did following the empathic rupture my remark caused, Patricia and I understood that my implicit expectations of changing her (not uncommon for therapists) paradoxically *interfered* with her ability to change. It was not my attempt to change her that would, in the end, help Patricia to grow, but instead my acceptance of who she was and my recognition of why she was that way, which would foster her development.

> In the session after my "interpretation," Patricia began a lengthy description of a binge-purge cycle, which, she said, was preceded by hysterical sobbing and a powerful need for sex. I asked what had occurred prior to the crying. She described an incident with her boyfriend in which she felt furious that he had not understood that she needed his attention and then immediately felt guilty and selfish for being so demanding. She then looked at me expectantly.
>
> My intervention in the prior session had been in the form of a suggestion that she might feel better if she could see things from her boyfriend's point of view. I now asked if she was afraid I was going to criticize her for not being more sympathetic to his needs. She began to cry. I asked her to try to tell me about her thoughts at the moment. Through her tears, she said that she was ashamed to be so selfish, that she was ashamed not to be able to see his side, but the problem was, she said, that she just couldn't see him as having needs at all—and not only that, she *needed* to see him as *not* having

needs. She needed him to be strong and invulnerable, she said, so that he could take care of her (one aspect of Kohut's idealized selfobject). "I know it's selfish," she sobbed. "I just can't help it." I nodded and said quietly, "I can understand that now. It's as though I was asking someone who was starving to share their small crust of bread with someone else. You can't give to someone else unless you feel you have something to give."

Patricia visibly pulled herself together. I could see that she now felt solid again, an impression she herself confirmed. Moreover, the next time she felt misunderstood or criticized by me, instead of binging and purging immediately, she was able to let me know that she was feeling inadequate and we quickly pinpointed the blow to her self-esteem caused by something I had said.

We came to understand her binging, purging, and promiscuous sexual activity as an attempt to soothe herself when she felt hurt, inadequate, and misunderstood, as well as when she felt ashamed of something she had revealed to me. She now had a new kind of knowledge about herself. One of her doors was open. This self-awareness did not, in and of itself, lead to change in her symptoms or personality. It was something that we reexperienced many times in the course of our work together, but each time it seemed easier to discover what had caused the dissolution of her sense of herself, or the damage to her self-esteem, and gradually she turned less and less to her bulimic symptoms as an automatic means of soothing herself.

Kohut believed that people never stop needing selfobjects. In his last book (1984), he suggests that analysis cures people by helping them to learn to find appropriate selfobjects and to use them appropriately.

The changes in Patricia's relationship with me gradually led to changes in her experience of herself, to the building of a stronger, more stable sense of herself, and to changes in her relationships with others. Only as a complex series of changes occurred in her self-perception and in her interactions with others was she able to stop utilizing binging and vomiting to maintain a sense of wholeness and autonomy.

Still, a large portion of her sense of self is dependent on others, and still, under crisis, she returns to the soothing mechanism of binging, vomiting, and sexual activity. Many therapists working with an eating-disordered individual become concerned over the linked issues of regression—in this case, return to symptoms—and resistance. From a self psychological perspective, many people with eating disorders have a fragile, vulnerable sense of self and need tools with which to pull themselves together after a narcissistic injury or other damage to self-esteem. Bulimia's symptomatic manifestations can be highly successful tools. Because they can only be abandoned when there are other, effective selfobjects available or when the individual has a strong enough sense of self to withstand blows to self-esteem without losing all good feelings about himself or herself, they are not easy to change. A self psychological perspective makes it easier for a therapist to handle some of the difficulties inherent in treating their patients (Jones 1985), including what at times may appear to be a resistance to the therapist or the therapy.

Patients let us know if our approach is working. In a recent session, Patricia began by saying that she did not know what to talk about, because everything was fine, and she felt that she should talk about problems in therapy. She went on to tell me several examples of feeling more "in herself" as she put it. She was reading a novel, something she could not remember doing before except when it was required in school, and she was enjoying it. She was writing a short story, something she had attempted many times before, but which she had never completed.

And she had recently had a fascinating conversation with the boyfriend of the empathic failure described above. He was no longer a lover, but simply a friend.

"He told me he wasn't crazy about his job," she told me with glee. I asked about the gleeful emotion.

"Well, I'm glad to know he has needs. It makes him more human. But at the same time, it frightens me."

"Why do you think it frightens you?" I wondered.

"Because I need him to be strong, stable. . . ."

"Do you know why that is?" I asked.

"Because I'm not."

I asked her to try to put into words why his being strong and stable was important—how it contrasted with her not being that way. It took the rest of the session, but she was able to articulate her belief that women are volatile, hysterical, and incompetent, and need men to be strong and hold them together. She was beginning to think that she could be competent and feel good about herself without a man's approval, and, to her surprise, she was feeling closer than ever before to some of the men in her life.

She told me, "I was always afraid that if I didn't need them, they wouldn't have any reason to connect with me, but I was always afraid that they wouldn't meet my needs, anyway. I think they like me more when I'm more competent and self-confident—but I still don't trust them to meet my needs."

Patricia, like many bulimics, continues to binge and purge at times of stress, but now she can often figure out why she does so. She no longer experiences the degree of self-hatred that used to increase the need to binge and purge, reinforcing a vicious cycle. Now, if she is unable to stop a binge-purge cycle, she is more accepting of herself, and does not further the punishment by continuing to binge and purge.

Patricia has developed some empathy for herself. She has begun to allow herself to feel what she feels, to think what she thinks, and to be who she is, without having to change herself in some way to make herself more "acceptable" or "likable." This is perhaps one of the most important contributions of self psychology to the therapeutic work with individuals with eating disorders. While different people who abuse food have different dynamics and different needs, the possibility for many of them is that, in some way, and to some extent, their symptoms are an attempt to repair damage to the sense of self. From this perspective, one goal of therapy may well be to help people to recognize who they are and to accept themselves fully, with all of their own characteristics—"good" and "bad."

CONCLUSION

Throughout his writings, Kohut maintains that it is the process of empathic rupture and healing that embodies the therapeutic work and leads to what he calls transmuting internalization and change. In his last book (1984), he divides the therapeutic work into two parts—understanding, and explaining or interpreting what one understands. Kohut suggests that with some patients, the entire work is done in the understanding phase. Although I think that the explaining phase can often go hand in glove with the understanding phase, understanding is an extremely important concept for the therapist working with eating-disordered patients, many of whom have never been understood or accepted for themselves and who do not understand or accept themselves as a result.

For many of these people, the therapist becomes an empathic selfobject who accepts unacceptable aspects of themselves (including the eating behavior), names unnameable feelings, and makes it safe to look at what G. Klein (1976) calls split-off self schema. As one bulimic woman said to me, "It's as if there were all these closed doors inside me. Doors that I was afraid to open, for fear of what might come out. With you, I've opened some of them. It's been okay, because I knew you'd let me close them if I needed to—even help me, if I couldn't do it myself—and that you'd help me sort through what I found in there, if I wanted to. Now I can open and close them myself. I feel more complete, more whole, more connected to myself." With such self acceptance, change is often spontaneous.

14

When a Parent
Is Abusive

Gail Wagner

The abuse and neglect of children are the cause of one of the most troublesome psychosocial problems of the 1980s, affecting over 1.3 percent of the underage population in the United States. In 1986, there were 2,086,000 documented reports of child abuse and neglect, 40 percent (834,400) of which were substantiated. This reflects an 8 percent increase over 1985 and a trend that has continued through 1987 and 1988 (American Humane Association 1988).

SEQUELAE TO CHILD ABUSE

Abuse and neglect of children represent a serious mental health problem, not only because the practice is so widespread and increasing, but because of its traumatic effects. There is increasing evidence that victims of childhood abuse and neglect will become psychiatric patients at some point in their lives. Clinical studies report a symptom picture of psychosomatic complaints, chronic low-grade depression, suicide, anger and aggression, shame and guilt, and self-hatred (Herman et al. 1986, Bryer et al. 1987). Several diagnostic categories have been identified in victims and abusers, including depression, borderline personality disorder, narcissistic personality disorder, post-traumatic stress disorder, and antisocial personality disorder.

TREATING PARENTS OF ABUSED
AND NEGLECTED CHILDREN

The problem of child abuse and neglect is present in all cultures and socioeconomic groups. There is, however, a pejorative attitude toward abusive parents that has interfered with the development of rational and effective treatment approaches. With such families much of the focus is on providing casework services to the child, such as day care, babysitting, homemakers, removal to foster homes, and/or adoption. Too often the developmental needs of the abusive parent(s) are ignored or neglected.

While traditionally parenting has been treated as a natural consequence of adulthood, self psychology emphasizes parenting as a function that has a relatively independent line of development. The roots of this development reach into the parents' own childhoods, which must be understood for their dysfunctions to be properly diagnosed and treated (Ornstein 1982).

Through the application of psychoanalytic principles and self psychology, child abuse and neglect can be seen as "a treatable syndrome resulting from a breakdown in the parent–child relationship" (Eldridge and Finnican 1985, p. 51).

PARENTING AS A DEVELOPMENTAL PHASE

Theresa Benedek (1959) viewed parenting as a developmental process that can bring about structural changes in both child and parent. The central aspect of this theory is "double identification," whereby the mother's identification with her own mother is reactivated when she becomes a mother herself. As the mother identifies with the baby's regressive needs she becomes both her own mother, who has cared for her, and her baby, who is the recipient of this care. "Since motherliness involves the repetition and working through of the primary, oral conflicts with the mother's own mother, the healthy, normal process of mothering allows for resolution of those conflicts, that is for intrapsychic 'reconciliation' with the mother" (p. 396). If the mother is overwhelmed with past conflicts, she will regress to a negative identification with her mother and child. She will become the "bad mother" of her child, and the "bad child" of her mother. Benedek suggested that the infant then becomes the "hated self" and also becomes, as her own mother once was, the needed and feared object. This concept of "double identification" helps us to understand how mothers who make a determined effort to care for their babies differently from the way they were cared for, often find that powerful unconscious identifications with their own mothers interfere with their intent. Steele (1970) noted that most abusive parents were brought up in the same fashion that they bring up their own children. In his work, he suggested that there is a pattern of child rearing that is characteristic of the abusive parent. "Basic in the abuser's attitude is the conviction, largely unconscious, that infants exist in order to satisfy parental needs" (p. 450). Children are expected to respond properly to parental needs and commands, with no regard for the child's own needs or whether the child is developmentally capable of responding properly. If the child meets the unrealistic expectations, the parent feels approval and love. If the child does not respond satisfactorily, the parent feels justified in physically or psychologically punishing the child to make him behave. When the child is uncooperative with the parental caretaking efforts, it confirms the parent's perception of being unloved and unworthy. Consequently, the child becomes a selfobject whose role is to fill the residual, unsatisfied, unresolved infantile needs of the parent that were unmet by their own parents (Kohut and Wolf 1978). Abusive parents use their children not only for the enhancement of their self-esteem but also for the establishment and/or maintainence of their self-cohesion. A role reversal is created in which children perform developmentally vital selfobject functions for their parents, rather than parents providing such functions for their children (Miller 1981). As children, abusive parents were expected to meet the needs of their own parents, often sacrificing their own needs and desires. Consequently, they were left with a sense of unworthiness and unimportance, which led to lowered self-esteem, anger, and a tendency toward self-fragmentation.

The defense, "identification with the aggressor" (Fraiberg 1975), is a central mechanism in parental dysfunctions. According to Fraiberg, abusive parents form an "identification with the aggressor" during their own traumatic childhoods. This adaptive defense protects them from overwhelming affects brought about by the abusive treatment of their (selfobject) parent. "The parent who does not remember his or her childhood pain and suffering (the affect) may find himself or herself in an unconscious alliance and identification with the fearsome figures from the past. In this way, the parental past is inflicted upon the child" (p. 419). This inability to be affectively connected with the early trauma of abuse and neglect, severely limits the parent's ability to be empathically responsive to childhood needs. Consequently, the development of healthy narcissism is thwarted.

NARCISSISTIC ISSUES OF THE ABUSIVE PARENT

The clinical picture of the abusive parent is characterized by deficits in self-esteem and failures in parental empathy. Kohut's contributions of self psychology to the understanding of narcissism clarifies the relationship between self-esteem issues and child abuse. "In . . . abusive parents we see relics of primitive narcissism and omnipotence, indicating a developmental fixation on . . . archaic selfobject configurations. The resulting adult personality is impoverished and threatened by the potential intrusions of archaic longings for the functions these selfobjects never provided" (Eldridge and Finnican 1985, p. 53). Anna Ornstein (1982) suggested that "development and personality organization [are] determined by the unique fit that [is] established between the infant's temperament and constitution on the one hand and his or her unique environment on the other" (p. 10). This "fit" between the child and environment is subject to modification throughout the child's life. Recent studies of infants have demonstrated that the infant is capable of drawing from the environment those social responses that are essential for its psychological survival and progressive development. Born with a "predictable genetic ground plan," the infant must be "assured of specific phase-appropriate environmental responses . . . to develop into a viable, vigorous, and hopefully creative human psyche" (p. 11). These phase-appropriate environmental responses are what self psychology refers to as "selfobject functions" (also "selfobject transferences") of mirroring, idealizing, and twinship.

The self evolves and becomes consolidated through the empathically responsive selfobjects. Developmentally, the concept of the selfobject corresponds to Winnicott's (1986) description of the infant experiencing the mother as a "subjective object." However, the similarity of the two concepts ends here, as both are from two different theoretical frames of reference. Winnicott's theory on development is based on the theories of object relations and drive, while Kohut's theory is based on deficits of the self. Kohut and Wolf (1978) defined selfobjects as "objects which we experience as part of our self . . ." (p. 414). The consolidation of the self occurs through the transmuting internalization of the selfobject functions that are provided by parents and others in the child's environment. These selfobject functions, when withdrawn gradually (optimal frustration), are transmuted into self functions whereby the self no longer has to rely on the selfobject for such functions.

The mirroring selfobject function involves affirmation and validation provided by selfobjects. Mirroring culminates in the acquisition of a reasonably stable self-esteem, a capacity for joy in the body and mind, and the ability to pursue one's goals and ambitions. Inappropriate responses "to the child's grandiosity and exhibitionism [may] lead to developmental arrests with fixations on archaic ambitions and archaic modes of exhibitionism" (A. Ornstein 1982, p. 13).

Idealizing refers to the function of calming, soothing, and protecting. The consolidation of this function leads to the capacity of the self to regulate tension and affects, provide self-soothing and self-calming, and to hold high goals and values. Failure to merge with the calmness and strength of the parent may lead to deficits in the capacity to calm and soothe the self.

The third selfobject function, twinship, is related to the unresolved need to experience the self as someone or something—"to be human among humans." Twinship needs, when gratified, facilitate the use of one's innate skills and potentials. Unmet twinship needs may lead to feelings of alienation, emptiness, and being different from others.

Self psychology informs us how empathic selfobjects perform caretaking functions that are then transmuted into self functions, the psychic structure of a cohesive self (Kohut 1971). "Parental response will determine whether the child will become driven or will form a cohesive nuclear self able to experience pleasure in his physical and mental attributes, capable of balancing this with his ideals in a manner which allows him to achieve goals he can define for himself" (Elson 1986, p. 8). Failure of the earlier selfobjects to perform caretaking functions often leads to deficits that give rise to driven behavior. The desperate need to engage selfobjects to perform certain functions (mirroring, idealizing, twinship) is indicative of where the structural deficit is, what kinds of needs exist, and where they emanated from in the past. It is a failure in empathy that leads to these deficits. In the therapeutic relationship, empathic responsiveness allows the gradual unfolding and working through of the selfobject transference.

SELF PSYCHOLOGICAL UNDERSTANDING
OF ABUSIVE PARENTS

Self psychology offers an explanation of the abusive parent's personality, focusing on the early development of the self. Pathogenic features of the parent and the atmosphere in which the child grows up explain the "maldevelopment" characterizing the adult personality. This "maldevelopment" (or psychopathology) is seen in the personality of child abusers who enlist an unsuspecting child unwittingly to participate in their (the abusing parents') struggle to maintain a sense of self. Often as children these parents were abused. Bereft of empathic selfobjects, they did not experience the optimal frustration and gratification necessary for the building of stable psychic structure. Subject to multiple traumatic empathic failures, they were unable to develop a cohesive sense of self.

The inability to respond to the mirroring, idealizing, and twinship needs of the developing self leaves the child with a painful sense of depletion, depression, and isolation. Unable to share in the soothing, calming, and strengthening qualities of the parent, the child will usually develop alternate means of soothing himself/herself to relieve the painful feelings of helplessness and isolation, such as rocking or head banging. To feel a sense of connectedness with the parent, these children often sacrifice their own needs.

These adaptive attempts at self-regulation without empathic support keep infantile needs and longings split off from the personality. The environment is experienced as hostile and ungratifying. As adults these children are prone to fragmentation and rage-filled outbreaks. They are unable to identify their affective needs, cue others to those needs, or tolerate any delay in response to those needs.

These adults, then, become parents who are unprepared for the tasks of parenthood. Their own unmet needs come forth in the process of trying to meet their child's needs. Parents who never experienced the empathic support of the environment as children are themselves narcissistically deprived. "Throughout their lives they are looking for what their own parents could not give them at the correct time—the presence of a person who is completely aware of them and takes them seriously, who admires and follows them" (Miller 1981, p. 7). They attempt to gratify these needs through substitute means (selfobjects), the most available of which are the parents' own children. The child, more likely than not, proves to be inadequate, unable to gratify the parent's needs. Perceiving the child as unresponsive, the parent feels injured and may respond with infantile rage.

Gunther (1980) noted that there are four qualities that accompany narcissistic rage: "(1) an expectation of absolute control over the object's behavior; (2) an expectation of perfection of response from the object; (3) an utter incapacity for empathy with the object, the object's behavior, or the object's motives; (4) an incapacity to distinguish the issue or problem from the object as a separate entity" (p. 178). This is the pattern described in the literature on child abuse, in which the parents who are struggling with infantile experiences of self deficits (rage reaction, rejection, feelings of worthlessness) erupt in violence toward their children.

Allyson

Allyson is a 25-year-old, single white woman, mother of two children, 3-year-old Jenni and 7-year-old Bobby. For the last four years her son has been in the permanent custody of one of Allyson's sisters due to excessive physical abuse. Allyson is involved with protective services, who initiated referral to the clinic after Allyson was hospitalized for depression and suicidal gestures. This was Allyson's fifth hospitalization for depression in four years. She is an alcoholic, in remission for four years, although she usually has a set-back just prior to each hospitalization.

Allyson was an abused child. She was physically and emotionally abused by her father, who was an alcoholic, while her mother, who suffered from depression, was unable to protect her. When her mother was hospitalized Allyson would stay with her maternal grandmother for a few weeks at a time. Beginning at age 1, Allyson spent six years with her grandmother. Then her grandmother died suddenly, and Allyson had to be returned to her parents.

When she was 13, Allyson was sexually abused by her father's best friend, but told no one for fear she would be blamed. Allyson describes her mother as passive and loving, because she would take beatings from her father that Allyson believes were meant for her. Allyson describes her father as a mean, cold-hearted man who told her she was no good. Up to the day he died, Allyson tried desperately to please him, but felt she was never good enough.

Allyson has primary child care and financial responsibility for herself and Jenni, with little or no support from family, friends, or community. Her father died two years ago, at which point her mother moved to another state. Allyson reports that she does not get along with her six siblings. Since she does not trust them she makes it a point to stay away from them. She also describes poor peer relationships, again because she has difficulty trusting. Allyson feels she needs to protect herself.

Dysfunctional relationships with her own parents led to an extremely fragile sense of self. Allyson seems resigned to her fate, convinced that "you get what you deserve in life." Her difficulty in acknowledging any feelings of anger stem from a pervasive guilt and self-loathing that render her own needs as unreasonable or illegitimate.

Allyson's current depressed state may be traced back to her inadequate, rejecting, chaotic childhood when she felt empty and alone. Unable to calm or soothe herself, under the stress of her multiple losses and medical problems, she needs external supports (alcohol, the hospital) to function.

Consistently deprived of the mirroring and confirming experiences that would allow for an internalized cohesive sense of self, Allyson faces mothering with a split-off and painfully needy self. She looks to her daughter Jenni, to gratify her needs. When Jenni is unable to gratify those needs, Allyson regresses to narcissistic rage, and physically attacks her. Allyson is unable to be empathically connected to either of her children. Out of her own inability to find inner soothing and self-love, Allyson is unable to provide these to her children. In an unconscious attempt to replicate unresolved aspects of her own selfobject relationships, Allyson recreates, through Jenni, her own selfobject failures.

Jenni was 2 years old when Allyson sent her to live with her grandmother. Allyson's own childhood traumas make it all but impossible for her to empathize with or to differentiate her own needs from those of her child.

While abusive parents yearn for understanding and acceptance, they are "plagued by a sense of inferiority and an inability to have any confidence in being loveable or in finding real understanding and help" (Steele 1970, p. 454). This slows the establishment of a therapeutic alliance and makes it more difficult.

Therapists must deal with their own feelings about the child-abusing parent. The self psychological position facilitates being value-neutral, because it puts in bold relief the parent's own treatment as a child. ". . . [A]n immersion into the child's inner world does not exclude the therapist from empathically encompassing

the psychic reality of the parents as well. We as therapists are not asked to take sides, we are asked to understand and explain" (A. Ornstein 1982, p. 19).
When working with abusive parents the emergence of the transference is of primary importance. From a self psychological perspective the narcissistically disturbed parent–patient looks to the therapist to meet those needs that were unfulfilled by earlier selfobjects. These are mirroring, idealizing, and twinship. In therapy, as those needs are met, parents become capable of soothing their children's distress, rather than turning to them for narcissistic gratification.

THERAPIST'S INTERVENTION

The therapist's noncritical acceptance and understanding of Allyson allowed idealizing and mirroring transferences to emerge.

> **Allyson** (with hostility): It was my DSS worker that sent me here. She thinks I'm not a good parent and that I can't take care of Jenni.
> **Therapist:** It must be difficult trying to manage a 2-year-old on your own, especially when you yourself are not feeling well.
> **Allyson:** The DSS doesn't think that way. No matter how bad I'm feeling, if I so much as raise a hand to my own daughter, they are right there. (Sullenly) Where were they when I was a kid?
> **Therapist:** You're wishing someone had been there to protect you and keep you safe when you were a child.

The therapist's responses to these previously unmet needs provide the soothing, strengthening, affirming, and validating selfobject functions necessary for Allyson to move beyond her rage to become an empathic parent.

> **Therapist:** I'm wondering why you said it might be wishful thinking about how you remember your grandmother.
> **Allyson:** I guess because I only remember good things.
> **Therapist:** What was it like at your parents'?

Allyson: At my grandmother's I was an only child and got lots of attention. I was good then. At my parents' I was bad and got punished a lot. I didn't get the attention I needed, or I should say *wanted.*

Therapist: You don't think you needed it?

Allyson: (Wrinkles her nose and looks down at her hands.)

Therapist: You had just lost someone very important to you, and moved back to a family you hadn't been with for six years and didn't really know, but you don't think you needed a little extra attention?

Allyson: (Shrugs sadly.)

Therapist: I think that was an understandable need, Allyson.

"Structure building, the establishment or restoration of a cohesive nuclear self, [takes] place by reason of myriad selfobject functions performed by [the] therapist" (Elson 1986, p. 136).

Fraiberg (1975) and A. Ornstein (1982) emphasized the importance of helping abusive parents to return psychologically to their own past to rework and refeel the lack of empathy with their own parents in order to help them become more empathically attuned to their own children. As Allyson was able to use the therapist as a selfobject to relive affectively the painful empathic failures in her own childhood, she was better able to respond empathically to Jenni.

Allyson: When I was at my grandmother's, I would dream of what it would be like to live with my mother. I never understood why she sent me away.

Therapist: What are your thoughts about that now?

Allyson: My mind tells me that my mother wasn't in a position to take care of me, but that doesn't make me feel any better.

Therapist: Can you tell me how it makes you feel?

Allyson: (Thinks, looking down at her hands, which she is wringing in her lap.) I guess I've always felt that I was bad, that I'd done something wrong so I was sent to my grandmother's. And when I came home I was always getting whacked by my father and punished.

Therapist: You felt that meant you were bad.

Allyson: (Gets teary-eyed.) I know in my heart that I wasn't bad, but my father told me I was so many times and beat me for it, that I really believed it. And my mom let him do it. (Asks angrily) Why did my mom let him do it?

(Later in the session)

Therapist: I wonder what it is like for you to see your mother take such good care of Jenni when she wasn't able to take care of you.

Allyson: At first it hurt a lot, but I know Jenni's getting the attention she needs. (Laughs nervously.) I'm just worried now that she won't want to come home.

Therapist: I'm wondering if part of your worries might be because in your own experience grandmothers have been better mothers.

Allyson: (Nods her head and begins to cry.) I want to be a good mother to Jenni, I miss her so much. You know, I realize now that she's probably feeling the same way I did, that she is bad. How can I let her know that she is not bad?

In the process of reliving her painful childhood the therapist helped Allyson recognize her affective needs, before she could even begin to express them. Earlier in treatment Allyson was unable to recognize or modulate these needs.

Allyson: I'm sorry I missed last week, I totally forgot—I've been really spacey lately.

Therapist: I understand that you forgot, but I'm wondering if there may have been something about our last session that was difficult for you.

Allyson: No. No there wasn't.

Therapist: I'm wondering if I may have pushed you to talk about some painful things that you weren't ready to talk about. Sometimes that is very frightening and makes you angry?

Allyson: I don't want to talk about it.

Later in treatment Allyson was better able to modulate her affective needs and endure delay in their gratification.

Therapist: So you picked up Jenni and brought her home last weekend. How are things going?

Allyson: They are going pretty well. Jenni is readjusting—a little slowly. You were right when we talked about how she might react after being away from me for so long. She wouldn't come near me for about four hours, and even now she hesitates before coming to me.

Therapist: How is that for you?

Allyson: It's pretty painful. I want her to trust me, and run to hug me like she used to. But I know that it may take her a while. I can wait though, I know why she is angry with me, and it's okay. I just keep telling her how much I love her.

Therapist: You are doing a great job recognizing Jenni's needs as well as your own, and knowing that they are not always the same needs.

Through focused empathic responsiveness Allyson began to feel understood, accepted, and legitimized. This then allowed her to merge with the therapist to express her needs more realistically, with less shame, and with a more tolerant understanding of her feelings.

Allyson: I have a difficult time making friends, and then once I do I can't seem to keep them. I could talk to anybody I just meet, you know the "Hi, how are you?" but I can't seem to get beyond that.

Therapist: What happens when a relationship moves beyond that superficial phase?

Allyson: I put up a wall.

Therapist: How do you understand that?

Allyson: If I don't open myself up to anyone, I won't get hurt.

Therapist: If you open yourself up you expose your vulnerabilities and pain . . .

Allyson: And then people know how they can hurt me.

Therapist: What are you afraid of?

Allyson: (Sadly, thoughtfully) I'm afraid of being abandoned.

Therapist: You have had a lot of losses.

Allyson: When I was 6 years old my best friend died, leaving me. Then my first boyfriend died—he was the first person I ever loved. My mother left me, and my grandmother left me. When my grandmother died I wanted to be buried with her.

Therapist: It feels like everyone you have gotten close to has left you in some way.

Allyson: (Nods her head sadly.) I'm also afraid of rejection.

Therapist: What is that like?

Allyson: I'm afraid that people will get to know me, and then not like me.

Therapist: So you don't let people know the real you, for fear they won't like you. I'm wondering, Allyson, if you like yourself?

Allyson: (Shakes her head, indicating a no.) I think I'm disgusting. I'm always trying to be like somebody else. I wish I would stop wanting to change and just try and improve on who I am.

Therapist: I wonder if your feeling badly about yourself is related to people deserting you. That you must be pretty bad if those you care about leave you.

Allyson: (Nods her head sadly.)

Therapist: You have talked a lot about fearing rejection and abandonment if you open yourself up to someone. How do you feel about my going on vacation at a time when you have been able to open yourself up with me?

Allyson: It's okay, because I know you are coming back.

As Allyson came to understand how her present feelings and situation relate to her past experiences, she enjoyed an increase in self-esteem. The increasing restoration of Allyson's parent-self went hand in hand with the increasing consolidation of Jenni's growing self. Allyson no longer needed to use Jenni as a selfobject but could mirror, confirm, and guide Jenni in response to the child's own needs.

Allyson: It is ironic that of all the girls in my family, I'm the only one who didn't want kids, and I'm the only one who has them.

Therapist: Children are a big responsibility; a lot of work.

Allyson: I didn't know the first thing about being a parent. I didn't think I had what it takes to be a parent, and there were so many things I didn't want to give up. I remember sobbing when Bobby was first placed in my arms.

Therapist: Tears for the lost childhood you never had.

Allyson: (Nods.) I thought I would feel differently when Jenni was born, but I was just as angry. I feel so bad when I think of how I felt about Jenni, even two years ago.

Therapist: What was that like?

Allyson: I didn't like her. I resented her for needing me so much. All my time was spent on Jenni.

Therapist: It is hard to take care of someone else's needs, when your own aren't being met.

Allyson: Now it is so different. I really like spending time with her. It is hard to send her to day-care in the mornings. But I know she loves it, and it is important for her to be with other kids, so I keep sending her.

Therapist: Good parents often put aside their own needs for their children. You certainly are aware of how important it is for Jenni to be in day-care, though I know you must miss her. You talked about how you felt about Jenni, even two years ago. What is different now?

Allyson: (Thinks for a few minutes.) I think it is because I feel more comfortable and confident in myself. I hardly ever get angry with Jenni the way I used to, and I haven't hit her in a long time. (Pauses, and chuckles.) You'll appreciate this one—the other day Jenni was hitting the other kids at the day-care, so I slapped her hand and told her, "Don't hit." I realized what I was saying and doing and thought Jenni must really be confused. (Therapist and Allyson laugh together.)

Therapist: Good for you, Allyson.

As Allyson began to feel more whole and integrated, her abusive attacks on Jenni decreased. She was better able to use other selfobjects appropriately, become much less distrusting of family and friends, and begin to build a support network for herself.

Allyson: I think that one of the things that is different is that I have a lot more supports.

Therapist: Yes, you do. Your family, and Jenni's father's family have been very supportive.

Allyson: You know, they probably have been all along and I just couldn't see it, or accept it.

Therapist: What's changed?

Allyson: I think that I'm a lot more receptive.

Therapist: You've let down your wall a bit.

Allyson: (Ponders this a minute.) Yeah, I have. You are right.

Therapist: What is it like to realize you have let down your wall a bit?

Allyson: (Smiles.) It feels okay. I'm feeling more comfortable with my family and with Jenni's father's family. We spend a lot of time with them on weekends. Jenni really loves it.

Therapist: From your expression, I'd say that you really enjoy that time as well.

Allyson: (Smiles and nods her head.)

The changes that Allyson was able to make throughout the therapeutic process have been in relation to the therapist as a selfobject. The defenses and resistance that she initially presented, in an attempt to preserve a vulnerable self, "dissipate through the therapeutic process of appropriate functions and responses performed by the new selfobject therapist" (Elson 1986, p. 142). As the therapist provides mirroring and soothing functions, and helps the abusive parent–patient anticipate and regulate her needs, she is able to internalize, or transmute, the therapist's selfobject functions into self-functions.

CONCLUSION

Using self psychology is effective with abusive parents. It does not place blame. The focus of treatment is on the developmental needs of these parents, and in understanding the gross empathic failures in these parents' own childhoods. What is basic to self psychology is the understanding that every individual, no matter the extent of deprivation, has a need to be confirmed, validated, and mirrored as worthwhile. The therapist as a new selfobject is in tune with such needs and wishes, and provides the emotional sustenance through which the individual can realize her potential for individuality and significance.

Self psychology involves "experience-near" phenomena, not asking anything more than what the patient is able to bring to the therapeutic relationship. The therapist does not attempt to undo the past empathic failures of these abusive parent–patients' earlier selfobjects. Rather, through the therapist's focused empathic attention, the abusive parent–patient has an opportunity to understand how the earlier failures and thwarted wishes give rise to the driven behavior that has led to the current impasse; and then to move beyond it.

Most important, in dealing with the population of abusive parents, self psychology provides a means of intervening in the destructive cycle of child abuse.

Contributors

Diane Barth, M.S.W., C.S.W.

Teaches and supervises at the Psychoanalytic Institute of the Post-graduate Center, the National Institute for the Psychotherapies, Inc., and the Institute for Contemporary Health in New York City. She is also affiliated with the Center for the Study of Anorexia and Bulimia, and is in private practice, with individuals and groups, in New York City.

Jeffrey Dietz, M.D.

Clinical instructor of psychiatry, Albert Einstein College of Medicine/Montefiore Medical Center in New York City. He is also in the private practice of psychiatry and psychoanalysis.

Susan Donner, Ph.D.

Field director and associate dean of the Smith College School for Social Work. She has an interest in and teaches graduate courses in self psychology, and is in private practice in Northampton, Massachusetts.

Miriam Elson, M.A., A.C.S.W.

Lecturer in the School of Social Service Administration, University of Chicago, and consultant at Children's Memorial Hospital in Chicago.

Lawrence Josephs, Ph.D.

Assistant professor of psychology at the Derner Institute of Advanced Psychological Studies of Adelphi University, and a supervisor and faculty member of the Psychoanalytic Institute of the Postgraduate Center for Mental Health in Garden City, New York. He is in private practice in New York City and Garden City.

Lawrence W. Lazarus, M.D.

Assistant professor of psychiatry, Rush Medical College, and director, Geriatric Psychiatry Fellowship Program, in Chicago.

Jerome Levin, Ph.D.

Director and on the faculty of the Alcohol and Substance Abuse Counselor Training Programs, New School for Social Research, New York City; on the faculty of the humanities department, the New School; and supervisor and on the faculty of the Post-Graduate Center for Mental Health and of the American Institute for Psychotherapy and Psychoanalysis in New York City. He has a private practice of counseling and psychotherapy, specializing in the treatment of alcoholism, in New York City and Riverhead, Long Island, New York.

Vincent J. Lynch, M.D.

Faculty member and director of continuing education at Boston College Graduate School of Social Work, Chestnut Hill, Massachusetts. He does extensive consultation and supervision to individual therapists and to clinics, hospitals, and agencies. He is in private psychotherapy practice in Newton and Littleton, Massachusetts.

Barbara L. Nicholson, Ph.D.

Assistant professor at Boston College School of Social Work, Chestnut Hill, Massachusetts. She is currently serving as National Institutes of Mental Health faculty scholar.

Anna Ornstein, M.D.

Professor of child psychiatry and attendant child psychiatrist, University of Cincinnati College of Medicine; Clinic of Child Psychiatry staff psychiatrist, outpatient department, University Hospital; staff child psychiatrist at the Child Psychiatry Center; co-director of the International Study Center; and psychoanalytic self psychologist at the University of Cincinnati Medical Center. She is also in private practice in Cincinnati, Ohio.

Jayne Patrick, Ph.D.

Associate professor, Department of Psychiatry, McMaster University, Hamilton, Ontario, Canada.

Marion F. Solomon, Ph.D.

Director of clinical training, Continuing Education Seminars in Los Angeles, California; program consultant, health sciences, humanities sciences, and social sciences at the UCLA Extension; and senior extension teacher, bio-behavioral sciences, at the UCLA Extension. She is also in private practice in Los Angeles.

Gail Wagner, LICSW

Currently supervising a joint investigation and treatment unit in the Eastern Middlesex Area office of the Department of Social Services in Malden, Massachusetts. She is also a member of the Tri-City Task Force for the Prevention of Child Abuse and Neglect.

Thomas M. Young, Ph.D.

Assistant professor at Portland State University in Portland, Oregon. He teaches treatment of children and adolescents from a self psychological perspective in the Graduate School of Social Work. He is also in private practice in Portland.

References

Adler, G. (1981). The borderline–narcissistic personality disorder continuum. *American Journal of Psychiatry* 138:1–50.

—— (1986). Psychotherapy of the narcissistic personality disorder patient: two contrasting approaches. *American Journal of Psychiatry* 143:430–436.

Alexander, F. (1961). *The Scope of Psychoanalysis.* New York: Basic Books.

American Psychiatric Association (1980). *Diagnostic and Statistical Manual of Mental Disorders* (3rd ed.). Washington, D.C.

—— (1987). *Diagnostic and Statistical Manual of Mental Disorders* (rev. ed.). Washington, D.C.

Andreasen, N. C. (1984). *The Broken Brain: The Biological Revolution in Psychiatry.* New York: Harper and Row.

Atchley, R. C. (1982). The aging self. *Psychotherapy, Therapy, Research and Practice* 19:388–396.

Bacal, H. (1985). Optimal responsiveness and therapeutic process. In *Progress in Self Psychology*, ed. A. Goldberg, pp. 202–227. New York: Guilford Press.

Baker, H., and Baker, M. (1987). Heinz Kohut's self psychology: an overview. *The American Journal of Psychiatry* 144:1.

Balint, M. (1979). *The Basic Fault: Therapeutic Aspects of Regression.* New York: Brunner/Mazel. (Originally published 1968.)

Bandler, L. (1979). The evolution of clinical social work. Proceedings of the Oxford Conference Challenge and renewal in psychodynamic social work. Northhampton, MA; Smith College School for Social Work, and London: The Group for Advancement of Psychotherapy in Social Work.

Basch, M. F. (1984a). The selfobject theory of motivation and the history of psychoanalysis. In *Kohut's Legacy: Contributions to Self Psychology*, ed. P. Stepansky and A. Goldberg, pp. 3–17. Hillside, NJ: The Analytic Press.

——— (1984b). Selfobjects, development, and psychotherapy. In *Kohut's Legacy: Contributions to Self Psychology*, ed. Stepansky and A. Goldberg, pp. 157–159. Hillside, NJ: The Analytic Press.

——— (1986). How does analysis cure? An appreciation. *Psychoanalytic Inquiry* 6:403–428.

Benedek, T. (1959). Parenthood as a developmental phase: a contribution to the libido theory. *Journal of the American Psychoanalytic Association* 7:389–417.

Berger, D. (1987). *Clinical Empathy*. Northvale, NJ: Jason Aronson.

Blanck, G., and Blanck, R. (1974). *Ego Psychology: Theory and Practice*. New York: Columbia University Press.

Bryer, J. B., Nelson, B. A., Miller, J. B., and Krol, P. A. (1987). Childhood sexual and physical abuse as factors in adult psychiatric illness. *American Journal of Psychiatry* 144:1426–1430.

Burgess, A. W., Hartman, C. R., and McCormack, A. (1987). Abused to abuser: antecedents of socially deviant behaviors. *American Journal of Psychiatry* 144:1431–1436.

Carmen, E., Rieker, P. P., and Mills, T. (1985). Victims of violence and psychiatric illness. *American Journal of Psychiatry* 141:378–383.

Cath, S. H. (1976). Functional disorders: an organismic view and attempt at reclassification. In *Geriatric Psychiatry: A Handbook for Psychiatry and Primary Care Physicians*, ed. L. Bellak and T. B. Karasu, pp. 141–172. New York: Grune and Stratton.

Chappell, P. F., and Sander, D. L. (1979). Mutual regulation of the neonatal, maternal interactive process. In *Before Speech—*

The Beginning of Interpersonal Communication, ed. M. Bullova, pp. 89-109. Cambridge, England: Cambridge University Press.

Chernin, K. (1985). The hungry self. In *Women, Eating and Identity*. New York: Harper and Row.

Chess, S., and Thomas, A. (1984). *Origins and Evolution of Behavior Disorders: From Infancy to Early Adult Life*. New York: Brunner/Mazel.

———— (1986). *Temperament and Clinical Practice*. New York: Guilford Press.

Chessick, R. D. (1985). Kohut's special clinical observations and classifications. *Psychology of the Self and the Treatment of Narcissism*, pp. 175-195. Northvale, NJ: Jason Aronson.

Cohler, B. (1980). Adult developmental psychology and reconstruction in psychoanalysis. In *The Course of Life*, ed. S. I. Greenspan and G. H. Pollock 3:149-200. Bethesda, MD: NIMH.

Demos, E. B. (1988). Affect and the development of the self: a new frontier. In *Frontiers in Self Psychology*, ed. A. Goldberg, pp. 27-53. Hillsdale, NJ: The Analytic Press.

Denzin, N. K. (1984). *On Understanding Emotion*. San Francisco: Jossey-Bass.

Dicks, H. V. (1967). *Marital Tensions*. London: Routledge and Kegan Paul.

Donner, S. (1988). Self psychology: implications for social work. *Social Casework* 69:1.

Dvorak-Peck, S. (1987). Social work and power: are they compatible? Paper presented at Smith College School for Social Work, Northampton, MA.

Eldridge, A., and Finnican, M. (1985). Applications of self psychology to the problem of child abuse. *Clinical Social Work Journal* 13:50-61.

Elson, M. (1984). Parenthood and the transformation of narcissism in parenthood. In *Parenthood: A Psychological Perspective*, ed. R. Cohen, B. Cohler, and S. Weissman, pp. 297-314. New York: Guilford Press.

———— (1986). *Self Psychology in Clinical Social Work*. New York: Norton.

Epstein, L. (1979). The therapeutic use of countertransference data with borderline patients. *Contemporary Psychoanalysis* 15:248–275.

Erikson, E. (1963). *Childhood and Society*, rev. ed. New York: Norton.

Fraiberg, S., Adelson, E., and Shapiro, V. (1975). Ghosts in the nursery. *American Academy of Child Psychiatry* 14:387–421.

Freud, A. (1958). Adolescence. *Psychoanalytic Study of the Child* 13:255–278. New York: International Universities Press.

—— (1965). *Normality and Pathology in Childhood: Assessments of Development*. New York: International Universities Press.

Freud, S. (1937). Constructions in analysis. *Standard Edition* 23:257–269.

—— (1961a). On narcissism: an introduction. *Standard Edition* 14:67–104.

—— (1961b). The ego and the id. *Standard Edition* 19:3–68.

—— (1961c). Inhibitions, symptoms, and anxiety. *Standard Edition* 20:77–128.

—— (1986). Introductory lectures on psychoanalysis. *Standard Edition* 15–16.

Garrett, A. (1958). Modern casework: the contributions of ego psychology. In *Ego Psychology and Dynamic Casework*, ed. H. Parad, pp. 38–52. New York: Family Service Association of America.

Gedo, J. (1979). *Beyond Interpretation: Towards a Revised Theory for Psychoanalysis*. New York: International Universities Press.

Geist, R. (1981). *Advances in Clinical Psychoanalysis*. New York: International Universities Press.

—— (1984). Therapeutic dilemmas in the treatment of anorexia nervosa: a self psychological perspective. *Contemporary Psychotherapy Review* 2:115–142.

Gill, M. (1951). Ego psychology and psychotherapy. *Psychoanalytic Quarterly* 20:62, 71.

Goldberg, A. (1973). Psychotherapy of narcissistic injuries. *Archives of General Psychiatry* 28:722–726.

―――― (1975). Narcissism and the readiness for psychotherapy termination. *Archives of General Psychiatry* 29:695–704.

―――― (1978a). A shift in emphasis: adolescent psychotherapy and the psychology of the self. *Journal of Youth and Adolescence* 7:119–132.

―――― (ed.) (1978b). *Advances in Self Psychology.* New York: International Universities Press.

Goodsitt, A. (1977). Narcissistic disturbances in anorexia nervosa. *Annuals of Adolescent Psychiatry* 5:304–312.

Greenberg, S. (1985). The supportive approach to therapy. *Clinic Social Work Journal* 13:6–13.

Gruenthal, R. From a panel discussion on different psychoanalytic theories. Unpublished.

Gunther, M. (1980). Aggression, self psychology and the concept of health. In *Advances in Self Psychology*, ed. A. Goldberg. New York: International Universities Press.

Hall, J. (1985). Idealizing transference: disruptions and repairs. In *Advances in Self Psychology*, vol. 1, ed. A. Goldberg, pp. 109–146. New York: International Universities Press.

Hartmann, H. (1958). *Ego Psychology and the Problem of Adaptation.* New York: International Universities Press.

Henderson, A. (1988). Theory and practice: a humanistic perspective. Unpublished manuscript.

Herman, J., Russell, D., and Trocki, K. (1986). Long-term effects of incestuous abuse in childhood. *American Journal of Psychiatry* 143:1293–1296.

Horowitz, M. (1976). *Stress Response Syndromes.* New York: Jason Aronson.

Hollis, F. (1958). Personality diagnosis in casework. In *Ego Psychology and Dynamic Casework*, ed. H. Parad, pp. 83–96. New York: Family Service Association of America.

Izard, C. E. (1972). *Patterns of Emotions: A New Analysis of Anxiety and Depression.* New York: Academic Press.

Jacobson, E. (1964). *The Self and the Object World.* New York: International Universities Press.

Jones, D. (1985). Bulimia: a false self-identity. *Clinical Social Work Journal* 13:305–316, 940.

Josephs, L. (1988). Witness to tragedy: A self psychological approach to the treatment of schizophrenia. *Bulletin of the Menninger Clinic* 52:134–144.

Josephs, L., and Josephs, L. (1986). Pursuing the kernel of truth in the psychotherapy of schizophrenia. *Psychoanalytic Psychology* 3:105–119.

Josephs, L., and Juman, L. (1985). The application of self psychology principles to long-term group therapy with schizophrenic inpatients. *Groups* 9:21–30.

Kernberg, O. (1975). *Borderline Conditions and Pathological Narcissism*. New York: Jason Aronson.

——— (1980). *Internal World and External Reality*. New York: Jason Aronson.

Klein, G. (1976). *Psychoanalytic Theory*. New York: International Universities Press.

Kohut, H. (1950). On the enjoyment of listening to music. *Psychoanalytic Quarterly* 19:64–87.

——— (1957). *Death in Venice* by Thomas Mann: a story about the disintegration of artistic sublimation. *Psychoanalytic Quarterly* 26:206–228.

——— (1959). Introspection, empathy, and psychoanalysis: an examination between mode of theory and observation. *Journal of the American Psychoanalytic Association* 14:459–483.

——— (1966). Forms and transformations of narcissism. *Journal of the American Psychoanalytic Association* 14:243–272.

——— (1968). Psychoanalytic treatment of narcissistic personality disturbances. *Psychoanalytic Study of the Child* 33:86–113. New Haven, CT: Yale University Press.

——— (1971). *The Analysis of the Self*. New York: International Universities Press.

——— (1972a). The two analyses of Mr. Z. *International Journal of Psycho-Analysis* 58:3–28.

——— (1972b). Thoughts on narcissism and narcissistic rage. *The Psychoanalytic Study of the Child* 27:360–400. New York: Quadrangle.

——— (1974). The self in history. In *Search for the Self*, ed. P. Ornstein, pp. 771–784. New York: International Universities Press.

———— (1977). *The Restoration of the Self.* New York: International Universities Press.

———— (1978a). *The Search for the Self: Selected Writings of Heinz Kohut, 1958–1978,* vols. 1 and 2, ed. P. Ornstein. New York: International Universities Press.

———— (1978b). Summarizing statement at the Chicago Conference on Self Psychology, Ritz Carlton Hotel.

———— (1980). Reflections. In *Advances in Self Psychology,* ed. A. Goldberg. New York: International Universities Press.

———— (1982). Introspection, empathy and the semi-circle of mental health. *International Journal of Psycho-Analysis* 63:395–407.

———— (1984). *How Does Analysis Cure?* Chicago: University of Chicago Press.

———— (1987). *The Kohut Seminars on Self Psychology and Psychotherapy with Adolescents and Young Adults.* New York: Norton.

Kohut H., and Goldberg, A. (1978). *Psychology of the Self: A Casebook.* New York: International Universities Press.

Kohut, H., and Wolf, E. (1978). The disorders of the self and their treatment: an outline. *International Journal of Psycho-Analysis* 59:413–425.

Lang, J. A. (1984). Notes toward a psychology of the feminine self. In *Kohut's Legacy: Contributions to Self Psychology,* ed. P. E. Stepansky and A. Goldberg. Hillside, NJ: The Analytic Press.

Lansky, M. (1989). Speech at Cedars-Sinai Medical Center, Los Angeles, California.

Lichtenberg, J. D. (1983). *Psychoanalysis and Infant Research.* Hillside, NJ: The Analytic Press.

Maas, H. S. (1958). Social casework. In *Concepts and Methods of Social Work,* ed. W. Freidlander, pp. 15–115. Englewood, NJ: Prentice Hall.

Malan, D. (1976). *Toward the Validation of Dynamic Psychotherapy: A Replication.* New York: Plenum.

Mann, J. (1973). *Time-limited Psychotherapy.* Cambridge, MA: Harvard University Press.

Meissner, W. W. (1976). Normal psychology of the aging process, revisited—I: Discussion. *Journal of Geriatric Psychiatry* 9:151–159.

—— (1979). Narcissistic personalities and borderline conditions: a differential diagnosis. *The Annual of Psychoanalysis* 7:171–202.

Miller, A. (1981). *Drama of the Gifted Child*. New York: Basic Books.

Minuchin, S., Rosman, B. L., and Baker, L. (1978). *Psychosomatic Families: Anorexia Nervosa in Context*. Cambridge, MA: Harvard University Press.

Modell, A. (1975). A narcissistic defense against affects and the illusion of self-sufficiency. *International Journal of Psycho-Analysis* 56:275–282.

—— (1976). The holding environment and the therapeutic action of psychoanalysis. *Journal of the American Psychoanalytic Association* 24:255–307.

Moos, R. H., and Fuhr, R. (1982). The clinical use of social-ecological concepts: the case of an adolescent girl. *American Journal of Orthopsychiatry*, 52:111–122.

Muslin, H. L., and Val, E. R. (1987). *The Psychotherapy of the Self*. New York: Brunner/Mazel.

Offer, D., and Offer, J. B. (1975). *From Teenage to Young Manhood: A Psychological Study*, 2nd ed. New York: Basic Books.

Orbach, S. (1978). *Fat is a Feminist Issue*. New York: Berkeley.

Ornstein, A. (1974). The dread to repeat and the new beginning: a contribution to the psychoanalysis of the narcissistic personality disorders. *The Annual of Psychoanalysis* 2:231–248. New York: International Universities Press.

—— (1982). Parental empathy and the troubled child. Family Counseling and Guidance Centers, Silver Jubilee Professional Symposium.

—— (1983a). An idealizing of the oedipal phase. In *Reflections on Self Psychology*. Hillside, NJ: The Analytic Press.

—— (1984). Psychoanalytic psychotherapy: a contemporary perspective. In *Kohut's Legacy: The Contributions of Self Psychology*, ed. P. E. Stepansky and A. Goldberg, pp. 171–181. New Jersey: The Analytic Press.

—— (1985). The function of play in the process of child therapy:

a contemporary perspective. *Annual of Psychoanalysis* 12–13:349–366.

—— (1986). Supportive psychotherapy: A contemporary view. *Clinical Social Work* 14:14–30.

Ornstein, P., ed. (1978a). *The Search for the Self*, vols. 1 and 2. New York: International Universities Press.

—— (1979). Self psychology and the concept of health. *Bulletin of the Association of Psychoanalytic Medicine* 19:14–21.

Ornstein, A., and Ornstein, P. (1984). Empathy and the therapeutic dialogue. Lydia Rappoport Lectures Program. Northampton, MA: Smith College School for Social Work.

Ornstein, P., and Ornstein, A. (1977). On the continuing evolution of psychoanalytic psychotherapy: reflections and predictions. *The Annual of Psychoanalysis* 5:329–370.

—— (1980). Self psychology and the process of regression. *Psychoanalytic Inquiry* 1:81–105.

—— (1983). Understanding and explaining: the empathic vantage point: progress in self-psychology, vol. 1, ed. A. Goldosy, pp. 43–61. New York: Guilford Press.

Palombo, J. (1985a). Self psychology and countertransference in the treatment of children. *Child and Adolescent Social Work Journal* 2:36–48.

—— (1985b). Depletion states and selfobject disorders. *Clinical Social Work Journal* 13:32–49.

Palombo, J., and Feigon, J. (1984). Borderline personality development in childhood and its relationship to neurocognitive deficits. *Child and Adolescent Social Work Journal* 1:18–33.

Reich, A. (1960). Pathological forms of self-esteem regulation. *Journal of the American Psychoanalytic Association* 15:215–232.

Rinsley, D. B. (1982). *Borderline and Other Self Disorders*. New York: Jason Aronson.

—— (1984). A comparison of borderline and narcissistic personality disorders. *Bulletin of the Menninger Clinic* 48:1–9.

Rochlin, G. (1965). *Griefs and Discontents: The Forces of Change*. Boston: Little, Brown.

Rogers, C. (1987). Rogers, Kohut, and Erikson: a personal perspective on some similarities and differences. In *Evolution* of *Psychotherapy*, ed. J. Zeig, pp. 179–188. New York: Brunner/Mazel.

Rosenfeld, H. (1971). A clinical approach to the psychoanalytic theory of life and death instincts: an investigation into the aggressive aspects of narcissism. *International Journal of Psycho-Analysis* 52:169–178.

Rosenman, S. (1981). Hypochondriasis and invidiousness: Two vicissitudes of narcissistic vulnerability. *Journal of the American Academy of Psychoanalysis* 9:51–70.

Rothstein, A. (1980). Toward a critique of the psychology of the self. *Psychoanalytic Quarterly* 49:132–455.

Saari, C. (1986). *Clinical Social Work Treatment*. New York: Gardner Press.

Sagar, C. J., Gundlach, R., and Kremer, J. (1968). The married in treatment. *Archives of General Psychiatry* 19:205–217.

Sander, L. (1977). The regulation of exchange in the infant–caretaker system, clinical reflections and considerations. *International Journal of Psycho-Analysis* 60:467–479.

Schafer, R. (1983). *The Analytic Attitude*. New York: Basic Books.

Schwaber, E. (1979). In the "self" within the matrix of analytic theory: some aspects in the context–content relationship. In *Interaction Conversation and the Development of Language*, ed. M. Lewis and L. Rosenbaum. New York: John Wiley.

———— (1980). Self psychology and the concept of psychopathology: a case presentation. In *Advances in Self Psychology*, ed. A. Goldberg, pp. 215–242. New York: International Universities Press.

———— (1983). To begin with: reflections on ontogony. In *Reflections on Self Psychology*, ed. J. Lichtenburg and S. Kaplan. Hillside, NJ: The Analytic Press.

Shane, D. N. (1984). Self psychology: a new conceptualization for the understanding of learning-disabled children. In *Kohut's Legacy: The Contributions of Self Psychology*, ed. P. E. Stepansky and A. Goldberg, pp. 191–201. Hillside, NJ: The Analytic Press.

Sifneos, P. E. (1972). *Short-term Psychotherapy and Emotional Crisis*. Cambridge, MA: Harvard University Press.

Solomon, M. (1989). *Narcissism and Intimacy*. New York: Norton.

Steele, B. F. (1970). Parental abuse of infants and small children. In *Parenthood: Its Psychology and Psychopathology*, ed. E. Anthony and T. Benedek, pp. 449–477. Boston: Little, Brown.

Stern, D. (1974). Mother and infant at play: the dyadic interaction involving facial, vocal, and gaze behaviors. In *The Effect of the Infant on Its Caregiver*, ed. M. Lewis and L. Rosenblum, pp. 187–213. New York: John Wiley.

―――― (1985). *The Interpersonal World of the Infant: A View from Psychoanalysis and Developmental Psychology*. New York: Basic Books.

Stern, D. N., Jaffe, J., Beebe, B., and Bennett, S. L. (1974). Vocalizing in unison and in alternation: two modes of communication within the mother–infant dyad. *Annals of New York Academy of Science* 263:89–100.

Stolorow, R. D. (1975). Toward a functional definition of narcissism. *International Journal of Psycho-Analysis* 56:179–185.

―――― (1986a). Narcissistic rage. *Psychiatric Annals* 16:489–490.

―――― (1986b). Critical reflections of the theory of self psychology: an inside view. *Psychoanalytic Inquiry* 6:387–402.

Stolorow, R., and Lachmann, F. (1980). *The Psychoanalysis of Developmental Arrests*. New York: International Universities Press.

Tittler, B. I., Frederim, S., Blothcy, A. D., and Stedrak, J. (1982). The influence of family variables on the ecologically-based treatment program for emotionally disturbed children. *American Journal of Orthopsychiatry* 52:123–130.

Tolpin, M. (1971). On the beginnings of a cohesive self. *Psychoanalytic Study of the Child* 26:316–354. New York: Quadrangle Books.

―――― (1980). The borderline personality: its makeup and analyzability. In *Advances in Self Psychology*, ed. A. Goldberg, pp. 299–316. New York: International Universities Press.

―――― (1983). A change in the self: the development and transformation of an idealizing transference. *International Journal of Psycho-Analysis* 64:461–483.

Tolpin, M., and Kohut, H. (1980). The disorders of the self: the psychopatholoy of the first year of life. In *The Course of Life: Psychoanalytic Contributions toward Understanding Person-*

ality Development, vol. 1, ed. S. I. Greenspan and G. H. Pollock, pp. 425–442. Bethesda, MD: National Institutes of Mental Health.

Tomkins, S. (1962). *Affect, Imagery, Consciousness*. Vol. 1: *The Positive Affects*. New York: Springer.

——— (1963). *Affect, Imagery, Consciousness*. Vol. 2: *The Negative Affects*. New York: Springer.

Treurniet, N. (1980). On the self. *International Journal of Psycho-Analysis* 61:325–333.

Waelder, R. (1936). The principle of multiple function: observations on overdetermination. *Psychoanalytic Quarterly* 5:45–62.

Wilson, C. P., ed. (1983). *Fear of Being Fat: The Treatment of Anorexia Nervosa and Bulimia*. New York: Jason Aronson.

Winnicott, D. W. (1960). Ego distortion in terms of true and false self. In *The Maturational Processes and the Facilitating Environment*, pp. 29–36. New York: International Universities Press.

——— (1965). *The Maturational Processes and the Facilitating Environment: Studies in the Theory of Emotional Development*. New York: International Universities Press.

——— (1986). *Playing and Reality*. London: Tavistock Publications.

Wolberg, L. R. (1965). *Short-term Psychotherapy*. New York: Grune and Stratton.

Wolf, E. S. (1980). On the developmental line of selfobject relations. In *Advances in Self Psychology*, ed. A. Goldberg, pp. 117–132. New York: International Universities Press.

——— (1980). Tomorrow's self: Heinz Kohut's contribution to adolescent psychiatry. *Adolescent Psychiatry* 8:41–50.

Wolf, E., Gedo, J., and Termon, D. (1972). On the adolescent process as a transformation of the self. *Journal of Youth and Adolescence* 1:257–272.

Young, T. M. (1990). Therapeutic case advocacy: a multi-level model for helping emotionally handicapped children and their families. *American Journal of Orthopsychiatry* 60:118–124.

Zimberg, S. (1978). Principles of alcoholism in psychotherapy. In *Practical Approaches to Alcoholism Therapy*, ed. A. Zimberg, J. Wallace, and S. B. Blume, pp. 1–18. New York: Plenum.

CREDITS

The editor and publisher gratefully acknowledge the following for permission to reprint material found in this book.

"When the Patient Is Psychotic" by Lawrence W. Josephs. Ph.D. Reprinted with permission from the *Bulletin of the Menninger Clinic*, Vol. 52, No. 2, pp. 134–144, March 1988. Copyright © 1988, The Menninger Foundation.

"Self Disorders in Adolescence" ("Adolescents") is reprinted from *Self Psychology in Clinical Social Work* by Miriam Elson, M.A., A.C.S.W., by permission of the author and W. W. Norton & Co., Inc. Copyright © 1986 by Miriam Elson.

"Therapeutic Response to Rage Reactions in the Treatment of Severely Disturbed Narcissistic Personality Disorders" ("When the Patient Exhibits Narcissistic Rage") by Jayne Patrick, Ph.D., reprinted with permission from *Dynamic Psychotherapy*, Vol. 4, No. 2, 151–158. Copyright © 1986 by Brunner/Mazel, Inc.

"Self Psychology—Its Application to Brief Psychotherapy with the Elderly" ("Elderly") by Lawrence W. Lazarus, M.D., from the *Journal of Geriatric Psychiatry*, Vol. 21 (2), 1988. Reprinted by permission of the author and the publisher, International Universities Press.

"Narcissism and Narcissistic Impairments: A Perspective from Self Psychology" ("Narcissism") by Barbara Nicholson, Ph.D., from *Psychotherapy in Private Practice*, Vol. 8 (1), 99–117 by permission of the Haworth Press, Inc. Copyright © 1990 by the Haworth Press, Inc.

"Differential Diagnosis and Assessment: A Perspective from Self Psychology" ("Narcissism") by Barbara Nicholson, Ph.D., from *Journal of Independent Social Work*, Vol. 4 (3) (in press) by permission of the Haworth Press, Inc. Copyright © 1991 by the Haworth Press, Inc.

INDEX